How to Live

Being Happy and Dealing with Moral Dilemmas

Mirko Bagaric

UNIVERSITY PRESS OF AMERICA,® INC.
Lanham • Boulder • New York • Toronto • Oxford

Copyright © 2006 by
University Press of America,® Inc.
4501 Forbes Boulevard
Suite 200
Lanham, Maryland 20706
UPA Acquisitions Department (301) 459-3366

PO Box 317
Oxford
OX2 9RU, UK

All rights reserved
Printed in the United States of America
British Library Cataloging in Publication Information Available

Library of Congress Control Number: 2006927254
ISBN-13: 978-0-7618-3532-5 (paperback : alk. paper)
ISBN-10: 0-7618-3532-6 (paperback : alk. paper)

∞™ The paper used in this publication meets the minimum
requirements of American National Standard for Information
Sciences—Permanence of Paper for Printed Library Materials,
ANSI Z39.48—1984

Contents

Preface   vii

PART A   THE MORAL FRAMEWORK

1 What is Morality?   3
    1.1 The Nature of Morality: It is the Most Important Standard   3
    1.2 Morality is Objective Not Subjective   4
    1.3 Overview of Moral Theories   8
    1.4 Non-consequentialist (Rights) Theories   8
    1.5 Consequentialism   13

2 The Things That Make us Happy   26
    2.1 Overview of the Convergence of the Human Condition   26
    2.2 What is Happiness?   27
    2.3 Why is Happiness Important   28
    2.4 What Makes People Happy?   29

PART B   PERSONAL ETHICS

3 Loyalty, Friendship and Love   47
    3.1 Overview of our preference towards those close to us   47
    3.2 The Nature of Loyalty   48
    3.3 The Tension Between Loyalty and Morality   49
    3.4 The Overlap Between Morality and Loyalty   51
    3.5 The Limits of Loyalty   55

4 Lying   59
    4.1 Introduction   59
    4.2 Different Types of Lies   61

4.3	The Moral Status of Lies	63
4.4	The Discord Between the Perception and the Reality of the Prohibition against Lying	69

PART C MEDICAL ETHICS

5 Eugenics: Should We Create Designer Babies? — 75
  5.1 Introduction — 75
  5.2 Whether Eugenics is Intrinsically Wrong — 77
  5.3 Bad Consequences and Slippery Slope Argument — 79
  5.4 Balancing all the considerations — 84

6 Stem Cell Research and Abortion — 87
  6.1 Introduction — 87
  6.2 The Potential Benefits of Stem Cell Research — 89
  6.3 The Moral Status of Stem Cell Research — 90
  6.4 The Central Issue: When Does Life Begin? — 93
  6.5 Ramifications for Morality of Stem Cell Research — 96
  6.6 Abortion — 98

7 Euthanasia — 102
  7.1 Overview and Definitional issues — 102
  7.2 Arguments favouring euthanasia — 104
  7.3 Arguments Against Euthanasia — 107
  7.4 Overview of Moral Status of Euthanasia — 113

PART D DEALING WITH WRONGDOERS

8 Punishment and Sentencing — 119
  8.1 Introduction — 119
  8.2 Pick a Theory of Punishment — 120
  8.3 Ignore Public Opinion — 121
  8.4 Identify the Objectives of Sentencing—Incapacitation, Deterrence and Rehabilitation? — 122
  8.5 Make the Punishment Fit the Crime — 123
  8.6 Aggravating and Mitigating Factors—Scrutinise each of them — 124
  8.7 On-Going Reform — 125

9 Terrorism — 128
  9.1 Terrorism: what is it? — 128
  9.2 Responses to Terrorism—Security Versus Liberty — 131
  9.3 The Types of Restrictive Laws That are Permissible — 134

9.4	The Right to Free Speech is Untrammeled—It is a weapon against terrorism	135
9.5	Broader solutions to terrorism	136

PART E DEALING WITH 'OTHER' PEOPLE AND ANIMALS

10 World Poverty — 141
- 10.1 The Enormity of World Suffering — 141
- 10.2 The Explanation For The Inadequate Response — 142
- 10.3 Conclusion — 146

11 Migrants — 148
- 11.1 Introduction and an Overview of Arguments Against Strict Migration Controls — 148
- 11.2 Sovereignty and the History of Migration Controls — 150
- 11.3 Arguments in Favour of Reduced Migration Controls — 155
- 11.4 Arguments in Favour of Strict Migration Controls — 161
- 11.5 Reform Proposals and Conclusion — 166

12 The Environment — 169
- 12.1 Introduction — 169
- 12.2 Growing Interest in Environmental Law—Lip Service Only? — 169
- 12.3 A Moral Environmental Duty is Not Self-Evident — 172
- 12.4 Grounding a Moral Environment Duty — 174
- 12.5 Practical Application: Should we Ratify the Kyoto Protocol — 176

13 Animals — 184
- 13.1 Overview of Chapter — 184
- 13.2 It is Morally Wrong to Treat Animals Cruelly — 185
- 13.3 Why Has There Not Been More Attempts to Prevent Cruelty to Animals? — 191

PART F BUSINESS ETHICS

14 The Social Responsibility of Corporations — 197
- 14.1 Introduction — 197
- 14.2 The Threshold Issue: Is There a Role For Ethical Considerations in Business — 198
- 14.3 Application of Moral Principle to Business Setting — 204
- 14.4 Additional Duties Imposed on Corporations—A Duty of Benevolence? — 206

	14.5 Extreme Wealth and Duty to Not Frustrate Access to Justice	212
	14.6 Summary	213
15	**Bribery and Networking**	**216**
	15.1 Introduction	216
	15.2 Definitions	217
	15.3 Moral Evaluation of Bribery	219
	15.4 Moral Evaluation of Networking	220
	15.5 Conclusion	225

Preface

This book examines over a dozen important contemporary moral issues. Some relate to matters which confront us daily, while others are more general issues, the proper resolution of which is central to the capacity for individuals and a society to flourish.

The issues discussed in the book are of considerable contemporary relevance and are approached from an interdisciplinary perspective (morality, psychology and law). In particular, moral theory and the implications that recent advances in well-being studies have on this area of thought are considered in detail. The framework of the book is set out in chapters one and two. The rest of the book applies this framework to the most important moral and social issues of our time.

Part A (chapters 1 and 2) sets the framework for the book. Chapter one examines the different streams of moral thought and concludes that the most sound theory is utilitarianism, which is the view that the ultimate moral duty is to maximise happiness. As an illustration of the different conclusions reached by the respective moral theories, I discuss the vexed issue of torture. Chapter two examines the notion of well-being and happiness and looks at the large amount of recent scientific and sociological literature in this area. It informs readers of the keys to happiness.

Part B (chapters 3 and 4) deals with personal ethics. First, I examine friendship and love. I conclude that even though morality requires that we act impartially, it is permissible (and in fact desirable) to form close relationships because loyalty is an important moral ideal and people are constituted in such a way that they obtain enormous pleasure from close relationships. Chapter four discusses the complex issue of lying. Despite the formal prohibition against lying, empirical data shows nearly all people lie regularly. I explain this anomaly and conclude that certain forms of lies are permissible, namely lies to protect others and some white lies.

Part C (chapters 5, 6 and 8) discusses the most pressing issues in medical ethics. In chapter 5, I argue that we should embrace medical developments that can improve the health and capacities of our children, despite the fact that potentially this can lead to a superior class of people. Stem cell research is discussed in chapter 6 where it is argued that we should prohibit embryonic stem research. This seems to violate the right to life and current medical data indicates that adult stem cells (which do not require destruction of an embryo) may be as equally functional as embryonic stem cells. The related issue of abortion is also considered in this chapter. Euthanasia is examined in chapter 7. I argue that the practice is morally unsound. Empirical data shows that if voluntary euthanasia is legalised it leads to non-voluntary euthanasia. Moreover, in relation to issues of life and death we should adopt a life-affirming approach.

Part D (chapters 8 and 9) examines how we should deal with wrongdoers. Punishment and sentencing is considered in section 8 where I conclude that the sentencing systems of most Western countries are too harsh. We need to adopt sentencing principles which lead to less harsh penalties and reduce the crime rate. This is followed by a discussion of how to deal with the terrorist threat. This requires tougher anti-terrorism laws, which involve incursions into some civil liberties. At the same time we need to work together and harmoniously with Muslim communities that live in Western countries – they are a component of the solution, not part of the problem.

Part E (chapters 10, 11, 12 and 13) looks at how we should treat 'distant' people and animals. Chapter 10 identifies the reasons that we are so stingy when it comes to tackling world poverty and indicates the measures that need to be taken to address preventable suffering in other parts of the world. This is followed, in chapter 11, by a discussion of migration controls which are strictly enforced by all Western nations. I argue that this is discriminatory and we need to move towards an open border policy. It is simply a matter of pot luck where a person is born and this should not exclude them from certain opportunities and privileges. The environment is considered in chapter 12, where I contend that the duty to future generations has been overstated. Entities that do not exist cannot have rights, thus we do not owe duties to them. Nevertheless, I identify a more modest basis for an environmental duty and discuss the implications of this for our daily lives. The chapter on animals argues that the appalling way we treat them will constitute the shame of our generation. Animals derive moral standing from the fact that they can feel pain. They are entitled to far more compassionate than they are currently accorded.

Part F (chapters 14 and 15) deals with business ethics. In chapter 14, I argue that the main duty of corporations is to comply with the law. However, if they are very successful in their money making endeavours they should pay a social dividend. Chapter 15 examines the seemingly innocuous practice of networking. Like bribery it involves trying to get an advantage for reasons other than merit or efficiency and hence distorts the market system. Like bribery it is also probably morally wrong.

Part A

THE MORAL FRAMEWORK

Chapter One

What is Morality?

1.1 THE NATURE OF MORALITY: IT IS THE MOST IMPORTANT STANDARD

Morality consists of the principles which dictate how serious conflict should be resolved in our lives. Morality does not govern every aspect of our lives. It does not dictate what colour shirt we should wear, who gets to watch their television show or what career we choose. Morality is not concerned with trivialities. It has nothing to do with the 'small stuff'. Rather it only comes into play in relation to the important decisions that we make. That is why the study of morality or *ethics* (the words are used interchangeably) is so central to the decisions we make in our day to day lives and the reason why it is important to have a coherent moral outlook.

When morality applies to a particular situation it does so in a decisive manner. Moral judgments trump all other types of principles. It is a settled social convention that moral prescriptions can be invoked to justify breaches of all other types of standards and rules, whether they relate to norms of business, sport, politics, etiquette or even law.

Thus, if you break the law but have acted in an ethical manner in doing so, you will not necessarily avoid legal punishment, but you will avoid the social embarrassment and stigma that is normally consequent upon legal wrongdoing. Many people are prepared to excuse even the murderer who euthanises another person and kills out of compassion and journalists who refuse to reveal the identity of informers who have tipped them off regarding stories of social importance are typically regarded as heroes as opposed to wrongdoers. In other domains, we do not condemn the politician who disregards party policy and casts a conscience vote on a morally important issue, such as abortion or stem cell research and it is permissible to break the social etiquette of queuing in order to get timely medical assistance to an injured person.

Another feature of morality is that it only relates to situations where there is an actual or potential conflict of interest between two or more parties—it (is used to) assesses and weighs the respective interests. In a perfect world, consisting of unlimited resources and no clashing interests, morality would be redundant.

A unique feature of morality is that moral judgments are by their nature motivational. This is what philosophers term the 'practicality' of moral judgments. Upon judging something as right or wrong we feel in a pull in accordance with that judgment. In a motivational sense we are never totally indifferent to our moral sentiments. Of course, we do not always end up acting in accordance with such judgements, but this is not because the motivation is absent. Rather, it is simply that a stronger conflicting desire or want outweighs our moral judgment.

The belief that it is good to feed starving animals provides us with a motivation to feed malnourished animals, at least when we come across them. We might not always act upon this judgement, because we might not have food with us or we might be rushing to an appointment and so on. Nevertheless the belief that starving animals should be fed provides us with a motivation to feed them. This is in contrast to other beliefs that we hold. The belief that a car is blue or that it is a sunny day does not necessarily drive us towards any type of action. The action guiding nature of morality provides another central reason why it is important for people to learn more about ethics. This book is about providing people with that knowledge.

It does so by setting out the moral framework in the first two chapters. The other chapters focus on applying the framework to important moral issues of our time. It is not possible to discuss every possible moral dilemma. This is not a shortcoming of the book. The moral compass set out in the first two chapters can be applied to all moral issues, allowing readers to make clear and sophisticated decisions in relation to moral dilemmas with which they are confronted.

I shortly commence discussing the framework. Prior to doing so, I discuss whether moral judgments are subjective or whether they have an objective core that applies to all people.

1.2 MORALITY IS OBJECTIVE NOT SUBJECTIVE

The relevance of morality as a tool for laying a road map to the important decisions in our lives is challenged by many commentators on the basis that it is supposedly a subjective concept, an expression of our tastes and preferences rather than a factual reality, and hence incapable of providing firm guidance on important issues.

Proponents of this view point to the diversity of moral standards across cultures, evolving moral standards over time and differences in moral sentiments that people have within the one culture.

These arguments can be broken down into two separate themes. There is no question that throughout time within the one society and across cultures at any point in time there is a considerable divergence in moral sentiment. Thus, we see that in the Western World today women have far greater rights and privileges than they did several decades ago. Women now are regarded as the equal of men and cannot be subordinated by them. Across cultures, there remains an enormous difference in moral standards. For example, in many parts of the world minority groups are discriminated against and have poor access to important opportunities and services, such as education, health and employment.

These observations, understandably, fuel the argument that morality is not objective, but rather a subjective practice, dependent on the society and period of time in question. This theory is called moral relativism.

The theory known as moral subjectivism is similar, but it focuses on divergent sentiments within the one society at a particular point in time. It focuses on the fact that at any one time in any group there is a rich diversity of views regarding what is right and wrong. In the Western World presently, there is intense disagreement regarding many important issues (some of which are discussed in this book), such as euthanasia, eugenics, stem cell research, the treatment of migrants, world poverty and the environment. With so many different views, how can morality possibly be an objective inquiry?

The counter to both moral subjectivism and relativism is similar. The fact that people disagree about the true state of affairs of a certain matter does not necessarily mean that the field of inquiry is devoid of an absolute truth. Practices, beliefs and theories in the areas of medicine, engineering and economics have changed massively over the ages and we have seen throughout history enormous differences in the way that societies have treated patients, built bridges and developed market structures. These differences are often just as manifest within a society at any given point in time. Different doctors in the same city will use different techniques for dealing with the same illness and financial advisers often provide conflicting advice about how to maximise wealth.

Yet these variances are not generally used to support arguments that endeavours such as medicine, economics and engineering are not objective fields of inquiry. Instead they are thought to be simply indicative of the fact that we are becoming smarter and more sophisticated and through experimentation or trial and error are getting closer to finding objective truths in these areas. The same can be said of moral judgments. The important point to note is that differences in standpoint do not necessarily mean a lack of objectivity in relation to the inquiry in question. It can equally be explained on the basis that we are moving towards a, yet as unascertained, objective truth.

In this regard it is important to be mindful of the fact that there seems to be a slow, but evident, convergence in the moral judgments that people endorse across most cultures. For example, slavery is now universally deplored, the plight of women has improved enormously in many parts of the world over the past two or three decades and more generally there is a growing acceptance that people are entitled to equal opportunities and privileges, and hence discrimination is widely deplored (though far from being stamped out).

More specifically, there are several principles upon which there is widespread consensus in most societies. They are:

1. Do not kill or otherwise violate the physical integrity of others;
2. Do not steal the property of others;
3. Do not lie (this includes keeping promises);
4. Assist others in serious trouble, when assistance would immensely help them at no or little inconvenience to oneself (the maxim of positive duty).

These rules are negative in character, apart from the maxim of positive duty —which is only remotely intrusive (and is discussed further in chapter 10). It is illuminating to note at this point, that it follows from these principles that according to widely shared moral standards we are free to do as we wish within the ambit of the rules. In this derivative fashion personal liberty is also an important virtue.

The manner in which we invoke moral language and discourse also supports the view that morality is objective. In relation to matters of pure taste or preference, we do not engage in serious debate. We use moral language to try to convince others that our standpoint is correct. This is even in relation to people from vastly different cultures. Cross cultural moral debate and argument is widespread. Parties from different cultures (and even more commonly from within the one culture) often debate moral issues, with each trying convince the other of the correctness of their view. The parties speak as if morality has universal standards; not as if it is akin to matters of personal taste in relation to which there is no objective right or wrong. If morality is not objective, such discourse is either futile or vastly different in character to the type of process which the surface nature of exchange indicates—it is not feasible to attempt to *logically* persuade another by a series of utterances or personal feelings.

The way in which we actually use moral language does not prove that it is objective. We could simply be wrong in alluding to an objective core or it could be the case that we are being (probably subconsciously) cunning in this regard. In order to impress our views on ours, we could be trying to objectify our comments. If we accepted that morality was simply a matter of personal preference we would not have a rational lever to try to convince others that our standpoint should be adopted. Our words would be devoid of persuasion — the rational response would be that we are simply venting our personal feelings which are no more valid or instructive than the feelings of others.

Ultimately whether morality is objective or subjective turns on whether there are sufficient similarities about the human condition such that the flourishing of all people would be enhanced by adherence to a set of defined principles. This would require evidence that due to some aspect of biology and/or evolution there is a degree of uniformity in the way people are built. In the following chapter we will see that despite ostensible differences between human beings, ultimately we are remarkably similar in relation to the matters that are conducive or detrimental to our well-being.

The objectivity of moral judgments stems from the fact that human nature, in terms of what makes us happy, is not random. 'Moral principles rest upon the basic general structure of the human predicament, and this does not change'.[1] Correct moral judgments are those that experience shows tend to increase net happiness.

Thus, morality is objective in the same sense as other biological and social sciences, such as economics. Economic theory does not exist outside human kind — economic principles do not transcend the parameters of human thought and human engagement. But this does not mean that there are not any economic principles which are right, and others that are wrong. The correct principles are those that will achieve the purpose of the discipline: to attain wealth; the wrong ones are those that will not promote this goal. So too in the case of morality.

The objectively correct moral principles are the ones that will serve the ultimate aims of the inquiry at hand, which is also the ultimate end of mankind — to be happy. If one adopts this as the starting premise, objectivity will follow. It is a matter of trial and practice and informed experimentation to ascertain which patterns of conduct will best promote this end. It seems that the above four secondary principles are all conducive of this. They are not context sensitive, applying equally in New York and Kenya. There may be others. Only experience will tell whether other virtues, such as loyalty, forgiveness and integrity also facilitate such an end. Such knowledge may be hard to acquire, but difficulties in ascertaining whether the earth was flat, round or otherwise did not prevent it being the subject matter of an objective truth.

I consider which moral theory will best enhance human well-being.

1.3 OVERVIEW OF MORAL THEORIES

More ink has been spilt on discussing moral theory—perhaps because of its cardinal status in evaluating human conduct—than probably any other social issue. It is not productive to systematically catalogue and analyse the main streams of moral thought and the critiques of them that have been made over the ages. However, some general observations in this area are appropriate. This will set the framework and provide a moral compass for analysing the dilemmas that are considered in this book.

Moral theories can be divided into two broad groups. *Consequentialist moral theories* claim that an act is right or wrong depending on its capacity to maximise a particular ideal, such as happiness. *Non-consequentialist* (or deontological) theories claim that the appropriateness of an action does not depend on its ability to produce particular ends, but follows from the intrinsic features of the act, in particular the extent to which the conduct conforms to pre-determined rules.[2]

Thus, the main difference between consequentialist and non-consequentialist moral theories is the emphasis that they give to consequences in determining whether an act is morally sound. Consequentialist theories look solely towards the effect that the conduct has on human flourishing, whereas this is at best a secondary consideration in relation to non-consequentialist theories. For example, some non-consequentialists believe that it is always wrong to lie, whereas for consequentialists lying is permissible if it will produce good consequences such as saving life. I now discuss the merits of these theories.

1.4 NON-CONSEQUENTIALIST (RIGHTS) THEORIES

1.4.1 Explanation of Rights Based Theories

The leading contemporary non-consequentialist theories are those which are framed in the language of rights. Following the Second World War, there has been an immense increase in 'rights talk',[3] both in number of supposed rights and in total volume. Rights doctrine has progressed a long way since its original aim of providing 'a legitimisation of . . . claims against tyrannical or exploiting regimes'.[4] As Tom Campbell points out:

> The human rights movement is based on the need for a counter-ideology to combat the abuses and misuses of political authority by those who invoke, as a justification for their activities, the need to subordinate the particular interests of individuals to the general good.[5]

What is Morality?

There is now, more than ever, a strong tendency to advance moral claims and arguments in terms of rights.[6] Assertion of rights has become the customary means to express our moral sentiments. As Sumner notes: 'there is virtually no area of public controversy in which rights are not to be found on at least one side of the question—and generally on both'.[7] The domination of rights talk is such that it is accurate to state that human rights have at least temporarily replaced maximising utility as the leading philosophical inspiration for political and social reform.[8]

1.4.2 The Emptiness of Rights Based Theories

Despite the dazzling veneer of deontological rights based theories, when examined closely they are unable to provide convincing answers to central issues such as: what is the justification for rights? How can we distinguish real from fanciful rights? Which right takes priority in the event of conflicting rights?

Such intractable difficulties stem from the fact that contemporary rights theories lack a coherent foundation. A non-consequentialist ethic provides no method for distinguishing between genuine and fanciful rights claims and is incapable of providing guidance regarding the ranking of rights in the event of a clash.

1.4.2.1 The Nonsense of Dignity

The most popular modern day rationale that is used in attempt to justify specific rights claims is dignity. For example, at the international law level numerous instruments employ the notion of dignity in an attempt to provide a basis for more specific rights claims. The concept of dignity gained considerable currency as a result of the egregious and widespread abuses that occurred during World War II. 'The idea of human dignity was decisively strengthened by developments after the Second World War. After the terrible crimes and contempt towards mankind by the Nazis, there was a sudden surge for stronger protection of human dignity'.[9] The preamble to the Universal Declaration of Human Rights, drafted shortly after the War, states:

> Whereas recognition of the inherent dignity and of the equal and inalienable rights of all members of the human family is the foundation of freedom, justice and peace in the world.

In this regard it has been noted that:

> It is the concept and term of 'the Inherent Dignity' that carries the whole burden of being the fountainhead from which the equal rights of man follows which leads us back to the deistic or theistic worldview.[10]

The influence of dignity on rights discourse and on the development of rights-based legal theories is so pronounced that it has acquired 'a resonance that leads it to be invoked widely as a legal and moral ground for protest against degrading and abusive treatment'.

However, the notion of dignity is incapable of providing a justification and basis for rights based moral claims. There is probably no such thing as dignity, and almost certainly no such thing that is uniquely the preserve of human beings.

The meaning of dignity is so indeterminate that it is often used (without a hint of incoherence) by advocates on both sides of a moral divide to press their arguments. For example, opponents of euthanasia argue that intentionally killing a person is the antithesis of respecting the patient's dignity. This view was adopted by the influential 18th century German Philosopher Immanuel Kant who believed that self-murder is contrary to human dignity because it involves treating oneself as a means. However, perhaps the most widely utilised argument by pro-euthanasia advocates is that allowing a patient to die in pain against his or her wishes is undignified. Famous contemporary modern day US philosopher Ronald Dworkin believes that a true appreciation of dignity requires respect for individual freedom and the ability for each person to make his or her own moral decisions including those relating to life and death. This highlights the open-ended nature of the concept. Argumentative devices that are so duplicitous are ultimately formless.

Moreover, there is no evidence that humans are imbued with such a 'noble' trait as dignity. If, as a species, we were so dignified, and this entailed us to some extra degree of concern and respect (beyond that of other species), presumably such an important trait would to some extent guide our values and conduct, leading us to on balance engage in 'dignified' acts. The opposite is true. On the wanton destruction register we are the most culpable creatures on earth—towards ourselves and all other life forms. If this is what does dignity leads one to, then perhaps we have overdosed.

Given that there is no ascertainable meaning of dignity, it is not an ideal that can be used to establish social policy. And certainly there is no other virtue that offers hope of grounding non-consequentialists rights claims.

1.4.2.2 *No Limits on Fabricating Rights Claims*

The emptiness of rights theories, stemming from an absence of a concrete foundation, has resulted in a proliferation of rights claims. The 'great' thing about rights is that you actually get to make them up as you go along without any danger of being accused of incoherency. This means that when they clash the winner is the person who yells loudest—the antithesis of a moral code.

From humble origins where they used to relate to important interests such as life and liberty, rights are today bloated like never before. A good example is the recent claim by the Australian Prime Minister that 'each child has the right to a mother and father'. In a similar vein, in light of the increasing world oil prices, it has been declared that this violates the 'right of Americans to cheap gasoline'. Greek soccer supporters in 2004, frustrated by the fact that coverage of the European Soccer Cup was only available on pay TV, were asserting a right to 'watch their team on free TV'. We can't blame too much Ouzo for that one. More likely they were fuelled by Article 25 of the Universal Declaration of Rights which reckons we have a right to 'rest and leisure'.

Due to the great expansion in rights talk, rights are now in danger of being labelled as mere rhetoric and are losing their cogent moral force. Or, as Sumner points out, rights become an 'argumentative device capable of justifying anything [which means they are] capable of justifying nothing'.[11]

Despite the fact that rights are nonsense, we like rights. They appeal to those of us who have a 'me, me, me' approach to moral issues. They are individualising interests and promise to confer benefits to people. Hence, simply labeling an interest as a right oxygenates the blood. A poll on whether we supported the 'right to unrestricted paid maternity leave'; 'a right for our children to attend university'; 'a right to the best possible health care'; and 'a right to high quality public housing' would receive widespread support.

But buried only slightly beneath such an approach are the inescapable realities that as people we live in communities; communities are merely the sum of a number of other individuals; and the actions of one person (exercising his or her rights) can have a (negative) effect on the interests of others. While rights seek to atomise people, the reality of the human conditions, as we shall see in chapter two, is that we do not and cannot function (happily) without the involvement of others.

The process of balancing competing rights claims is not a task commonly undertaken by rights proponents. While we might yearn for the above rights, the enthusiasm would start to wane the moment the cost—in the form of a mega increased taxation hit—was disclosed. Sure we like to the idea of unlimited access to education, health and other goods and services, but the attractiveness dissipates when it becomes apparent that it would require massive increases in community resources, which can in the end only be gained by working longer and longer hours.

Without an acute awareness of the conflicting nature of rights claims and a mechanism for rationally resolving these claims, we will get distorted outcomes where lower order interests trump higher order human concerns and the common good is further removed from our consciousness. Rights worship does this. Thus, we see, for example, that minor interests such as the right to privacy are prone to trump high order rights, such as the right to life.

A good example is the misguided concern at the recent Supreme Court ruling in Victoria in July 2005 that a woman's right to privacy does not prevent information being released about a termination she had at 32 weeks after learning that the child might be born with dwarfism. As a community of course we need to know about the circumstances in which the right to life is being potentially violated—how can such a low order interest such as privacy come even close to trumping the right to life? It can only do so because of the rights fog within which modern day Western societies operate.

A month later, we see another example in the same State of the unduly trumping power accorded to privacy. Residents in an outer Melbourne suburb (Sunbury) were aghast that they were not informed that a notorious pedophile who had sexually abused over 20 young boys, Charles Alan Smith, was living in their suburb, a couple of blocks from primary and secondary schools.

The residents of Sunbury were so incensed about their new neighbour that they were literally protesting in the streets—in particular in his street—about the fact that they had a known pedophile in their midst.

The Government would not tell the residents where other pedophiles were living, nor confirm the location of Smith, because it did not want to infringe their supposed right to privacy. The Government also was of the view that revealing the identity and location of pedophiles would set back their interests, making it harder for them to integrate back into society.

Lost in this analysis was the fundamental principle of justice that the rights of the innocent take priority over those of wrongdoers. Indeed, the pedophiles have done their time, but nevertheless it is their dysfunctional mindset that makes them an ongoing risk to others in society. They are the problem. Innocent people should not be required to accept increased risks to their safety to protect people from problems of their doing.

Notions of personal responsibility require that it is the pedophiles who wear the potential adverse consequences of their appalling conduct. These consequences should not be thrust onto the rest of the community.

Moreover, we all have a fundamental right to protect ourselves and those close to us. We can only exercise this right if we have knowledge of the risks that confront us. Thus, we are entitled to know if there are hazardous or noxious substances in our neighbourhood. The same applies in relation to risks presented by people whose past behaviour indicates they have dangerous tendencies.

The above analysis may seem to be unduly dismissive of rights based theories and pay inadequate regard to the considerable moral reforms that have occurred against the backdrop of rights talk over the past half-century. There is no doubt that rights claims have proved to be an effective lever in bringing about social change. As Campbell correctly notes, rights have provided 'a constant source of inspiration for the protection of individual liberty'.[12] For example, recognition of the (universal) right to liberty resulted in the abolition of slavery; more recently the right of equality has been used as an effective weapon by women and other disenfranchised groups.

For this reason, it is accepted that there is an ongoing need for moral discourse in the form of rights. This is so even if deontological rights-based moral theories (with their absolutist overtones) are incapable of providing answers to questions such as the existence and content of proposed rights, and even if rights are difficult to defend intellectually or are seen to be culturally biased. There is a need for rights-talk, at least at the 'edges of civilisation and in the tangle of international politics'.[13] Still, the significant changes to the moral landscape for which non-consequentialist rights have provided the catalyst must be accounted for.

There are several responses to this. Firstly, the fact that a belief or judgment is capable of moving and guiding human conduct says little about its truth—the widespread practice of burning 'witches' being a case in point. Secondly, at the descriptive level, the intuitive appeal of rights claims, and the absolutist and forceful manner in which they are expressed, has heretofore been sufficient to mask over fundamental logical deficiencies associated with the concept of rights. Finally, and perhaps most importantly, I do not believe that there is no role in moral discourse for rights claims. Simply, that (as we shall see shortly) the only manner in which rights can be substantiated is in the context of a consequentialist ethic.

1.5 CONSEQUENTIALISM

1.5.1 The Utilitarian Theory

A more promising tack for constructing and justifying a ladder of human interest is to ground the analysis in a consequentialist ethic. The most popular consequentialist moral theory is utilitarianism. Several different forms of utilitarianism have been advanced. The most cogent (and certainly the most influential in moral and political discourse) is hedonistic act utilitarianism, which provides that the morally right action is that which produces the greatest amount of happiness or pleasure and the least amount of pain or unhappiness. This theory selects the avoidance of pain, and the corollary, the attainment of happiness, as the ultimate goals of morality. The splendour of utilitarianism is that each person's interest carries exactly the same weight. It provides that when we are faced with moral choices we must perform the action that will maximise the amount of happiness in the world. In this equation we must include the interests of all parties that are directly and indirectly affected by our decision. This includes our family, friends, work colleagues and even strangers and people in distant parts of the world.

Despite the appealing simplicity of utilitarianism and its egalitarian nature, it has received a lot of bad press over the past few decades, resulting in its demise as the leading normative theory. The criticisms of utilitarianism come in two main forms.

1.5.2 Horror Consequences Are Acceptable

The first is that utilitarianism fails to protect basic individual interests (such as rights and integrity[14]) and since it does not prohibit anything per se, condones horrendous outcomes, such as punishing the innocent[15] and forcing organ donations where the donations would maximise happiness by saving the lives of many or assisting those most in need.[16]

However, on closer reflection, many of the appalling conclusions utilitarianism supposedly commits us to, do not *really* insurmountably trouble us on a post-philosophical level to the extent that one is justified in arguing that any theory which approves of such outcomes must necessarily be flawed.[17] The horror scenarios which it is claimed utilitarians are committed to are in fact consistent with the decisions we as individuals and societies as a whole readily have made and continue to make when faced with extreme and desperate circumstances. Once we accept that our decisions in extreme situations will be confined to desperate predicaments and will not serve to henceforth diminish the high regard we normally have for important individual concerns and interests, we find that when placed between a rock and a hard place we do and *should*, though perhaps somewhat begrudgingly, take the utilitarian option. In the face of extreme situations we are quite ready to accept that one should, or even must, sacrifice oneself or others for the good of the whole.

A pointed example is the decision by the English Prime Minister of the day, Winston Churchill, to sacrifice the lives of the residents of Coventry in order to not alert the Germans that the English had deciphered German radio messages. On 14 November, 1940 the English decoded plans that the Germans were about to air bomb Coventry. If Coventry were evacuated or its inhabitants advised to take special precautions against the raid the Germans would know that their code had been cracked, and the English would be unable to obtain future information about the intentions of its enemy. Churchill elected not to warn the citizens of Coventry, and many hundreds were killed in the raid which followed. The lives were sacrificed in order not to reveal the secret that would hopefully save many more lives in the future.[18]

A famous modern day example which comes closest to the dilemma of choosing whether to frame the innocent or tolerate massive abuses of rights followed the Rodney King beating in Los Angeles in 3 March 1991. The four police officers who beat King were acquitted under State law of any offence regarding the incident. Riots ensued, resulting in widespread looting, damage to property, and dozens of deaths. Shortly afterwards, the Federal Government announced the almost unprecedented step that the police officers, who one must remember were found not guilty of any offence, would be tried on federal civil rights charges relating to the incident. Two of the police officers were duly found guilty for violating King's civil rights, despite the apparent double jeopardy involved, and were sentenced to thirty months' imprisonment. Whatever one's view of the government's motivation for committing the police officers on federal charges, it seems that justice took a back seat—for a while.[19]

What we actually do does not necessarily justify what *ought* to be done. Morality is normative, not descriptive in nature: an 'ought' cannot be derived from an 'is'.[20] Nevertheless, the above account is telling because the force of the objection that utilitarianism commits us to horrendous consequences lies in the fact that the utilitarian outcomes so trouble our moral consciousness that utilitarianism can thereby be dismissed on the basis that 'there must be a mistake somewhere'. However, the objection loses its force when it is shown that the consequences utilitarianism commits us to are in fact no worse than other activities we condone.

Further, the horror scenario or extreme moral crisis criticism cuts both ways. While rights philosophers have gained much mileage from conjuring up extreme examples which supposedly commit utilitarians to perverse conclusions, it is not difficult to cite examples which demonstrate the total impotence of rights based theories to resolve moral dilemmas. A recent example is the outcome and reasoning in the case of *A (Children)*[21]—the Jodie and Mary Siamese Twins case.

1.5.3 Only Utilitarianism Can Deal with Hard Cases

In *A (Children)* the English Court of Appeal was confronted with what it understandably termed the truly agonising dilemma of what ought to be done in the case of conjoined twins: Mary and Jodie.[22] They each had their own brain, heart and lungs and other vital organs and they each had arms and legs. They were joined at the lower abdomen, and could be separated. But the operation would kill the weaker twin, Mary. That is because her lungs and heart were too deficient to oxygenate and pump blood through her body. Had she been born a singleton, she would not have been viable and resuscitation would have been abandoned. She would have died shortly after her birth. She was alive only because a common artery enabled her sister, who was stronger, to circulate life sustaining oxygenated blood for both of them. Separation would have required the clamping and then the severing of that common artery. Within minutes of doing so Mary would die (and ultimately—following the operation—did so). Yet if the operation did not take place, both would have died within about three to six months.

The parents refused to consent to the operation. The twins were equal in their eyes and they could not agree to kill one even to save the other. As devout Roman Catholics they sincerely believed that it is God's will that their children were afflicted as they are and they must be left in God's hands. The doctors believed that they could carry out the operation so as to give Jodie a life which would be in most respects relatively normal.

In the circumstances, the hospital sought a declaration that the operation may be lawfully carried out. Johnson J in exercise of the inherent jurisdiction of the High Court granted it on 25 August 2000. The parents applied to the Court of Appeal for leave to appeal against his order. The Court, while granting permission to appeal, unanimously dismissed the appeal.

The judgment in *A (Children)* is over 100 pages in length. The justificatory rationale adopted by two of the Lord Justices, Ward and Brooke LJJ, is found in about a dozen words. After considering a plethora of 'relevant' rights claims, including the right to life and the parents right to choose and getting no closer to a solution, the answer was only forthcoming when the Lord Justices eventually got around to looking at the situation from a utilitarian perspective. In the end, they resolved the matter 'by choosing the lesser of the two evils and so finding the least detrimental alternative'.[23]

Of course it is theoretically possible to *attempt* to resolve such dilemmas on the basis of rights theory alone, but his can lead to somewhat curious results. In an attempt to buttress his view that surgery would be in Mary's best interests, Walker LJ stated:

> [That surgery would also be in the] best interests of Mary, since for the twins to remain alive and conjoined in the way they are would be to deprive them of the bodily integrity and human dignity which is the right of each of them.[24]

The conclusion reached by Walker LJ is quite remarkable when one remembers that he is talking about the interests of Mary, whom the operation will kill. Bodily integrity and human dignity sound like fine ideals, and undoubtedly the more the better, but they would not seem to be of much value in the grave. Surely a pre-condition to the splendour of such virtues is one's

1.5.4 Utilitarian Rights

The other main criticism of utilitarianism is that it cannot protect any individual interest. However, on closer analysis, rights have a place in a utilitarian ethic, and what is more, it is only against this background that rights can be explained and their source justified. Utilitarianism provides a sounder foundation for rights than any other competing theory. For the utilitarian, the answer to why rights exist is simple: recognition of them best promotes general utility. Their content is discovered through empirical observations regarding the patterns of behaviour which best advance the utilitarian cause.

Difficulties in performing the utilitarian calculus regarding each decision make it desirable that we ascribe certain rights and interests to people, which evidence shows tend to maximise happiness[25] — even more happiness than if decisions were made without such guidelines. Rights save time and energy by serving as shortcuts to assist us in attaining desirable consequences. By labelling certain interests as rights, we are spared the tedious task of establishing the importance of a particular interest as a first premise in practical arguments.[26]

1.5.5 No Absolute Rights—Case Example: Torture

Thus utilitarianism is able to explain the existence and importance of rights. It is just that rights do not have a life of their own (they are derivative, not foundational) as is the case with deontological theories. Due to the derivative character of utilitarian rights, they do not carry the same degree of absolutism or 'must be doneness' as those based on deontological theories. However, this is not a criticism of a utilitarian model of rights, since it is farcical to claim that rights are absolute. The absurdity of absolute rights is illustrated by the extreme lengths some have gone to in order to attempt to justify such a notion. For example, in search of an absolute right it has been stated that 'the right of a mother not to be tortured to death by her son is absolute'.[27] However even such extravagant examples fail. One could hardly begrudge a son torturing his mother to death if this is the only way to save the lives of all his other relatives whom the mother is about to unjustifiably kill.

Indeed incidence of mistreatment by US officials of enemy combatants during their occupation of Iraq and Afghanistan in the early to mid 2000s led to widespread debate regarding the morality of torture. Most commentators stated that there should be an absolute prohibition on torture. Torture is in fact prohibited at international law and is not officially sanctioned by the domestic law of any country. Despite this, it is widely used. Contrary to widespread belief, torture is not the preserve of despot military regimes in third world nations. It is widely assumed that the United States tortured senior Al Qaeda leader Khalid Shaikh Mohammad. There is irrefutable evidence that it tortured large numbers of Iraqi prisoners and there is strong evidence that it tortured prisoners at Guantanamo Bay prison in Cuba, where suspected Al Qaeda terrorists are held.

The belief that torture is *always* wrong is, however, misguided and symptomatic of the alarmist and reflexive responses typically emanating from social commentators who do not have a coherent moral theory from which they can make sound moral judgments.[28] A supposed absolute ban on torture is this type of absolutist and shallow rhetoric that lies at the core of many distorted moral judgments that we as a community continue to make, resulting in an enormous amount of injustice and suffering in our society and far beyond our borders. It is the reason why there is often a void between good intentions and good consequences. This gulf is considered at length in this book, but first a little more about torture.

Consider the following example, a terrorist network has activated a large bomb on one of hundreds of commercial planes carrying over three hundred passengers that is flying somewhere in the world at any point in time. The bomb is set to explode in 30 minutes. The leader of the terrorist organisation announces this via a statement on the Internet. He states that the bomb was planted by one of his colleagues at one of the major airports in the world in the past few hours. No details are provided regarding the location of the plane where the bomb is located. Unbeknown to him, he was under police surveillance and is immediately apprehended by police. The terrorist leader refuses to answer any questions to police, declaring that the passengers must die and will shortly.

Who in the world would deny that all possible means should be used to extract the details of the plane and the location of the bomb? The answer is very few. Claims that there is an absolute proscription against torture would run very hollow. The passengers, their relatives and friends and society in general would expect that all means should be used to extract the information, even if the pain and suffering imposed on the terrorist resulted in his annihilation. Given this, it is illogical to insist on a blanket prohibition against torture.

The reason that torture in such a case is defensible and necessary is because the justification manifests from the closest thing we have to inviolable right: the right to self defence (which has as its underpinnings the legal notion of 'necessity'), which extends to the defence of another. Given the choice between inflicting a relatively small level of harm on a wrongdoer and saving an innocent person, it is verging on moral indecency to prefer the interests of the wrongdoer.

The analogy with self-defence is further sharpened by considering the paradigm hostage taking scenario, where a wrongdoer takes a hostage and points a gun to the hostage's head threatening to kill the hostage unless a certain (unreasonable) demand is met. In such a case it is not only permissible, but desirable for police to shoot (and kill) the wrongdoer if they can get a 'clear shot'. This is especially the case if it is known that the wrongdoer has a history of serious violence—and hence is more likely to carry out the threat.

There is no logical or moral difference between this scenario and one where there is overwhelming evidence that a wrongdoer has kidnapped an innocent person and informs police that the victim will suffocate or be decapitated by a co-offender if certain demands are not met. In the first scenario, it is universally accepted that it is permissible to violate the right to life of the aggressor to save an innocent person. How can it be wrong to violate an even less important right (the right to physical integrity) by torturing the aggressor in order to save an innocent life in the second scenario? The scenarios are morally equivalent.

Torture is permissible where the evidence suggests that this is the only means, due to the immediacy of the situation, to save the life of an innocent agent. What level of harm can be inflicted to save the innocent person? As with self-defence, lethal force is justifiable. Obviously people cannot provide information if they are killed and hence torture should not be used in a way that aims to have this outcome. However, this is a risk that is inherent whenever one inflicts harm on others. It is a risk that is worth taking if it is the only means available to save innocent lives.

It is important to note that the only situation where torture is justifiable is where it is the only means available to avert a moral catastrophe and save innocent lives. Thus of course I do not condone any of the recent claims of torture which were apparently undertaken as punitive measures or in a bid to acquire information where there was no evidence of an immediate risk to the life of an innocent person.

The examples above are hypothetical but the force of the argument cannot be dismissed on that basis. Fantastic examples play an important role in the evaluation of moral principles and theories since they sharpen the contrasts between them and illuminate the logical conclusions of the respective principles and in this way test the true strength of our commitment to the principles. Moreover, given the extreme measure that some disgruntled groups around the world are now taking to advance their causes, it is not difficult to envisage the community being faced with such a reality. We should be prepared for that and appoint a small number of officials who are competent to issue 'torture warrants' to police. Indeed in November 2005, the US Vice President, Dick Cheney, made an appeal to Republican senators to allow the CIA to torture suspects in US custody where this was necessary to prevent a terrorist attack.[29]

There are three main counter arguments to the proposal to allow torture in limited circumstances. The first is the slippery slope argument: 'if you start allowing torture in a limited context, the situations in which it will be used will increase'.

The slippery slope or the dangerous precedent argument (also often run under the banners of 'thin end of the wedge'; 'the tip of the iceberg' or the 'floodgates argument'), is often invoked in relation to acts which in themselves are justified, but which have similarities with objectionable practices, and urges that in morally appraising an action we must not only consider its intrinsic features but also the likelihood of it being used as a basis for condoning similar, but in fact relevantly different undesirable practices.

The slippery slope argument has been criticised on the basis that it logically prevents change and advancement. It amounts to the principle, so the argument runs, that:

> You should not now do an admittedly right action for fear that you . . . should not have the courage to do the right thing in some future case, which ex hypothesi is essentially different, but superficially resembles the present one. Every public action which is not customary, either is wrong, or, if it is right, is a dangerous precedent. It follows that nothing should ever be done for the first time.[30]

This, however, fails to recognise the real force behind the slippery slope argument, which lies in our propensity to justify 'progress' by analogising from one situation to another, and our fallibility in discerning the relevant and significant factors about the practices we are comparing. There are two versions of the slippery slope argument: the logical and empirical.

The logical form of the argument is the view that the clear boundaries cannot be drawn around the practice under consideration. In the context of torture, this form of the argument is unconvincing. The *reasons* advanced in favour of limited torture, namely the compassionate desire to save an innocent life are not logically capable of condoning torture in wider circumstances. None of the known incidence of torture that have ever been committed throughout the history of humankind would seem to fit within the criteria set out above. A very bright line can be drawn between using torture as a last resort to save innocent lives, as opposed to using torture as an act of suppression, domination or cruelty.

The empirical version of the argument provides that if torture is condoned in any circumstances, it will as a matter of fact, lead to a greater preparedness to use it in other circumstances where it is not justifiable. This version rests on the view that any torture would desensitise the human condition to such acts, leading to the greater use of torture.

This argument also fails. First, the floodgates are already open- torture is used widely, despite the absolute legal prohibition against it. Amnesty International has recently reported that they had received, during 2003, reports of torture and ill-treatment from 132 countries, including the United States, Canada, Japan, France, Italy, Spain and Germany. It is, in fact, arguable that it is the existence of an unrealistic 'absolute' ban on torture that has driven torture 'beneath the radar screen of accountability' and that the legalization of torture in very rare circumstances would in fact reduce the instances of torture because of the increased level of accountability.

Moreover, often there is no such thing as a slippery slope, thin end of the wedge or tip of the ice berg. As we shall see in chapters 6 and 7, floodgates arguments only work where there is evidence that a practice once sanctioned has in fact expanded in its scope of application. This is not the case with the proposal to use torture as a means to save lives. Torture has never been used in such a context. It is most unlikely that if torture was sanctioned in the extremely limited circumstance above that the floodgates would burst open, just as the use of state sanctioned killing (capital punishment) did not result in a greater inclination to kill by the State to kill its citizenry. Thus, critics of the proposal to legalise torture in limited circumstances need to address the suggestion that is being advanced not avoid the issue by the inappropriate use of their imagination.

The second main argument against a limited use of torture is that it will 'dehumanise' society as a whole. This is no more true in the case of torture in the circumstances outlined above than as a result of our tolerance towards self-defence in general. The contrary is in fact true; a society that elects to favour the interests of wrongdoers over those of the innocent, when a choice must be made between the respective interests of two, is morally warped and in need of serious ethical re-wiring. Those who favour the absolute ban of torture are in effect saying that we should not do all that is possible to save the destruction of innocent lives and that it is less bad to allow innocent people to be killed than to violate the physical integrity of wrongdoers. It is at this point that the irrationality of their position becomes clear—there is no underlying theory that justifies the view that death is a less serious harm than physical pain.

A third reason why some people support a complete ban on torture is that we can never be totally sure that torturing a person will in fact result in us saving an innocent life. In particular, it has been argued that torture often does not work—suspects will not provide the relevant information. This, however, is the same situation as in all cases of self-defence. Reverting to the above hostage example, the gun might in fact be empty. Still it is permissible to shoot. Like all decisions we must base them on the best evidence at the time. Absence of perfect information regarding the outcome of a proposed form of conduct is never a good reason not to act, otherwise we would never leave our houses—we might get a hit by a car on the way to work.

Sometimes torture will not work, but anecdotal evidence that it often works is found in the large amount of court cases where confessions by accused people are ruled inadmissible because they were extracted by police beatings. If people are willing to betray themselves as a result of physical persuasion, surely many would be willing to betray their causes when placed under similar types of pressure. Further there are many examples of suspects yielding to torture. Marcy Strauss gives the example of famous terrorist Abu Nidel who was 'broken' by Jordan officials and the 1993 World Trade Centre bombings which were cracked by the Philippines when they threatened a suspect that they would send him for torture.[31]

Against this is evidence from some people that have observed torture and claim that it does not work. This does not rebut my proposal. Previous incidents of 'failed' torture have no relevance to the discussion at hand. They were invariably crude practices, not undertaken in a controlled clinical environment where there were safeguards to ensure that the suspect did in fact have the requisite knowledge. They were 'fishing expeditions' often motivated by a punitive desire, in the 'hope' that the suspect may divulge some information. This has no similarity with the torture performed in a clinical environment only upon people known to have life saving information. In such circumstances, we obviously cannot be guaranteed that torture will work, but we can be virtually certain that doing nothing will fail when we are faced with an imminent catastrophe.

Thus, in fact torture in the circumstances advocated above is a humanistic, life –affirming, approach. Opponents of this view are committed to the absurd view that we should prefer the physical integrity of wrongdoers over the lives of innocent people. This is logically flawed and morally reprehensible. The baroness of their argument is highlighted by considering what they could possibly say to the relatives of the victims of the plane bombing in the above example if they decided not to torture the suspect in an attempt to save the lives of the passengers. They would need to do better than sending them copies (albeit framed) of the Convention against torture—but there is nothing else.

Will a real life situation actually occur where the only option is between torturing a wrongdoer or saving an innocent person? Perhaps not. Nevertheless, the above argument in favour of torture in limited circumstances highlights several failings of rights based theories. First, it shows that no right or interest is absolute. Secondly, rights must always yield to consequences, which are the ultimate criteria upon which the soundness of a decision is gauged. Lost lives hurt a lot more than bent 'principles'. Thirdly, we must take responsibility not only for the things that we do, but also for the things that we can, but fail to prevent. The retort that we are not responsible for the lives lost as a decision not to torture a wrongdoer because we did not 'create' the situation, is code for moral indifference.

As noted above, at the core of the utilitarian theory is the notion of happiness. A common criticism of utilitarianism is that given the diversity of human nature, it is too vague to provide guidance on importance matters. As we shall see in the next chapter, wide-ranging recent research into the human condition has shown that we are not unique after all. As a species, despite ostensible differences, we are very similar in terms of the things that promote our common good.

NOTES

1. J L Mackie, *Inventing Right and Wrong* (1977), 122–3.

2. Thus, the morality I am alluding to is not in the sense that it is independent to the existence of human beings. There are no moral truths 'out there' that exist outside the human condition. This does not undercut the claim to objectivity. The same analysis applies in relation to the statement that it is (objectively) true that knives kill people. Change the way people are constructed, you change the truth of the statement. However, we still feel that the statement that 'knives kill people' is objective in a meaningful sense. So too, the normative ethic I describe. It is meaningful simply because we have an external reference by which moral judgments can be evaluated: whether they serve to promote overall human happiness.

3. See T Campbell, *The Legal Theory of Ethical Positivism* (1996) 161–88, who discusses the near universal trend towards Bills of Rights and constitutional rights as a focus for political choice.

4. S I Benn, 'Human rights—For Whom and For What?', in E Kamenka and A E Tay (eds), *Human Rights* (1978) 59, 61.

5. T Campbell, 'Realizing Human Rights', in T Campbell et al (eds), *Human Rights: From Rhetoric to Reality* (1996) 1, 13.

6. Almost to the point where it is not unthinkable to propose that the 'escalation of rights rhetoric is out of control': see L W Sumner, *The Moral Foundation of Rights* (1987) 1.

7. Ibid.
8. H L A Hart, *Essays in Jurisprudence and Philosophy* (1983), 196–7.
9. J Eckert, 'Legal Roots of Human Dignity in German Law' in D Kretzmer and K Eckart (eds), *The Concept of Human Dignity in Human Rights Discourse* (2002) 41, 52.
10. Y Arieli, 'The Emergence of the Doctrine of the Human Dignity of Man' in D Kretzmer and K Eckart (eds), *The Concept of Human Dignity in Human Rights Discourse* (2002) 1, 8.
11. Sumner, above n 6, 8–9.
12. Campbell, *The Legal Theory of Ethical Positivism*, above n 23, 165.
13. Ibid.
14. For example, see Williams' famous Jim, Pedro and the Indians example: B Williams, 'A Critique of Utilitarianism', in J C C Smart and B Williams (eds), *Utilitarianism: For and Against* (1973) 99.
15. For example, see the small town sheriff example, in H J McCloskey, *Meta-Ethics and Normative Ethics* (1969) 180–1.
16. R Nozick, *Anarchy State and Utopia* (1974) 206–7.
17. The distinction I am making between intuitive moral judgements and those formed after due reflection is similar to that made by R M Hare between intuitive and critical levels of moral thinking: see R M Hare, *Moral Thinking: Its Levels, Methods and Point* (1981).
18. See M Velasquez and C Rostankowski, 'Utilitarian Ethics' in M Velasquez and C Rostankowski (eds), *Ethics: Theory and Practice* (1985) ch 4.
19. For an account of these events, see J Gibbs, *Race and Justice* (1996); D Cole, *No Equal Justice: Race and Class in the American Justice System* (1999) 23.
20. This has been used as an argument against a naturalistic view of morality. However, see C R Pigden, 'Naturalism' in P Singer (ed), *A Companion to Ethics* (1991) 421, 422–6, where he points that this phenomenon simply reflects the conservative nature of logic—you cannot get out of it, what you do not put in.
21. B1/2000/2969, 22 September 2000: http://www.courtservice.gov.uk/judgments/judg-home.htm (henceforth *A (Children)*. All pages numbers refer to the page number of the document printed from this site.
22. The facts are taken from the judgment of Ward LJ, 7–8.
23. See Ward LJ at 42.
24. Ibid, 98.
25. These rights, however, are never decisive and must be disregarded where they would not cause net happiness (otherwise this would be to go down the rule utilitarianism track).
26. See J Raz, *Morality of Freedom* (1986), 191. Raz also provides that rights are useful because they enable us to settle on shared intermediary conclusions, despite considerable dispute regarding the grounds for the conclusions. See also, A Marmor, 'On the Limits of Rights' (1997) 16 *Law and Philosophy* 1, 17.
27. A Gewirth, *Human Rights: Essays on Justification and Applications* (1982) 232.

28. For further comments on the torture debate, see M Bagaric and J Clarke, 'Not enough (official) torture in the world? The circumstances in which torture is morally justifiable' (2005) 39 *University of San Francisco Law Review* 581.

29. D Espo, L Sidoti, 'Cheney bid for torture ban exemption', *The Age*, 6 November 9.

30. F M Cornford, *The Microcosmographia Academica* (Cambridge University Press, 1908) 23.

31. M Strauss 'Torture' (2004) 48 *NYL Sch L Rev* 201.

Chapter Two

The Things That Make us Happy

2.1 OVERVIEW OF THE CONVERGENCE OF THE HUMAN CONDITION

As we saw in the previous chapter a key issue regarding the objectivity and nature of morality is whether the human condition is sufficiently convergent to make some general, yet instructive, conclusions regarding the matters that are conducive to human flourishing.

The capacity to establish moral standards founded on the notion of happiness has been severely curtailed over the ages because happiness has been viewed as being too vague and subjective to provide pointed answers regarding the things that are important for human flourishing. While it is obvious that people need food, shelter, health care and a sense of personal security, beyond this the general view has been that the conditions that promote happiness vary from person to person. This is supported by the almost infinite number of activities and projects that people choose to pursue. The richness and diversity of the human species seems to militate against the idea that there is even approximate convergence concerning the things that are conducive to happiness. Hence, moral reformers and commentators have largely bypassed empirical data in framing moral standards.

In the past few decades, however, there has been an explosion in the amount of studies conducted into human happiness and well-being. Happiness has increasingly become a scientific rather than theoretical concept. The overriding pursuit of happiness is now a psychological truism rather than a 'heady' aspirational objective. There is now a dedicated international journal, the 'Journal of Happiness Studies' which is devoted to articles based on empirical studies of what makes people happy (or indeed unhappy), and over the last few years there has been a number of important works looking at what makes people happy, and in particular looking at whether there is a positive or negative correlation between happiness and wealth creation. Most recently, in January 2005 *Time* Magazine devoted a whole edition to exploring 'The New Science of Happiness'.

While noting the diversity in the range of activities through which people choose to express themselves, the studies show that at the base we are not that different after all. At the core, humans are wired pretty much the same. While some people prefer singing in a choir as opposed to boxing in a ring, and others prefer repairing motor vehicles to writing poetry, we should not allow these superficial differences to divert us from the fact that we have the same basal needs and our well-being is promoted by the same type of things.

We can now confidently identify the things that make us happy. We have the same basic wants and needs and it is possible to develop a road map to happiness. There will no doubt be sceptics who will remain slaves to unsubstantiated economic and social objectives, such as the pursuit of economic rationalism or an esoteric form of justice (as most versions of justice tend to be), despite the emerging evidence of what it is that really matters to people. To this end, it is important to point out that the scientific methodology used to ascertain the results relating to human well-being is the same as that used to obtain medical and biological information about people. Thus, a denial that, for example, money does not cause happiness is just as specious as the claim that excess alcohol does not cause sclerosis of the liver. In this respect it is particularly important to note that one or two counter-examples do not disprove a general point. The claim that some people are happier after they make lots of money no more disproves the point that money does not make people happy, than the fact that one has a relative who drank two bottles of wine a day and lived until he or she was 95 years of age disproves the link between alcohol and liver damage.

In the next section, I discuss the nature of happiness and its importance to human beings. I then discuss the results of happiness studies and spell out the activities which promote happiness. This is followed by a discussion of the relevance of the studies to the development of moral standards.

2.2 WHAT IS HAPPINESS?

In *Nicomachean Ethics*, Aristotle wrote that happiness is 'the whole aim and end of human existence'. According to Aristotle:

> Happiness is an activity; and activity plainly comes into being and is not present at the start like a piece of property . . . happiness is good activity, not amusement

> ... for, in a word, everything that we choose we choose for the sake of something else—except happiness, which is an end ... for happiness does not lie in such occupations, but, as we have said before, in virtuous activities ... Happiness extends, then, just so far as contemplation does, and those to whom contemplation more fully belongs are more truly happy, not as a mere concomitant but in virtue of the contemplation; for this is in itself precious. Happiness, therefore, must be some form of contemplation.

For the ancient Greeks and Romans, to be happy was to live serenely, above the world's swings of passion and material fortune.[1] For Epicurus, happiness derived from life's sustainable pleasures, such as tranquil peace of the mind.[2]

Numerous other definitions have been put forward over the centuries, however, in essence happiness is:

> A pervasive sense that life is good. Well-being outlasts yesterday's moment of elation, today's buoyant mood, and tomorrow's hard time; it is an ongoing perception that this time of one's life, or even life as a whole, is fulfilling, meaningful, and pleasant.[3]

As we shall see below happiness can be further broken into different types of sentiments, namely gratifications and pleasures. Moreover, we shall also see that not only can happiness be defined, but it can be scientifically measured by means of devices that detect brain activity.

2.3 WHY HAPPINESS IS IMPORTANT

There are two levels where the issue of why happiness is important becomes relevant. The first is at the level of personal motivation and desire, it being suggested that happiness is the ultimate aim of mankind. However, what proof is there of this?

2.3.1 As an Empirical Fact People Desire Happiness Most

Accordingly to Jeremy Bentham, this premise that people desire happiness most is incapable of proof. For him, it was the ultimate principle, which could not be proved by another principle: 'is it susceptible of any direct proof? It should seem not: for that which is used to prove every thing else, cannot itself be proved: a chain of proofs must have their commencement somewhere'.[4]

Nevertheless, something more beyond the assertion of the premise can be said. The evidence in favour of this premise is the incongruity in the assertion that 'I don't want to be happy'. Such a statement normally prompts puzzlement and requires an explanation—far more so than the denial of any other desire. It normally leads to a suspicion that the person is either confused, irrational or disingenuous. The same degree of suspicion does not attach to a denial of other desires, which are often regarded as being highly pervasive, such as the desire to be wealthy, wise, famous, beautiful, or even healthy. This observation supports the view that in the end the thing which we desire most is to be happy.

In addition to this, apart from the intrinsic benefit stemming from happiness, there are derivative benefits flowing from this. The benefits of happiness go beyond the psychic sensation. Happy people report less aches and pains and are more energetic, decisive and flexible. They also tolerate more frustration and are less likely to be abusive. They are more forgiving and are good to have around because they are more willing to help those in need.[5] 'The feel-good, do-good phenomenon' is genuine. Thus, 'human happiness is both an end—better to live fulfilled, with joy—and a means to a better caring and healthy society'.[6]

2.3.2 At the Normative Level People Cannot Be Expected To Ignore Their Basic Wants

Secondly, happiness is important at the normative level. In this regard there is a total synergy between what we want and what we should be doing. Given that soundest moral theory is utilitarianism, morality and human nature both urge us to act in a manner that promotes happiness.

This is a welcome overlap. If moral theory required of us to desist from pursuing happiness, as a matter of psychological reality, it would become self-defeating. If the ultimate principle guiding our conduct fails to reflect our ultimate desire, it would become redundant very quickly. Human discipline is not such that we are capable of suppressing our fundamental desires, especially those that are not inherently harmful to the interests of others, for prolonged periods of time.

2.4 WHAT MAKES PEOPLE HAPPY?

So what is that makes people happy?

The starting point is one of the most interesting and important books of the late 20th century, *The Pursuit of Happiness*, by David Myers in which he draws together the results of hundreds of surveys on human well being in search of common variables that make people happy.

2.4.1 Methodology

The methodology used in the surveys reported in David Myers' book is the same as that adopted in relation to most scientific experiments. A hypothesis is developed and is then tested through experimentation involving a representative and a statistically significant number of respondents. This method is far more accurate than haphazard sampling.[7]

To ascertain people's sense of well-being, respondents were asked to report their feelings of happiness or unhappiness along with their thoughts of how satisfying their lives were.[8] The results were, not surprisingly, that people who feel happy also think their lives are satisfying. Sometimes this was probed according to a single measure, on other occasions researchers probed with multi-item measures. One method which was used to gauge the impact of suspected variables on happiness was to give two equivalent groups an experience that differed only in that factor. Thus, in order to determine if people are happier by accumulating wealth, people were randomly assigned to either experience or not experience this factor.[9]

In terms of how happiness is tested, happiness is obviously a state of mind and the ultimate and only judge is the individual. If you feel happy, you are happy. Despite this, there is obviously the problem that people may be disingenuous in their self-reports of happiness. And indeed, there is a distinct tendency for people to over-report good feelings.[10] However, this does not undermine the accuracy of the studies. This is because happiness is ultimately measured by the sensations felt by the individual in question.

> To discover who is happiest, and why, we need only assume that those who say they are "very happy" or "completely satisfied" do experience greater well-being than those who say they are unhappy or dissatisfied.[11]

Another possible bias in the results is the momentary moods of people. This does not, however, impugn the validity of the results. People tend to attribute judgements of well-being to their overall situation as opposed to transient feelings. It is noteworthy that the happiness level of people is remarkably consistent over their lifetime. Also, people experience both good and bad transient mood altering experiences. Thus, to the extent these experiences impact on subjective feelings of well-being they will in a properly selected sample of people cancel each other out in terms of the overall result. Further, when comparing across samples each sample will have approximately equal numbers of people in good and bad moods at the time of the respective studies.

It follows that the same empirical techniques that have been used to test scientific truths apply here. The findings, therefore, are as equally valid as

2.4.2 The Results—The Things That Make People Happy

2.4.2.1 Participation and Freedom

Myers found that people function best in circumstances of democracy and personal freedom. Involvement and a sense of contribution and control over the activities that impact on one's life are key ingredients to a sense of well-being. The connection between participation, control and happiness manifests in many sorts of domains: 'study after study finds that when workers have more control—when they can help define their own goals and hours and when they can participate in decision making—their job satisfaction rises'.[12]

In a slightly different context, a study by Judith Rodin encouraged nursing home patients to contribute more to the policies determining their environment in the nursing home. Ninety three per cent became more alert, active and happy.[13] Myers notes that 'similar results have been obtained after allowing prisoners to move chairs and control the room lights and the TV'.[14] Another interesting point to emerge is that the more developed the institutions of direct democracy, the happier the individuals are, *irrespective* of the outcome of the democratic process.[15]

2.4.2.2 Pursing Projects and Goals

People need to be active in pursuing projects. The more challenged a person is, whether by a job, hobby or sport, the happier he or she is likely to be.[16] To this extent happiness results from intellectual and physical challenges, not mindless passivity—such as watching television. Studies have found that in general 'the less expensive (and generally more involving) a leisure activity, the happier people are doing it. Most people are happier gardening than power boating, talking to a friend than watching TV'.[17] TV in particular is inimical to happiness. The message here is clear—get off the couch and get active, do something! One proviso to this is that while work can be a source of satisfaction, it should not be over done. Regular periods of relaxation are conducive to happiness.[18] In order for people to participate in activities and maintain a semblance of control in their lives it is important that people enjoy a large degree of personal autonomy and hence autonomy ranks highly on the happiness barometer.

2.4.2.3 Happiness Does Not Wildly Fluctuate

One of the other more interesting findings is that objective life circumstances have only a small part to play in one's sense of well being. Human beings are remarkably adaptable and resilient. The consistent (and astonishing) result is that people who experience the worst possible catastrophes (such as paralysis or being diagnosed with a life threatening illness) recover from these experiences to a point where their current mood is within a relatively short period of time more affected by the day's ordinary events than by the tragedy.[19] The converse situation applies regarding dramatically positive events. For example, wining the lottery provides only a short term boost and in fact in the long run most lottery winners are less happy after winning the lottery than before the win.[20]

These results are supported by a study of lottery winners by Philip Brickman.[21] In this study, twenty-two individuals who had recently won large amounts of money in the Illinois state lottery were compared with a group of people who lived near the recently rich individuals. All study participants were asked about their general happiness and how much pleasure they derived from everyday experiences, such as talking with a friend, eating breakfast, hearing a funny joke, and the like. The happiness of lottery winners was no different from that of people who had not experienced a large increase in their wealth, and the lottery winners actually reported being *less* pleased with everyday events.

However, it is important to note that we are not slaves to our pasts and inbred dispositions. Our traits and attitudes follow our behaviour. 'We are as likely to act ourselves into a new way of thinking as to think ourselves into a new way of acting'.[22] In fact 'going through the motions [and telling yourself that you are happy] can trigger the emotion'.[23]

2.4.2.4 Age is Irrelevant

Happiness is not age dependent. While people think that adolescents and the elderly are the unhappiest, this is not true. People of all ages report similar feelings of well-being.[24] In particular there is no evidence to support the supposed mid life crisis phenomena. Middle age people are no more dissatisfied than other people and there is no evidence of high levels of turmoil in this group of people.[25] The only related finding was that as we get older our feelings mellow. Average happiness stays about the same, but as we age we are less often very excited or very sad,[26] and as we age our priorities change. For example, older people report less satisfaction with their jobs and better align their aspirations with their attainments.[27]

2.4.2.5 Health and Gender as Predictors of Happiness

Health and fitness is a particularly important predictor of happiness across all ages: 'more than a hundred studies confirm that for adults of all age

... one predictor of happiness is health and physical fitness'.[28] Gender also has a role to play as a predictor of happiness. While men and women experience the same average happiness, women are twice as vulnerable to depression.[29]

2.4.2.5 Self-esteem is Good, but PeopleOverestimate Their Worth

Studies also report a number of interesting traits that are relevant to happiness. One in particular is our tendency to hold self-serving biases. People accept more responsibility for good deeds than bad events, and for successes than for failures.[30] On most subjective and socially desirable dimensions people see themselves as better than average.[31] People have an inflated confidence in the accuracy of their beliefs and judgments and are quicker to believe flattering descriptions of themselves than unflattering ones. We also engage in group pride—believing our group is better than another group.[32] However, this is not necessarily negative. Positive self illusions, which most of us have, protect us against anxiety and depression. Hence self-esteem is conducive to happiness.

2.4.2.6 Close Personal Connections are Important

Close friendships are also important to health and happiness.[33] Moreover, married people are normally happier than singles.[34] More generally, individualist societies are less collectively happy than communal societies. It seems that the rights wave is an illusion: personal identity, which encourages people to pursue such behaviour as leaving home when opportunity strikes and not to compromise themselves, is self-defeating. Being deprived of familiar attachments prompts a sense of meaninglessness:

> People in competitive, individualist cultures such as the United States, have more independence, make more money, take more pride in personal achievements, are less geographically bound near elderly parents, are less likely to prejudge those outside their groups, and enjoy more privacy. . . But compared to collectivists, individualists are also lonlier, more alienated, less likely to feel romantic love, more likely to divorce, more homicidal, and more vulnerable to stress related diseases.[35]'

Ultimately, Myers notes that totalitarianism, materialism and self-reliant individualism have deluded us with false promises of well-being.[36] In addition to this, there is a link between optimism and happiness. Optimists are healthier and enjoy greater success.[37] Another trait of happy people is that they are more outgoing. Extroverts, in study after study, report greater happiness and satisfaction with life.[38]

2.4.2.7 Money and Happiness

One of the most interesting aspects of the research reported by Myers involved the association between money and happiness. Empirical studies consistently show that there is only a modest connection between wealth and happiness. Following what is probably the most extensive and expansive assessment of well-being ever conducted—with representative samples of 170,000 people in a number of different countries, Ronald Inglehart notes that there are significant national differences in the levels of happiness experienced by people.[39] For example, year after year, the Danes, Irish and Dutch are happier and more satisfied with life than the French, Greeks and Italians. The results of this study showed that a nation's well-being correlated only modestly with national affluence. There seemed to be a far stronger connection between democracy and happiness. Interpreting these results David Myers states:

> Moreover, the surveyed nations differ in ways other than affluence, making it hard to disentangle cause and effect. For one thing, the most prosperous nations have enjoyed stable democratic governments, and there is a striking link between a history of stable democracy and national well-being. The thirteen nations that have maintained democratic institutions continuously since 1920 all enjoy higher life satisfaction levels than do the nations whose democracies developed after World War II or have not yet fully emerged.[40]

Thus, across countries there is not a strong link between happiness and wealth. Similar results emerge within countries. It is not the case that within any country that the happiest people are the rich.[41] This led Myers to conclude:

> So, whether we base our conclusions on self-reported happiness, rates of depression, or teen problems, our becoming better off over the past thirty years has not been accompanied by one iota of increased happiness or life satisfaction . . . Once beyond poverty, further economic growth does not appreciably improve [human happiness].[42]

It seems that 'if not wracked by hunger or hurt, people at all income levels can enjoy one another and experience comparable joy'.[43] Another interesting finding is that happiness is relevant to the attainment of others: we feel good or bad depending on whom we compare ourselves to.[44]

> Happiness shrivels with the gap between what we have and what we want, what we have and what we expected to have by now, what we have and what our neighbours have.[45]

This explains the reason that happiness increases when a person escapes poverty, but societies do not become happier as they progress from relative poverty to affluence.[46]

A fundamental issue which emerges is what is the point of diminishing returns beyond which more money no longer meaningfully contributes to our lives? In absolute terms the answer is the level of income that is necessary to provide one with the means necessary to provide for the essentials of living—food, shelter, and basic health care and education. Happiness also has a relative component. People who have less than their neighbours are unhappy about this. Thus, money ceases to have a significant effect on one's sense of well-being once they derive an average level of income.

In July 2005, the Australia Institute released a report, *Why Australians will Never Be Prosperous*, which shows that Australians may in fact become *less happy* when they have more income to play with. According to the report's authors, Dr Clive Hamilton and Claire Barboto, 21.2 per cent of surveyed individuals in the lowest income group (0–$25,000) indicated that they were totally satisfied with life whereas only 12.7 per cent of surveyed individuals in the highest income group ($100,001+) indicated that they were totally satisfied.

This disassociation between wealth and happiness was confirmed in a study about a decade later by Tim Kasser. Tim Kasser's, *The High Price of Materialism*, published in 2002,[47] provides a useful scientific explanation as to why personal well-being is not connected to the accumulation of wealth, but rather depends on basic core needs—our indicators of happiness. The book provides a 'psychological theory of materialism' and describes the research that supports it. This book is important due to the extensive research conducted by Kasser and his colleagues over a significant period of time. His research involved empirical studies, both clinical and laboratory that he and his colleagues conducted, as well as by other psychologists and social scientists, from countries around the globe. Importantly, the population samples included preschoolers, college students and adults from all around the world.

Kasser's study not only confirms previous studies in the area which have shown that beyond satisfying basic needs (such as food, shelter and clothing), further material gain does little to improve our overall well-being, but shows that people who focus on the accumulation of wealth and material possessions are actually *more likely to be unhappy*, and will experience anxiety, depression, low self-esteem and other problems. Materialistic values, according to Kasser, are counter-productive as over time they heighten insecurity which is one of the primary causes of unhappiness.

> Desires to have more and more material goods drive us into an ever more frantic pace of life. Not only must we work harder, but, once possessing the goods,

we have to maintain, upgrade, replace, insure, and constantly manage them. Thus, in the journey of life, materialists end up carrying an ever-heavier load, one that expends the energy necessary for living, loving, and learning—the really satisfying aspects of that journey. Thus materialism, although promoting happiness, actually creates strain and stress.[48]

He further notes:

> In recent years, scientific investigators working in a variety of fields have begun to tally the cost of a materialistic lifestyle. Although the body of empirical literature on materialism is not large, especially compared with what we know about topics such as depression, stereotyping, neurons, and memory, its findings are quite consistent. Indeed, what stands out across the studies is a simple fact: people who strongly value the pursuit of wealth and possessions report lower psychological well-being than those who are less concerned with such aims.

Kasser points out that a number of other investigators studying materialism have reached exactly the same conclusion as he did: that materialistic values are associated with low well-being.[49] Kasser refers, for example, to an Australian study by Shaun Saunders and Don Munro that found that a materialistic outlook in Australian students was associated with increased feelings of anger, anxiety, and depression, along with decreased life satisfaction.

Kasser writes that materialism as a value can quickly lose its persuasiveness when it is shown that materialism is really a coping mechanism to respond to insecurity (caused by non-nurturing parents, anxiety, poverty etc), but which in the long-term leaves people feeling more insecure. According to Kasser:

> My understanding of the connection among insecurity, a materialistic value orientation, and well-being is that sometimes people experience circumstances (non-nurturing parents, poverty, death anxiety) that lead them to feel insecure. This causes unhappiness and dissatisfaction, as security needs must be satisfied for good psychological health. At the same time, insecurity also makes it likely that people will pursue materialistic aims, as both inner predispositions and external consumer culture suggest that resources can purchase security. Thus, materialistic values are both a symptom of an underlying insecurity and a coping strategy taken on in an attempt to alleviate problems and satisfy needs.[50]

Happiness scientists also explain the quest for materialism as demonstrating our capacity for 'miswanting'. Daniel Gilbert of Harvard University's psychology department, working with a team including psychologist Tim Watson and Nobel laureate in economics, Daniel Kahneman, found from their study that our work in acquiring [material] things—such as homes, children, careers and wealth—is all based on how happy we predict they will make us. However, we overestimate the intensity of the happiness that these things bring, due to underestimating our capacity to adjust. For example, the new BMW will probably make us happy for a couple of weeks, or even months, but within about six months it will have become like wallpaper in our lives: there, but no longer able to provide the charge of joy it gave us initially.[51]

2.4.2.8 Overview of Happiness Studies

Thus in a nutshell the things that are conducive to happiness are fit and healthy bodies, realistic goals, self-esteem, optimism, an outgoing personality, a sense of control, close relationships, challenging work and active leisure, punctuated by adequate rest and a faith that entails communal support, purpose and acceptance. Myths about happiness include that it is bought by money and that religious faith suppresses happiness.

Kasser forms similar conclusions to Myers regarding the things that are necessary for happiness. He states that there are four sets of 'psychological needs' that are necessary for the motivation, functioning and well-being of all humans: (1) safety, security and sustenance—the human desire to remain alive and avoid early death—ie roof over our heads, food on the table, clothing to protect us ('the essentials of life'); (2) competence, efficacy and self-esteem 'involves a feeling that we are capable of doing what we set out to do and of obtaining the things we value. Competence and esteem needs also entail a desire to have a more positive than negative view of ourselves and to like ourselves. In essence, to fulfil these needs each of us must feel like a competent and worthy person'; (3) connectedness—the human desire for intimacy and closeness with others—'these needs lead us to belong to larger groups, such as churches, neighbourhood organizations, and teams. We need to feel that we belong and are connected with others' lives, be it as parents, friends, neighbours, or co-workers'; and (4) autonomy and authenticity—a desire for freedom to act on one's own and to have a feeling that one is self-directed, 'rather than feeling pressured or burdened by our circumstances, we need to pursue activities that provide us with challenge, interest and enjoyment. By doing so, we can feel ownership of our own behaviour, and thus feel both authentic and autonomous'.[52]

According to Kasser, 'well-being and quality of life increase when these four sets of needs are satisfied and decrease when they are not'.[53] Kasser refers to these psychological needs as 'intrinsic' values, which are 'based in people's real psychological needs, support their growth and development, and are inherently satisfying to pursue'. Kasser states that:

> Compared with materialistic people, those who believe intrinsic values are relatively important report greater happiness, enhanced psychological health, better

interpersonal relationships, more personal contribution to the community, and more concern for ecological issues. These findings are substantiated by work of researchers using different value measures, and by research conducted with various age and cultural groups.[54]

2.4.2.9 Positive Psychology—Types of Happiness Pleasures and Gratifications

The findings of Myers and Kasser are developed further by Martin Seligman who confers the label 'positive psychology' to the science of ascertaining the matters that are conducive to happiness.

Seligman in his book, *Authentic Happiness*, explains that his positive psychology consists of 'three pillars'.

> First is the study of positive emotion. Second is the study of positive traits, foremost among them the strengths and virtues, but also the "abilities" such as intelligence and athleticism. Third is the study of the positive institutions, such as democracy, strong families, and free inquiry, that support the virtues, which in turn support the positive emotions.[55]

According to positive psychologists there is a very strong correlation between the level of effort that people put into an activity, and the level of pleasure and happiness that they experience from the activity. Seligman examines intensively the concept of happiness, and believes that it embraces two very 'distinct kinds of things': pleasures and gratifications.

'Pleasures' have very clear positive sensory and emotional components: ecstasy, thrills, delight, mirth, exuberance, and comfort. They involve very little thinking, and thereby are essentially passive. In philosophy, these sensations are referred to as 'raw feels'. Gratifications, on the other hand, involve next to no 'raw feels', instead we become fully immersed and absorbed in the activity, through having to use our personal strengths to meet the challenge of fulfilling the action. Examples given by Seligman are rock climbing, reading a book, dancing and making a slam dunk. According to Seligman, the 'gratifications last longer than the pleasures, they involve quite a lot of thinking and interpretation, they do not habituate easily, and they are under-girdled by our strengths and virtues'.[56] These findings are consistent with those of Myers which suggest that the pursuit of challenging endeavours (typically and characteristically, long term projects) is conducive to happiness.

Seligman goes on to explore the distinction between gratifications (long term pleasures) and pleasures (short term 'treats'):

> [Gratification] is part and parcel of right action. It cannot be derived from bodily pleasure, nor is it a state that can be chemically induced or attained by any shortcuts. It can only be had by activity consonant with noble purpose. . . . The

pleasures can be discovered, nurtured, and amplified . . . but the gratifications cannot. The pleasures are about the senses and the emotions. The gratifications, in contrast, are about enacting personal strengths and weaknesses.[57]

Based on this dichotomy, Seligman outlines the agenda and role of positive psychology:

> The right question is the one Aristotle posed two thousand five hundred years ago: "What is the good life?" My main purpose in marking the gratifications off from the pleasures is to ask this great question anew, then provide a fresh and scientifically grounded answer. My answer is tied up in the identification and the use of your signature strengths.[58]

Importantly, to highlight the practical difference between gratifications and pleasures in terms of which is conducive to real happiness, Seligman refers to a study by Mike Csikzentmihalyi involving the experience sampling method (ESM).[59] ESM involves given pagers to those being surveyed, which beep during different times of the day and night. Each time the pager beeped, participants were asked to record what they were doing at that moment — what they were thinking, what emotions they were feeling, and how engaged they were. The overall finding was that participants recorded a much higher level of psychological well-being (including self-esteem and engagement) from participating in active events, and mild depression when involved in more passive pursuits, such as watching television.

In *Authentic Happiness*, Seligman also considers the rise of depression in the United States and suggests that, contrary to other explanations for this development over the last few decades, the main reason for this depression is an increase in the amount of passive, as opposed to active, consumption by Americans and greater reliance on 'short term pleasures':

> Depression is now ten times as prevalent as it was in 1960, and it strikes at a much younger age. . . . This is a paradox, since every objective indicator of well-being — purchasing power, amount of education, availability of music, and nutrition — has been going north, while every indicator of subjective well-being has been going south. How is this epidemic to be explained? . . .

> I have theorized that an ethos that builds unwarranted self-esteem, espouses victimology, and encourages rampant individualism has contributed to the subject . . . [however] there is another factor that looms as a cause of the epidemic: the over-reliance on short-cuts to happiness. Every wealthy nation creates more and more shortcuts to pleasure: television, drugs, shopping, loveless sex, spectator sports, and chocolate to name but a few. . . .

> What would happen if my entire life were made up of such easy pleasures, never calling on my strengths, never presenting challenges? Such a life sets one up for

depression. The strengths and virtues may wither during a life of taking shortcuts rather than choosing a life made full through the pursuit of gratifications.[60]

When we engage in pleasures, we are perhaps just consuming. The smell of perfume, the taste of raspberries, and the sensuality of a scalp rub are all high momentary delights, but they do not build anything for the future. . . . Pleasure marks the achievement of biological satiation, whereas gratification marks the achievement of psychological growth.[61]

It is important to note, however, that Van Boven and Gilovich make clear in their article that they are not suggesting that material purchases are simply not capable of making people happy. They make clear that 'the careful and measured acquisition of materials can no doubt advance one's happiness'.[62] They go on: 'our findings suggest, simply, that a person would be happier by investing in life experiences more than material possessions.' More generally, this study adds to the growing body of evidence suggesting that we are remarkably similar in the terms of the things that make us happy.

2.5 SCIENTIFIC MEASUREMENT OF HAPPINESS

The view that happiness can be objectively verified is supported by recent developments in brain research. A recent article published in the *New York Times*, 'Finding Happiness: Cajole Your Brain to Lean to the Left',[63] notes the work of brain researcher Dr Richard Davidson, director of the Laboratory for Affective Neuroscience at the University of Wisconsin, who in recent research using functional M.R.I. and advanced EEG analysis, has identified an index for the brain's set point for moods.

The images show that when people are emotionally distressed (anxious, angry or depressed), the most active sites in the brain are circuitry converging on the amygdala (part of the brain's emotional centres) and the right prefrontal cortex. When people are in positive moods those sites are quiet and there is heightened activity in the left prefrontal cortex.

Davidson believes a ready way to ascertain a person's typical mood range is to read the baseline levels of activity in these right and left prefrontal areas. That ratio predicts daily moods with surprising accuracy. The more the ratio tilts to the left the more happy a person actually is.

By taking readings on hundreds of people, Davidson has established a bell curve distribution, with most people in the middle, having a mix of good and bad moods. The data suggests that biology has a strong influence on the set point for our emotional range. One finding, for instance (which confirms earlier work noted above), is that 'both for people lucky enough to win a lottery and those unlucky souls who become paraplegic from an accident, by a year or so after the events their daily moods are about the same as before the momentous occurrences'. However, one's happiness set point is not beyond change, we are not slaves to our genes.

Davidson tested the left-right ratio on a senior Tibetan lama and he turned out to have the most extreme value to the left of the 175 people measured to that point. Moreover, happiness training is promising. A study by Davidson and Dr Jon Kabat-Zinn, founder of the Mindfulness-Based Stress Reduction Clinic at the University of Massachusetts Medical School in Worcester, reports the effects of training in mindfulness meditation. Mindfulness was taught to workers in a high-pressure biotech business for approximately two months. After the training, on average, the workers ratio shifted leftward and reported feeling more energized and less anxious. Thus, the results suggest that the emotion set point can shift, given the proper training.[64]

The results of the above studies confirm the objective reality of happiness and its potential to guide the development of moral standards. There is still much to be learnt about the precise conditions that are *most* conducive to human happiness. Even at this relatively early point, however, we still know a considerable degree about the circumstances in which people flourish most. The rest of this book applies the moral theory set out in chapter one and the known facts about what is important to human flourishing to the important moral issues of our time. In relation to certain moral issues, rights based theories continue to dominate societal judgements. Where this is the case, despite my reservations about the validity of such theories, I discuss the relevance of rights based theories to the issues at hand.

NOTES

1. D Myers, *The Pursuit of Happiness* (1992) 16.
2. Ibid, 16.
3. Ibid, 24.
4. Jeremy Bentham, 'An Introduction to the Principles of Morals and Legislation', in *Works 2* (TJ Bowring ed.,1843)
5. See Myers, above n 1, 20–21.
6. Ibid.
7. Ibid, 17.
8. Ibid, 24.
9. Ibid, 18–19.
10. Ibid, 27.
11. Ibid, 28.
12. Myers, above n 1, 130.

13. J Roden, 'Aging and Health: Effect of a Sense of Control' 1271 (1986) *Science* 233.
14. Myers, above n 1, at 115.
15. D S Frey, 'Happiness Prospers in Democracy' 1 (2000) *Journal of Happiness Studies* 79.
16. The study was conducted by Professor M Argyle and is reported in Tom Reid, 'Some Research that May Bring You a Degree of Happiness' *The Age* (Melbourne) 6 October 1998.
17. Myers, above n 1, 137
18. Ibid, 139.
19. Ibid, 48.
20. Ibid, 50–51.
21. This study is reported in Kasser, *The High Price of Materialism* (2002), 44.
22. Myer, above n 1, 123.
23. Ibid, 125.
24. Ibid, 69.
25. Ibid, 72–73.
26. Ibid, 73.
27. Ibid, 74–75.
28. Ibid, 76.
29. Ibid, 83.
30. Ibid, 110.
31. Ibid, 111.
32. Ibid, 111.
33. Ibid, 144.
34. Ibid, Ch 9.
35. Ibid, 147–48.
36. Ibid, 207.
37. Ibid, 117.
38. Ibid, 120.
39. R Inglehart, *Cultural Shift In Advanced Industrial Society* (1990).
40. Myers, above n 1, 36.
41. Ibid, 39.
42. Ibid, 43–44.
43. Ibid, 39.
44. Ibid, 56.
45. Ibid, 57.
46. Ibid, 56.
47. T Kasser, *The High Price of Materialism* (2002).
48. Ibid, xi.
49. Ibid, 21.
50. Ibid, 42.
51. See J Macken, 'Hunt for Happiness', *The Australian Financial Review*, 24 October 2003.
52. Kasser, above n 47, 24–25.

53. Ibid, 98.
54. Ibid, 98.
55. M Seligman, *Authentic Happiness* (2002), 102.
56. Ibid, xiii.
57. Ibid, 112.
58. Ibid, 121.
59. Ibid, 117.
60. Ibid, 118.
61. Ibid, 116–17.
62. Ibid, 120–1.
63. Daniel Coleman, 'Finding Happiness: Cajole Your Brain to Lean to the Left', *New York Times*, 4 February, 2003.
64. Another benefit for the workers, Davidson reported, was that mindfulness seemed to improve the robustness of their immune systems, as gauged by the amount of flu antibodies in their blood after receiving a flue shot. This supports the observations noted above concerning the link between happiness and physical health.

Part B

PERSONAL ETHICS

Chapter Three

Friendship, Love, Personal Projects and Loyalty

3.1 OVERVIEW OF OUR PREFERENCE TOWARDS THOSE CLOSE TO US

In our day to day lives we constantly make decisions that affect people close to us: our parents, spouses, children and friends. In doing so we often face conflicting demands. We have a natural preference towards those close to us, but often morality seems to command that we act impartially. The fact that we happen to be a familiar with a particular person is often merely a happenstance and should not, arguably, entitle that individual to preferential treatment. The $100 we spend on our child's Christmas present could sustain a starving infant in Africa for several months.

Yet as a practical reality most of us still have a strong bias towards those close to us. The history of human kind shows that people have an unwavering and constant tendency to prefer the interests of those they have a familial or other relational connection with. We are far more deeply affected by the plight of our relatives and friends than that of other people. But if morality mandates that all people count equally how can we possibly justify this preference?

Morality, on its face, requires us treat all people equally without reference to whether or not they happen to fall inside our circle of family and friends. This stems from a fundamental feature of morality—moral judgments are universalisable. A judgment is universalisable if the acceptance of it in a particular situation entails that one is logically committed to accepting the same judgment in all other similar situations. Accordingly, whenever one judges a certain action or thing (situation) as having a particular moral status then one is logically committed to the same judgment about any relevantly similar action or situation.[1]

If an action is morally good or bad, then it is so in all *relevantly* similar situations in which that action is performed. The context in which an action is performed does not appear to constitute a relevant difference. Deliberately lying to another person is (usually) wrong irrespective of whether it is done in private or in the context of sport, politics or other fields of human endeavour. Moreover, in forming moral judgments it has been suggested that numerical differences are irrelevant. This refers to specific descriptions of the person, relation or situation. Thus, the fact that the judgment relates to a particular person (such as John Smith), place (such as New York), relation (John's mother) is irrelevant. Also irrelevant are generic differences: tastes, preferences, and desires.

This entails that when we are making decisions regarding, for example, the allocation of resources we should not have a preference for those close to us. We should treat all people equally in this regard and therefore, seemingly, confer our disposable income, and the like, to those that need it most, as opposed to our loved ones.

If indeed we are blocked from extending preferential treatment to those close to us, this would make for a vastly different societal structure. We would not be able to extend preferences to our family and friends and in instead in relation to each decision we made would have to act impartially—giving our family no more weight than strangers.

However, as we shall see in this chapter, in fact morality is not so impersonal. It does allow considerable space for us to show preferences to those close to us and even to indulge in our personal projects and goals. In short, this is because otherwise our lives would be almost intolerable and significantly reduced in happiness. To see why requires an analysis of the ideal which underpins and guides much of our conduct regarding those close to us, whether they be our friends, family or colleagues. The same virtue also underpins our commitment to the goals and projects through which we often define ourselves. It is called loyalty.

3.2 THE NATURE OF LOYALTY

Loyalty is a concept that has received surprisingly little philosophical analysis. This is peculiar given the important role that loyalty has in influencing human behaviour. It has been proclaimed that loyalty is the basis of all moral judgments: 'in loyalty, when loyalty is properly defined, is the fulfillment of the whole of morality'.[2] For some people, loyalty is such a powerful force that it moves them to willingly lose their life for their country or their friend. In less dramatic contexts, loyalty is the force that sees many make great personal sacrifices, by caring for sick or infirm relatives or friends. As noted by Oldenquist, the breadth and intensity of loyalty is virtually limitless:

> It is the most common thing in the world for a person to decide that he should (or should not) do so-and-so on grounds of loyalty to his friend, family, organization, community, country, or species. Indeed it is likely that loyalties ground more of the principled, self-sacrificing, and other kinds of non-selfish behaviour in which people engage than do moral principles and ideals.[3]

Any analysis of loyalty must begin with an appreciation of the nature of the idea itself. The first thing to note is that loyalty is an imprecise concept:

> Loyalty, as the term is popularly used, is a mixed bag that includes both petty and profound attachments of wildly varying strengths. The loyalty that moves martyrs is of a far different order than the loyalty that prompts a sports fan to root for a particular team.[4]

Secondly, it is important to note that loyalty is a term of relation as it must be directed toward an object.[5] The potential objects of loyalty are numerous. People espouse loyalty to living creatures (their family, friends and pets) as well as causes (their country, sporting club or favourite charity).[6] What is more difficult to establish is whether there are limits to the type of objects to which one can act loyally. For instance, can loyalty exist between a person and an inanimate object? It seems nonsensical to avow loyalty to one's car, house or a rock. While such a relation could be seen to evoke loyalty, it would be stretching the concept too thin to say that devotion, or care, is akin to loyalty. In the same vein, one cannot be loyal to oneself. To proclaim loyalty to oneself is simply a misguided expression of egoism or other form of self-interest. Thus, although there must be relationship for loyalty to exist, there are some boundaries.

Accordingly, it follows that loyalty can be described as an obligation or preference[7] which one assumes towards a living object or a cause.[8]

3.3 THE TENSION BETWEEN LOYALTY AND MORALITY

As noted at the start of this chapter, it has been suggested that loyalty and morality are conflicting ideals. Loyalty, so the argument runs, is a sentiment that stands outside morality. To this end, moral philosophers have charged that 'loyalty changes the moral equation for deciding on a proper course of action';[9] 'at the level of philosophical theory, it may be difficult to make the case for the ethic of loyalty';[10] and that 'loyalties generally lead people to suspend judgment about right and wrong.'[11] Oldenquist states that loyalty falls somewhere between self-interest and impersonal morality (according to him, loyalty is a third category of the normative):

> Reasons of loyalty have a general appeal among members of a society whereas a self-interested reason appeals only to the agent. But neither is loyalty impersonal morality, since an obligation of loyalty depends on viewing a thing as one's own.[12]

It is true that the unbridled pursuit of loyalty can lead to morally unacceptable outcomes. Loyalty to an individual or group can often encourage or endorse morally repugnant behaviour. The 'brotherhood syndrome', identified in many police departments, is a classic illustration. Police members fail to disclose the unlawful behaviour of other officers through a sense of loyalty to both their colleagues and the 'cause' of policing. Moreover, as is noted by McChrystal, loyalty has been used to justify deception and unfairness, such as advice on tax avoidance, or how to use a technical defense to defeat an otherwise valid claim.[13] Loyalty to one's friends can lead to a total indifference to the plight of others. Pursued to its limits it can lead to a refusal to provide urgent assistance to an accident victim in order to avoid been later for a gathering with a friend.

This fact that loyalty can lead to bad outcomes does not necessarily mean, however, that it is antagonistic with morality. It is merely an illustration of the fact that, as we saw in chapter one, there are no moral absolutes. There are situations where observance of even widely accepted fundamental moral norms leads to undesirable consequences. A decision not to kill an aggressor can lead to the death of many innocent people.

Thus the mere fact that allegiance to loyalty does not *always* produce morally acceptable outcomes, neither proves nor disproves whether loyalty is a moral norm. An inquiry into whether the concept of loyalty has a moral justification is now made against a background of a utilitarian ethic.

As was saw in chapter one, uilitarianism is a maximising interpersonal theory, and on its face would appear to pay no heed to personal preferences or goals associated with loyalty. The ostensible tension between utilitarianism and loyalty is noted by Oldenquist, who argues that 'our duty is to Humanity and . . . doing what benefits your neighbourhood or country is wrong if it prevents a greater good for a larger whole.'[14]

Utilitarianism supposedly endorses impartiality and equality as its central tenets and hence the fact that, say, a person happens to be my friend or my spouse adds nothing to the utilitarian calculus. Some of the most persuasive criticisms that have been levelled against utilitarianism have focused on the impartial aggregative nature of utilitarianism. The nature and force of such objections is encapsulated by the famous 'archbishop and chambermaid' example by William Godwin.

In Godwin's example, Archbishop Fenelon's palace is in flames and a rescuer who comes upon the scene is only able to save one of either the Archbishop or his chambermaid. Who should it be? To Godwin, it ought to be the Archbishop. This is so even if the chambermaid is the rescuer's mother. It is argued that the utilitarian is committed to this course of action despite the strong love and affection towards one's mother, because decisions must be governed by the principle of maximising happiness for the whole of humankind.[15]

This example attempts to illustrate the de-humanising aspect of utilitarianism, which supposedly requires people to make purely clinical ethical decisions, totally detached from their personal preferences and sentiments. Given the intrapersonal nature of loyalty, if these criticisms are right there is no room for loyalty in such an ethic.

3.4 THE OVERLAP BETWEEN MORALITY AND LOYALTY

There are three central ways of addressing these criticisms and showing why there is considerable room for fixing loyalty within a utilitarian ethic. Firstly, loyalty is a fundamental aspect of human nature. Secondly, loyalty derives from the notion of liberty. Finally, loyalty is instrumental to the forging of bonds which are conducive to the attainment of important goals.

3.4.1 Loyalty and Human Nature

There is a strong pragmatic reason for recognising at least some role for loyalty in our moral decision making. An ethical theory that prescribed that people must at every point abandon their subjective preferences when there is a chance that pursuit of them would not maximise happiness would risk becoming obsolete. Such a requirement is fundamentally contradictory to an important aspect of human nature. Despite the ostensibly divergent nature of the many things that go toward promoting happiness, as we saw in chapter two, human beings place enormous importance on the pursuit of personal objectives, including the fostering and maintenance of relationships with other people. Close relationships are important to happiness. Additionally, the more challenged a person is, whether by a job, hobby or sport, the happier he or she is likely to be.

Thus, it seems that as a result of the manner in which humans are built, there is a strong innate desire to fulfil personal wants and pursue personal loyalties. This mirrors a common sense understanding of human nature. Loyalty is 'an obligation implied in every person's sense of being historically rooted in a set of defining familial, institutional, and national relationships.'[16] In light of this, a normative ethic which compelled us to disavow completely our personal pursuits would readily become unworkable. While the manner in which people behave is not decisive of how they should behave, pervasive aspects of human nature must nevertheless be factored into the types of prescriptions that form the content of a normative ethic, otherwise the whole project lacks any humanity at all, and could be equally (ineffectively) applied to a dog or a fish.

Even if the need to engage in personal projects and give effect to our subjective preferences is not so innate to be unchangeable, there are two other reasons why loyalty should be encouraged, in its relationship with ideas of liberty and human bonds.

3.4.2 Loyalty and Liberty

Loyalties often appear to lead to behaviour that is contrary to the common good. Looked at in isolation, for instance, it could be argued that the world would be a happier place if the funds spent on a birthday present for one's child were instead donated to a fund for starving children; better if instead of treating a spouse to dinner, time was spent helping to build a shelter for the homeless; or even if the archbishop was saved instead of his chambermaid.

All these examples fail to recognise that although pursuit of our subjective preferences, such as our projects and loyalties, may not be the most direct path to maximising overall happiness, net happiness consists of the aggregate level of happiness experienced by *each* individual. The most effective means of achieving the ultimate goal may be for each agent to generally pursue that which makes him or her happy. Thus, the pursuit of loyalty may have a place within a utilitarian ethic if the best way to achieve maximum happiness does not require a direct pursuit of this goal, and if it can be established that people with projects and attachments are generally happier than those without.

This is a point acknowledged by philosopher Bernard Williams. But for him this response is inadequate because he thinks that ultimately our ability to pursue our own projects is subject to the innumerable projects and demands of others which our actions may affect:

> It is absurd to demand ... of a man, when the sums come in from the utility network which the projects of others have in part determined, that he should just step aside from his own project and decision and acknowledge the decision which utilitarian calculation requires. It is to alienate him in a real sense from his actions and the source of his action in his own convictions. It is to make him into a channel between the input of everyone's projects, including his own, and

an output of optimistic decision. . . . [The utilitarian approach] is to neglect the extent to which [one's] actions and his decisions have to be seen as the actions and decisions which flow from the projects and attitudes with which he is most closely identified. It is thus, in the most literal sense, an attack on his integrity.[17]

At the heart of Williams' objection is that generally we should only be responsible for the consequences we have orchestrated, and that we cannot be expected to drop or compromise projects which may be defining of our lives simply because the utilitarian sum may happen to come down against us.

This is not a significant objection, as utilitarianism gives considerable weight to such considerations, even more than Williams is prepared to accept. The direct pursuit of overall happiness is often likely to fail. We cannot at every single point be expected to save the world: we simply do not know how, and an attempt to do so would likely be self-defeating. But one thing we do know is what works for each of us. The collective pursuit of our individual aims is, therefore, at most points likely to be the best method of maximising happiness. A pre-condition to the attainment of individual happiness is the ability to lead a life governed by one's own desires. In this way utilitarianism attaches an enormous amount of weight to personal liberty.

Once this is established, it becomes simpler to extend into the notion that people ought to be permitted to pursue the goals and endeavours which fulfil them unless it is obvious that this will not maximise happiness. To this end, there is little doubt that people obtain an enormous amount of happiness by pursuing their projects and loyalties. In this sense, loyalty receives at least partial justification from notion of personal liberty.[18]

3.4.3 Loyalty and the Bonds of Co-operation

Further, the desirability of loyalty goes beyond its derivative association with liberty—it is in fact better recognised as a moral virtue its own right. Difficulties in performing the utilitarian calculus regarding each decision necessitate that the general desirability of certain virtues, which evidence shows tend to maximise happiness, be acknowledged. As we saw in chapter one, in the context of rights, creating these kinds of guidelines saves time and energy by providing us with short cuts which will assist in attaining desirable consequences. By labelling certain virtues or interests as being morally desirable, we are spared the tedious task of establishing the importance of a particular interest as a first premise in practical arguments.

There is more information concerning exactly what it is that makes those around us happy, and hence our efforts are unlikely to be wasted. It is a far more effective process for achieving overall happiness than performing a utilitarian calculus in relation to each important decision we make. The capacity to gather and process information is restricted by a large number of factors, including lack of time, indifference to the matter at hand, defects in reasoning, and so on. It is often not possible to assess all the alternatives and to determine the likely impact upon general happiness stemming from each alternative. The ability to make the correct decision will be greatly assisted by narrowing down the range of relevant factors in light of pre-determined guidelines.[19]

Loyalty is conducive to happiness because the bonds that are forged by it play an important role in creating an environment where people can flourish. Loyalty assists in the establishment and maintenance of many of the virtues that stem from the rule of law. Loyalty secures predictability and certainty and gives people the confidence to enter into mutually beneficial projects, commitments and enterprises which would be impossible in a dispassionate world.[20] People would not nurture and cultivate a marriage (and enjoy all of the benefits flowing from such an enterprise) if they felt that their partner would leave them at the first sign of hard times. Loyalty is the force that holds 'lovers or friends in a bond that transcends temporary disaffection'.[21] More generally, absent loyalty, rational agents might well pursue short-term goals and cease striving for the higher pleasures which stem from long term co-operative activities: '[t]o foreswear fidelity is to open yourself up to other ideas, other thoughts, about what love is, what desire is, what happiness is, and what commitment is.'[22]

The good consequences that we claim are brought about by loyalty are similar to those that have been previously claimed to stem from the trust. This is not surprising, given that, as is noted by Petit, loyalty is one of the foundations of trust.[23] Trust is:

> A mechanism that reduces complexity and enables people to cope with the high levels of uncertainty and complexity of contemporary life. Trust makes the uncertainty and complexity tolerable because it enables us to focus on a few possible alternatives. Humans, if faced with a full range of alternatives, if forced to acknowledge and calculate all possible outcomes of all possible decision nodes, would freeze in uncertainty and indecision. In this state, we might never be able to act in situations that call for action and decisiveness. In trusting, Luhmann says, 'one engages in an action as though there were only certain possibilities in the future.' Trust, further, enables, 'co-operative action and individual but coordinated action: trust, by the reduction of complexity, discloses possibilities for action which would have remained improbable and unattractive without trust—which would not, in other words, have been pursued.' According to this account, trust expands people's capacity to successfully relate to a world whose complexity, in reality, is far greater than anything we are capable of taking in.[24]

Beyond this are other instrumental goods which are brought about by loyalty. Loyalty is a means of overcoming alienation (or a sense of lacking ownership), which Oldenquist claims is responsible for such destructive activities as exploitation of social services and leads to behaviours classified as criminal.[25] In the view of one of loyalty's chief proponents, it 'gives life meaning and direction'.[26]

In sum, loyalty is a virtue that has considerable moral weight because it tends to promote general happiness.

3.5 THE LIMITS OF LOYALTY

Thus there is a place for loyalty in our moral judgments and behavior. However, there are limits to how far we should go in acting upon our loyalties. One is to note that loyalty is not intrinsically valuable—it is a derivative, not foundational, good. This means that it is not the case that all loyalties should be given equal moral weight. Loyalties to people or causes which are clearly destructive to the common good, such as a loyalty to Hitler or the Ku Klux Klan, although carrying some weight on the utilitarian scales, will never come up trumps, since it is almost certain that whatever pleasure an agent obtains in expressing such loyalties will be outweighed by the harm the object of the loyalty will cause to others. This is not, however, a significant limitation as few objects of loyalty are demonstrably so damaging to the common good.

Secondly, like every other virtue or principle in a utilitarian ethic, loyalty is not absolute. Due to the derivative character of utilitarian secondary moral principles, they must be overridden where pursuit of them is contrary to the common good. The difficulty is determining the point at which loyalty should be subordinated to other principles. Given the important role that loyalty plays in the pursuit of happiness, arguably the scales need to be heavily tilted against it before one is morally required to abandon his or her loyalty.

In order to provide clearer guidance regarding when loyalties must be abandoned, an analogy can be drawn with the scope of the right to liberty. To this end, as we saw in chapter one, in addition to the negative postulates of morality (such as do not kill or lie) there is one very important positive attribute of liberty, that of assisting others in serious trouble, when assistance would immensely help them at little or no inconvenience to the rescuer.[27]

This maxim of positive duty (which is examined at length in chapter 10) provides that a person can engage in whatever behaviour he or she wishes (so long as it is not directly injurious to others) except where an alternative course of conduct would immensely assist another. This same broad criterion could govern the parameters of personal loyalty. Thus, two considerations are relevant in determining how much weight should be accorded to a particular loyalty. First is the strength of the loyalty and second is the good that is done by acting in accordance with it. In this way, we should always be free to express our preference towards our family, friends or sporting teams, except where to do so would be at the expense of not assisting another in serious trouble whom we could easily help.

Finally, in judging the correctness of an act, including that of loyalty, it is necessary to look beyond the immediate effects. This is best explored by returning to the archbishop and chambermaid example. In this case, loyalty provides a strong reason for saving the chambermaid, while the maxim of positive duty does not provide a countervailing reason for choosing the archbishop—he could only be saved at significant (physical) inconvenience and risk to ourselves. Like all guidelines in a utilitarian ethic, however, loyalty and the maxim of positive duty are not absolute. It therefore becomes necessary to save the archbishop if this is the course of action that will definitely promote the greater good, when all of the relevant variables, including distant and more speculative effects are considered.

This broader perspective, however, does not seem to alter the preference in favour of the chambermaid. While the world may initially be a better place if the archbishop was saved, condoning such a course of conduct may weaken the commitment to loyalty and to the general rule that utility is maximised when each takes care of his or her own. Not taking this weakening tendency into account may lead to disturbing results. For example, the next rescuer placed in a similar situation, except instead of an archbishop, is faced with the quandary of whether to rescue a doctor, engineer, plumber, lawyer, graphic designer, car salesman, nightclub promoter or his mother, and remembering the lesson that was learned from the previous rescuer saving the archbishop, may be inclined to think, instead of dashing in and going straight to his mother, 'who should I save?'

Given that moral judgments are universalisable, the rescuer in the new scene must now save the other, upstanding, party unless there is a *relevant* difference between the archbishop and that party. However, due to the vagaries involved with identifying 'relevant differences' there is a high risk that the rescuer will pick the wrong person. In the end, it works out that it is best to go for the 'sure thing' and save the mother. Speculative goods carry considerably less weight on a moral cost and benefit analysis than certain goods.

Thus, loyalty has a strong ethical foundation. The ability to express loyalty is integral to the capacity for human beings to flourish. Loyalty is thus a virtue that should be generally encouraged. We are free to actively engage in meaningful relationships with others and should be encouraged to do so.

Moreover, we should enthusiastically pursue our individual goals and projects. We should only waiver from these endeavours where there is demonstrable evidence that our energies will confer considerable benefits on others and this does not require a significant detour from our goals and passions. The situations when this occurs are discussed further in chapter 10.

NOTES

1. See John L Mackie, *Ethics: Inventing Right and Wrong* (1977) 83–102.
2. J Royce, *The Philosophy of Loyalty* (Hafner publishing, New York, 1908, 1971 reprint) 15.
3. A Oldenquist, 'Loyalties' (1982) LXXIX *The Journal of Philosophy* 173.
4. M K McChrystal, 'Lawyers and Loyalty' [1992] 33 *William and Mary Law Review* 367, 370. It has been argued that loyalty to causes may be more uncompromising than loyalty to people: ibid, 372–386.
5. Ibid, 370.
6. Royce suggested that the only proper objects of loyalty are causes that have social significance (or that remain 'loyal to loyalty'), in that they have value independent to that which the loyal person attaches to it, above n 2, 20; whereas Oldenquist regards loyalty as principally a relation between people: above n 2, 175–181. According to Oldenquist the types of causes stipulated by Royce are more in the form of ideals, rather than ideas: Oldenquist, above n 3, 175. However, neither provides persuasive reasons why loyalty should be viewed in such a counter intuitive fashion; see also McChrystal, above n 3, 375.
7. The notion of a preference is also emphasised by M Baron, *The Moral Status of Loyalty* (1984) 4.
8. See also McChrystal, above n 4, 386, where he defines loyalty as 'a term of relation, and the possible objects of loyalty are both people and causes'.
9. McChrystal, above n 4, however, ultimately accepts that loyalty does carry moral weight: 395–406.
10. Fletcher, *Loyalty* (1993), 163.
11. Ibid 36.
12. Oldenquist, above n 3, 176. He ultimately argues that all of social morality may depend on loyalties.
13. McChrystal, above n 4, 368.
14. Oldenquist, above n 3, 180.
15. W Godwin, 'The Archbishop and the Chambermaid' in P Singer (ed), *Ethics* (Oxford University Press, Oxford, 1994) 312.
16. Fletcher, above n 10, 21.
17. Ibid 116–7.
18. See also C Fried, 'The Lawyer as Friend: The Moral Foundations of the Lawyer-Client Relation' (1975) 85 *Yale Law Journal* 1060, who argues that our right to befriend whomever we choose is a product of our individual autonomy.

19. This, however, does not lead to a form of rule utilitarianism. As is discussed below, the guideline or rule should be abandoned where it is clear that its observance in a particular situation will not maximise happiness.

20. Ibid.

21. G Fletcher, *Loyalty* (1993) 5.

22. J Smiley, 'Why Marriage? Matrimony at the millennium offers solace to capitalism' (2000) 300 *Harpers*, 151, 154–5.

23. See P Petit, 'The Cunning of Trust' (1995) 24 *Philosophy & Public Affairs* 202, 211 where he provides that 'to be loyal or virtuous or even prudent is, in an obvious sense of the term, is to be trustworthy. It is to be reliable under trust and to be reliable, in particular, because of possessing a desirable trait.'

24. H Nissenbaum, 'Can Trust be Secured Online? A theoretical perspective' (1999) *Etica & Politica*: http://www.univ.trieste.it/~dipfilo-/etica_e_politica/1999_2 (citations omitted).

25. Oldenquist, above n 3, 189.

26. Royce, above n 2, 25–33.

27. See M Bagaric, 'Active and Passive Euthanasia: Is There a Moral Distinction and Should There be a Legal Difference' (1997) *Journal of Law and Medicine* 143, 147–150.

Chapter Four

Lying

4.1 INTRODUCTION

Liars deliberately mislead others with a view to getting other people to believe in a false state of affairs.[1] Lying aims to give a person a false impression of the way that things actually are.

Lies are almost universally deplored. Many believe that lying is inherently wrong. For them, lying is inexcusable and never justifiable. Moreover, lying often leads to bad consequences. People often act in reliance on lies and structure much of what is important to their lives based on a misrepresentation, and find important interests and concerns crumbling around them when the lie is uncovered.

People can lose their life savings upon being duped to enter into shonky investment schemes, they can lose their lives on the basis of being lied to about the sobriety of the driver of a vehicle and can spend many years in a loveless relationship with a cheating partner.

Liars often also get an advantage over others by making themselves appear 'better' (smarter, more skilled and experienced, more resourceful or virtuous) than they really are. Fabricating one's educational and work qualifications and experience can lead to undue rewards being conferred on the liar at the expense of more meritorious candidates.

Despite the fact that there are so many obviously bad aspects associated with lying, empirical data reveals that lying is very commonplace — most of us do it many times each day. A recent study by University of Massachusetts psychologist Robert S Feldman showed that most people lie in normal conversation when they are trying to appear competent and likeable (which is often the case).[2] According to the study, 60 per cent of people lied at least once during the course of a ten minute conversation. The average number of lies told during this time period was two or three. A further interesting finding to emerge was that while men and women told about the same amount of lies they differed in terms of their motivation. Men most often told self-serving lies, which were designed to make themselves look better. Women mainly told lies that aimed to make the person they were speaking to feel better.

Another recent survey by Psychologist Jeff Hancock of Cornell University showed that respondents lied during a quarter of their social interactions. The lies varied according to the medium through which the communication was transmitted. Telephone conversations accounted for 37 percent of the deception; face to face conversations included lies 27 percent of the time; the figure was 21 per cent for instant messages and only 14 percent for email. It is easier to lie over the telephone because others cannot see the expressions of the liar. Email invokes the most honesty because it leaves a permanent record.[3]

On reflection the results of such studies are not surprising. When asked by our friends or colleagues whether they look good in their shiny new attire the answer is invariably yes, no matter how ill fitting it may be, we compliment the host of a dinner party on his or her cooking prowess irrespective of how difficult the dinner has been to swallow, let alone stomach, and we rarely give a blunt evaluation of true performance and capabilities of our employees and colleagues—most of us fear finding the reaction too jarring.

Then of course there are the more cunning and calculated lies. People often lie to avoid responsibility for their harmful actions (an accused person charged with a criminal offence in the witness box is the classic example) and in some cases even blame others for their misdeeds. More generally, the acceptance of lying is so widespread that in some contexts it has become institutionalised. Thus the use of undercover police operatives is standard practice in most countries, as is the use of placebos in medical science research.

The frequency with which people lie provides a startling paradox. Perhaps in no area of moral theory is the gap between the surface language and the reality so great. The irony is that people who claim to never lie are perhaps the most profound liars of all. The frequency of lies, in reality, is accepted by nearly all people.

> In law and in journalism, in government and in the social sciences, deception is taken for granted when it is felt to be excusable by those who tell lies and who tend also to make the rules. Government officials and those who run for elections often deceive when they can get away with it and when they can assume that the true state of affairs is beyond the comprehension of citizens. Social scientists condone deceptive experimentation on the ground that the knowledge gained will be worth having. Lawyers manipulate the truth in court on behalf of

their clients. Those in selling, advertising, or any form of advocacy may mislead the public and their competitors in order to achieve their goals. Psychiatrists may distort information about their former patients to preserve confidentiality or to keep them out of military service. And journalists, police investigators, and so-called intelligence operators often have little compunction in using falsehoods to gain the knowledge they seek.[4]

Yet the charade continues. People who come out and publicly state that it is permissible to lie in some circumstances are typically viewed with a high degree of suspicion and hostility. So why the discord between the level of opprobrium towards liars and the reality about how much we actually lie? I consider this in section 4.4, after first analysing the moral status of lying.

4.2 DIFFERENT TYPES OF LIES

As we shall see, the moral status of lies varies considerably depending on the nature of the lie. There are broadly three different types of lies. The first, and most innocuous, are lies that are aimed to prevent unnecessary confrontation or sometimes merely discussion with others or that are designed to prevent hurt to others. Lies are often social lubricants and aim to allow us and others to lead efficient and harmonious lives. Life would become all the more tedious if the 'Good morning/afternoon/evening, how are you?' greeting was met with anything other than the token 'good' retort—no matter how badly the respondent is travelling. An honest response could turn the formal greeting into a half hour epilogue about the misfortunes that one has been struck with. Lies allow us to circumvent this inefficiency. Of course, if we start telling people how we are actually going in response to the 'how are you' greeting it could readily spell the death knell for this convention, but no doubt many of us would slip up from time and time, only to be confronted with the tedious details of the respondent's recent mishaps.

It is for similar reasons that when our partner asks us 'Does my bottom look big in this new dress? or 'Is my new haircut nice?' that we invariably say no and yes, respectively. This is irrespective of how many kilograms they have piled on recently or how ill-suiting the hair style actually is. There is usually no upside to honesty in relation to such matters. It can only serve to minimise our partner's confidence and self-esteem. She cannot take back the hair cut and is likely to wear the dress in any event. She might as well think that her appearance is enhanced. And if our partner believes that, and acts confidently, in fact he or she will be more appealing to others. In the looks stakes attitude counts for much—Mick Jagger and Madonna are testament to this.

These types of lies fall into the category of what are typically referred to as white lies. The key aspect of white lies is that they are not done for personal gain or advantage, nor are they motivated by a desire to harm another person. In fact often the opposite is true—they generally spring from benevolent considerations. These sorts of lies are very common.

> Though some lies produce interpersonal friction, others may actually serve as a kind of harmless social lubricant. "They make it easier for people to get along," says DePaulo, noting that in the diary study one in every four of the participants' lies were told solely for the benefit of another person. In fact, "fake positive" lies—those in which people pretend to like someone or something more than they actually do ("Your muffins are the best ever")—are about 10 to 20 times more common than "false negative" lies in which people pretend to like someone or something less ("That two-faced rat will never get my vote").[5]

The motivation behind white lies contrasts with the next two types of lies. Many lies are motivated by a desire to project oneself in an unduly favourable light. I call these 'embellishment lies'. Many people yearn for recognition. We want other people to think well of us. There are relatively well defined (though albeit perhaps flawed) criteria regarding the traits and goals that society encourages people to aspire to. Thus, we are taught to be virtuous and of good character (which roughly means to be ethical people), to be hard working and successful. To impress others many people fabricate or embellish information regarding their achievements or endeavours in relation to such matters. Thus, many people boast about how honest they are, exaggerate the importance of their job and the size of their bank balance, overstate their sporting prowess and educational achievements. These lies are designed to increase the level of acceptance that the individual receives from others. This can be either be at the personal level or in the professional sense where they are designed to assist the liar to secure new or higher level employment. As adverted to above, research shows that men are much more likely to tell embellishment lies than women.

> Not surprisingly, research also confirms that the closer we are to someone, the more likely it is that the lies we tell them will be altruistic ones. This is particularly true of women; although the sexes lie with equal frequency, women are especially likely to stretch the truth in order to protect someone else's feelings, DePaulo reports. Men, on the other hand, are more prone to lying about themselves—the typical conversation between two guys contains about eight times as many self-oriented lies as it does falsehoods about other people.[6]

The last type of lie ('undermining lies') refers to untruths which attempt to impugn or undermine others. People sometimes wish to harm others. This can be motivated by considerations of hatred or revenge. Lies can be a particularly effective technique for pursuing these motivations. They are boundless in scope and content, easy to invent and promulgate and normally attract less accountability than direct forms of harm that one can inflict on others, such as the infliction of physical pain or the deprivation of liberty or taking one's property.

These sorts of lies, while having the effect of undermining others are often motivated by less harmful motives. As noted previously, people have a desire to advance their interests. They typically do this by participating in worthwhile and challenging projects and thereby achieving worthwhile ends. Unfortunately that is not always the case. Laziness, apathy and lack of confidence sometimes stifle such pursuits. Yet, the desire to progress at the personal level remains. Personal progress is a relative concept—we compare ourselves with the achievements of others. In this regard we can get ahead two ways. First, we can progress by objective standards: getting a better job, running a marathon, learning a new skill or having another child. Another way is to stand still while the people in the world around us go backwards: they commit a crime, blow their fortune, cheat on their partner or engage in our other types of disreputable conduct.

In some societies, this is known as 'schaedenfraude': pleasure in another person's misfortune. In the Anglo-Saxon culture, a similar phenomenon is the tall poppy syndrome—we try to bring down successful people, or at least take some pleasure in being informed of their demise. The tendency to want to get ahead not by progressing ourselves, but while others around us go backwards is a fertile cause for lies that are aimed at undermining others.

I now morally evaluate lies.

4.3 THE MORAL STATUS OF LIES

The most straightforward approach to lying is that it is wrong—always so and there are no exceptions. This view was most famously advanced by Kant, who stated that:

> Truthfulness in statements which cannot be avoided is the formal duty of an individual to everyone, however great may be the disadvantage accruing to himself or to another.[7]

This view has been persuasively refuted on the basis that more important considerations, such as the right to life, can conflict with the duty not to lie. The classic counter example to Kant's absolute prohibition against lying is where a would-be murderer inquires about the location of his victim who is hiding in the next room. Most people reject the suggestion that we should not lie about the location of the potential victim. According to Kant, we must tell the killer the truth and this response is made more acceptable by the fact that we are not responsible for the murder because in being honest we have done nothing wrong. Responsibility for the murder supposedly rests solely with the killer.

This narrow take on personal responsibility, however, is flawed. It runs foul of the maxim of positive duty, which requires us to assist others when it would greatly assist them at least inconvenience to ourselves. Additionally, when evaluating the moral status of the act there is no basis for arbitrarily excluding the interests of an individual affected by the act. We cannot look at the scenario merely through the prism of the murderer and person being questioned. The fact that the respondent supposedly has no responsibility for the murder will give no comfort to the victim whose right to life is at stake.

Thus, it is obvious that lies are permissible in some situations, such as to protect or save others. They are no less permissible to protect oneself. This means, for example, that gay people living in countries run by totalitarian regimes which mete out harsh practices for homosexual behaviour are justified in lying about their sexual preference. The notion of self defence (which includes defence of another) extends beyond inflicting physical harm on wrongdoers to neutralising their threats by lies.

Given that it is implausible to suggest an absolute prohibition against lying, in the remaining part of the chapter I discuss the circumstances where lying is permissible. Prior to distinguishing between the three categories of lies, I look at the adverse effects associated with most forms of lies.

In order for us to plan, coordinate and structure our activities it is necessary to have an accurate understanding of the state of affairs in the world that impact on us and the cause and effect systems in the world. Absent this our plans and projects would be constantly frustrated. Lies undermine our capacity to effectively and efficiently achieve our goals and projects. This is so whether they relate to the traits and characteristics of people or the operation of systems and processes in the world. We could bypass the opportunity to form mutually advantageous friendships and associations with people if they have been unfairly maligned by others. Our plans to catch the morning train, attend important appointments and meet work and other deadlines could be derailed by misrepresentations regarding these matters. If things are not the way they have been portrayed, our goals would be constantly frustrated.

As noted in the previous chapter, it is especially important that we can trust other people. People live in communities and hence there is a strong interdependency regarding our activities. This is deeper and wider than most of us realise. Even those of us who live the most mundane lifestyles rely on large numbers of people in our daily lives to act in predictable and orderly ways so that we can accomplish basic tasks. We assume that statements and commitments made by others are truthful. The depth of this expectation is highlighted by the fact that we place significant reliance even on anonymous strangers whose actions impact on our lives. This rests largely on the assumption that others will act honestly consistent with widely shared, often implied, obligations and expectations. We assume that the person who made our morning cereal and coffee used the proper ingredients, and especially that the ingredients were not harmful to our health, that other motorists will stop at red lights and not stray onto our side of the road and that the operators of our energy stations will turn up and perform their expected day's work and so on.

The same point is emphasised by Sissela Bok in her seminal book on the issue of lies, *Lying*:

> Were all statements randomly truthful or deceptive, action and choice would be undermined from the outset. There must be a minimal degree of trust in communication for language and action to be more than stabs in the dark. This is why some level of truthfulness has always been seen as essential to human society, no matter how deficient the observance of other moral principle. . . . A society . . . whose members were unable to distinguish truthful messages from deceptive ones, would collapse. But even before such a society a general collapse, individual choice and survival would be imperiled. The search for food and shelter could depend on no expectations from others. A warning that a well was poisoned or a plea for help in an accident would come to be ignored unless independent confirmation could be found.[8]

In a similar vein is the following observation by G J Warnock:

> [Lies] undermine trust; and to the extent that trust is undermined, all co-operative undertakings, in which what one person can do or has reason to do is dependent on what others have done, are doing, or are going to do, must tend to break down. I cannot reasonably be expected to go over the edge of a cliff on a rope, for however vital an object, if I cannot trust you to keep hold of the other end of it; there is no sense in my asking you for your opinion on some point, if I do not suppose that your answer will actually express your opinion.[9]

Thus, lying ultimately limits personal liberty. If we are deceived our capacity to make informed choices and achieve our goals is significantly curtailed.

In addition to this, as Bok points out, the victims of lies (upon uncovering the lie), especially in relation to important matters, often feel resentful, betrayed, suspicious or let down. Even in relation to relatively trivial lies, hurt and loss of confidence can still occur because there is often little basis for confidence that liars will confine themselves to small lies and this leads victims to be wary about all forms of deceit.[10]

Given the connection between honesty and the bonds of cooperation, which are so important to our individual capacity to pursue and achieve our individual goals and projects, and the hurt that lies often cause to the deceived there is a presumption that lying is morally undesirable. In certain circumstances, however, this presumption can by overridden. In this regard, I look at each category of lying separately.

The third category of lies (undermining lies) is clearly the most damaging. The only redeeming aspect related to these lies is that promulgation of the lie may in fact please the liar. He or she may get satisfaction out of undermining the person who is the subject of the lie. The liar's feelings of hatred, revenge or jealousy may be placated. However, satisfaction of these feelings will in most circumstances be grossly outweighed by the damage done to the subject of the liar. Lies can often have a devastating effect on the lives of others. They can ruin relationships, careers and friendships. Even if the lie is ultimately uncovered, it can cause of a lot of pain in the short to mid term until the lie is uncovered.

It would be rare if ever that the short-term psychic boost to the liar outweighed the negative, often tangible, effects on the liar.

The second type of lies (embellishment lies) are typically less damaging, but nevertheless normally reprehensible. As noted above, these lies sometimes lead to undeserved opportunities and benefits being conferred on the liar at the expense of more virtuous individuals. There is yet another downside to these sorts of lies. They invariably prove to be personally self destructive. It is difficult to maintain a false reality for an extended period of time. Even the period of time while the lie is not uncovered is innately stress ridden. The liar is normally aware that their fantasy may be shattered by a dose of reality. When it is they must deal with the opprobrium that stems from being uncovered as a fraud.

Further, lying about one's achievements and attributes consigns one to living in a fiction. This is nearly always personally self-defeating and destructive. Reality is the only solid currency on the happiness front—it is certainly the only setting in which humans have been known to prosper. That is why rational people tend to ignore their dreams. Also, our wishes and aspirations unmet are no cause for joy. Living in a fool's land gives temporary comfort but at the same time inhibits people from pursuing the projects and goals that give life genuine meaning.

White lies may seem innocuous, but they are also often harmful. Often lost in the altruistic perspective of the liar are the long-term effects of lying, namely, the reduction of social cohesive stemming from a diminution in trust.[11] Moreover whenever any lie is uncovered (and there is nearly always the chance that this will occur) this diminishes the credibility of the liar and his or her opportunity to influence or guide the actions of others. Even if the lie is not uncovered, there is always the risk of this occurring (which is prone to induce a level of anxiety in most people). Lies, of whatever kind, when uncovered potentially reduce social cohesion.

According to Bok, it is for these reasons that even benevolent lies are often undesirable.

> [People who engage in white lies] are much more willing, in particular, to exonerate a well intentioned lie in their own part. . . . But in this benevolent self-evaluation by the liar of the lies he might tell, certain kinds of disadvantage and harm are most always overlooked. Liar usually weigh only the immediate harm to others from the lie against the benefits they want to achieve. The flaw in such an outlook is that it ignore or underestimates two additional kinds of harms — the harm that lying does to the liars themselves and the harm done to the general level of trust and social cooperation.[12]

According to Bok, the liars are harmed by their own lies in several ways. Apart from the chance that they will be caught out, there is also the risk that in their own eyes their integrity will diminish.

Bok accepts that the occasional white lie might not hurt the speaker, but contends that this perspective is often not realistic because few lies are solitary. Once a single lie has been stated, she believes that the psychological barriers are lowered and people are then far more prone to tell more lie — often in relation to more important issues.[13] She believes that 'those who begin with white lies can come to resort to more frequent and more serious ones. . . Because lines are so hard to draw, the indiscriminate use of such lies can lead to other deceptive practices'.[14]

The last two downsides of white lies identified by Bok are, however, not persuasive. The argument that those who pervade white lies are at risk of suffering personal integrity crisis assumes too much. This argument begs the question, given that the moral status of such lies is the very point in issue — if white lies are morally sound there can be no scope for a diminution in personal integrity.

The slippery slope argument assumes too much. There is no empirical evidence that people who lie for benevolent reasons are prone to extend this practice for other sorts of motives. As we have seen, lies have a qualitative as well as quantitative aspect. There are vastly different sorts of lies and it may be that people can neatly compartmentalise the lies that they are prepared to tell. This is certainly the situation in relation to many other forms of ostensibly harmful practices in which people engage. Rescuers and surgeons often inflict considerable bodily injury. This is motivated by the desire to assist their subjects and patients and there is no evidence to suggest that they are in other contexts more prone to cause harm to others. Thus it seems that benevolent motives do not necessarily spill over into broader patterns of conduct where such motives are absent.

Nevertheless, white lies are undesirable because they have the capacity to slightly diminish social cohesion. This means that unless there are pressing considerations to the contrary they ought to be avoided. Rather than complimenting the bad cook on his culinary skills better to acknowledge his (genuinely) nice attire or cute dog and instead of underplaying your husband's expanding waistline it is preferable to talk up his witty sense of humour or generosity.[15]

This does not mean that white lies ought to be totally avoided. It is often preferable to tell would-be visitors that you have another engagement rather than convey to them all the reasons that you find their company trying or objectionable. Continual knock backs will in time send a clear rejection message to people who have even a modicum of self awareness. The subtleness of this message is often less confronting and damaging than a blunt character assessment.

Ultimately, in evaluating the moral status of lies, there is a need to revert basic moral principles. We have seen that no principles are absolute and that they are universalisable. Normally the person whose interests are most adversely affected by lies is the duped party. Hence, an important consideration in evaluating the propriety of lies is whether the duped party, if he or she was aware of the all of the relevant facts, would agree that it was justifiable to lie in the given circumstances. Roughly this means that lies are permissible where one would not mind if he or she was duped.

An important caveat to this is that lies are always justifiable where they would maximise happiness. In performing this calculus, it is important to factor-in not only the direct harm that lost most lies cause to the duped and sometimes the liar but also the wider perspective in terms of negative impact that lies have on community trust and social cohesion.

This means that undermining and embellishment lies are almost always repugnant. As a general rule, lies are only justifiable in the following circumstances:

(1) In order to protect unjust attacks (on or violations of) higher order interests, such as the right to life, liberty and physical integrity. To this end parallels can be drawn with the right to self defence. This entails that lies are only justifiable in these circumstances were the threat is relatively im-

minent and there is no other lawful means to readily neutralise the risk. In applying this standard, higher order interests of the victim of the lie must not be ignored. Thus, it is permissible to tell a would-be suicide victim who is distraught at the loss of losing his job that his or her boss has reconsidered the decision if this is the only apparent way to get the sacked employee off the building ledge.

(2) To achieve important social goods which cannot be secured (at all or at least not very effectively) through open and transparent means. Thus, covert law enforcement practices and investigative journalism are sound practices.

(3) White lies are permissible where the topic of lie cannot be readily avoided and it is done with the principal motivation to spare a person's feelings. Thus it is permissible to tell an overweight person that they do not look fat in response to their question whether they look flabby, but it is not desirable to make the same remark if it has not been promoted by the fat person. White lies are also permissible where they act as social lubricants, obviating the need to engage in likely drawn out character evaluations and the like. In theory character appraisals have their benefits—hopefully they will lead to positive attitudinal reform. But this rarely happens. In relation to such fundamental matters most people seem to be very much stuck in their ways and often react negatively and sometimes in a hostile manner to criticism. Thus, it is preferable to decline a dinner invite on the basis that one has something else on rather than to tell them all the reasons you find them repugnant. To this end, the persistent invitor can obviously be draining. In such cases, a dose of measured reality may be necessary.

4.4 THE DISCORD BETWEEN THE PERCEPTION AND THE REALITY OF THE PROHIBITION AGAINST LYING

Having noted the frequency with which people lie and that lies are sometimes permissible there remains the paradox mentioned at the start of this chapter concerning the discord between the frequency of lies and public acceptance of them. As a psychological reality it seems that as a species we find it difficult to openly accept that lying is commonplace, that we all lie at some points and that lying is sometimes necessary and desirable. Thus, it would seem that as a community we engage in a consensual widespread deception on each other. We all know that lying is permissible in some circumstances but few of us are prepared to publicly acknowledge this fact.

The reason for the chasm between the pretence and truth about lying is unclear. However, speculating for one moment, the answer might rest in the fact that in order for the bonds of cooperation to subsist we need to at least pretend that lying is always bad. Overt acceptance to the contrary might weaken the bonds by making us look more suspiciously at every statement that is conveyed to us. Additionally, we might be reluctant to state that lying is permissible in some circumstances because of a fear that it will make it less likely that others will believe us in the future. If we admit lying in one context, there is a risk that others might think that we are pathological liars and hence are always to be distrusted.

Whether this collective con is desirable is not clear. Although the above discussion has shown that lying is permissible in some circumstances, it may yet be the case that we are better off pretending that it is inexcusable. After all this is just another lie. It might not be the 'mother' of all lies, but still a lie nevertheless. Ultimately whether or not we should maintain the illusion of the near absolute wrongness associated with lying or collectively adopt a more honest and pragmatic approach about the prohibition against lying turns on which approach is more likely to minimise the damage associated with lying.

An open recognition of the fact that lying is sometimes permissible would enable more accurate and efficient judgments to be made regarding the nature of lies which are uncovered. It might, however, have the side effect of encouraging more lies, many of which not fit within the accepted exceptions to the prohibition against lying. Thus, perhaps the policy of an ostensible total prohibition is best.

If this is the case, can we actually flourish in a world where some of the important rules are in fact shams? The answer would seem to be yes. In fact one of the leading recent ethicists, John L Mackie contented that the whole of moral discourse is illusory. This does not, according to Mackie, undercut its effectiveness as a means of guiding human behaviour. So long as we think or all pretend that it is objective it can properly guide our conduct.

In the case of lies, however, there is no evidence to suggest that we need to engage in a collective delusion in order to maintain social cohesion. As we have seen, sound arguments can be made why a person that lies in one context should not be viewed with suspicion regarding all their statements. There is no demonstrable slippery slope in the case of lying which turns whiter liars into pathological liars. There is a (rebuttable) presumption that they are bad. The lie that it is never permissible to lie should be viewed in the same light. We need to openly acknowledge that at times we all fib a little. This will lead to honest and open dialogue regarding the moral status of lies and sharpen the circumstances in which it is permissible to tell even bigger fibs.

NOTES

1. In her seminal work, S Bok, *Lying* (1978), 14, defines a lie as 'any intentionally deceptive message which is stated'.

2. Paradoxically, these results emerged from a study where the participants were themselves lied to regarding the purpose of the study—they were told that the purpose of the study was to examine how individuals interact when they meet someone new: (2002) *Journal of Basic and Applied Social Psychology*. For a summary of the findings see: http://www.eurekalert.org/pub_releases/2002-06/uoma-urf061002.php

3. A summary of the study can be found at: 'Study Shows Phone Calls are Ideal Fibbing Media': http://abcnews.go.com/Technology/story?id=99576.

4. S Bok, *Lying* (1978), xvii.

5. Allison Kornett: 'Deception is rampant—and sometimes we tell the biggest lies to those we love most': http://cms.psychologytoday.com/articles/pto-19970501-000033.html.

6. Ibid.

7. I Kant, *On A supposed Right to Lie From Altruistic Motives*, as extracted in Bok, at 285.

8. S Bok, above n 1, 19–20.

9. G J Warnock, The object of Morality (1971) as cited in Bok, ibid, 307.

10. Bok, above n 1, 21–22.

11. Ibid, 24.

12. Ibid, 25.

13. Ibid, 26–27

14. Ibid, 63.

15. A similar point is made by Bok, ibid.

Part C

MEDICAL ETHICS

Chapter Five

EUGENICS: SHOULD WE CREATE DESIGNER BABIES?

5.1 INTRODUCTION

Humankind is on the verge of a scientific revolution that has the potential to eradicate many human weaknesses and frailties that over the centuries have been the cause of an unthinkable amount of suffering. The human genome project, which involves mapping and sequencing the entire range of genetic materials found in human beings, has succeeded in providing at least a partial description of the genetic code of human beings. The potential benefits to humankind from the genome project are almost unlimited.

> Knowing how to control the human genome and how to change human genes is the most important piece of knowledge available for the twenty-first century, if not the third millennium. The improvement of man himself, the improvement of woman herself, is the most important improvement that humans have approached.[1]

In a similar vein, it has been observed that:

> [The Human Genome] Project has had a dramatic impact on medicine, and ... genetics will be "overwhelming" for medicine within 10 years. Virtually every month a new disease is identified as having "genetic roots." Once diseases are correlated with the genetic code, altering the relevant sequences through genetic engineering becomes an option. ... Many have a great deal of faith that we could connect DNA to "happiness and misery [and] the meaning of human existence" .... [The] effort underway is unlike anything ever before attempted ... If successful, it could lead to our ultimate control of human disease, aging, and death (references omitted).[2]

In this chapter, I examine the moral status of eugenics: the science that seeks to improve the human race through the control of hereditary factors. Eugenics promises to remove much of the luck involved in the birth process.

> Every newborn baby is dealt a genetic hand of cards which helps to determine how long he or she will be allowed to play the game of life. There are good cards, which predispose those who have them to a long and healthy existence, and there are bad cards, which predispose people to high blood pressure, say, or heart disease. Occasionally, cards are dealt out that doom their holders to an early and debilitating death. In the past, people never knew exactly which cards—in other words, which genes—they had been dealt. They could guess at the future only by looking at the kind of health problems experienced by their parents or grandparents (who provide the metaphorical pack from which the cards are dealt). Genetic testing, which makes it possible to probe for dangerous genes, has changed all this.[3]

Eugenics aims to go further than simply weeding out or identifying genes that cause or predispose people to certain diseases.[4] It can also be used for enhancement purposes.[5] It raises the prospect of identifying and using 'super genes' in the procreation process. Offspring produced with the aid of gene technology will in all probability be physically, aesthetically and intellectually superior to the rest of the community. Advances in eugenics may make it possible for each child to have the looks of Paris Hilton, the athletic ability of Lance Armstrong and the intelligence of Stephen W Hawking—all rolled into the one rather neat package.

Put simply, the human genome project promises to take eugenics from a clumsy trial and error process to a precise science, therefore opening up the way for far greater and more certain benefits to be derived in terms of the traits that can be conferred onto future generations. This coupled with the intense desire by parents for their children to have the best possible opportunity to succeed in life will invariably reinvigorate interest in eugenics. Pressure to utilise the knowledge gained from the human genome project in this way will also come from the apparently pervasive human desire to modify and change natural processes to its benefit.

Despite the initial attraction of eugenics, there are the 'spoilers': those that want to resist the scientific developments that promise to make many of the illnesses and limitations that stifle human flourishing a thing of the past. Given the enormous potential benefits of eugenics it is opportune to reflect on its moral status. The next part of this chapter discusses whether eugenics is intrinsically wrong. This is followed by a consideration of what I consider to be the two most persuasive objections against eugenics. First, it has been argued that eugenics will result in a vast disparity in the level of opportunity afforded to citizens. Secondly, opponents of eugenics point to the lessons of Nazi Germany as a reason for desisting from deliberate intervention with the procreation process.

I argue that neither of these perceived dangers constitutes a convincing reason for turning our backs on eugenics. Fortunately, the number of 'good genes' is not finite. Hence, a widespread eugenics program would in fact promote equality. Further, the slippery slope dangers associated with gene therapy have probably been overrated. The world has progressed significantly in a moral and legal sense over the past six decades or so. The type of belief and value system which underpinned the atrocities in Nazi Germany appears to have been firmly disavowed by most (at least Western) communities.

5.2 WHETHER EUGENICS IS INTRINSICALLY WRONG

In relation to most morally questionable practices, there are broadly two types of objections that can be raised. First, it can be argued that the practice is intrinsically wrong. The other type of argument is that the practice is wrong due to incidental bad consequences which will flow from it. This is an important distinction. Once opposition to a practice is grounded merely in possible adverse side effects stemming from it, the door is left open for proponents of the practice to irresistibly press their case by implementing safeguards nullifying the possible collateral harm.

Thus, the first line of attack, and potentially the strongest, available to those who oppose eugenics is to argue that eugenics necessarily violates some important norm — making it inherently morally wrong. As is discussed below, opponents of eugenics have generally employed the bad consequences argument as their main sword. Despite this, it is worth exploring whether they have dug their trenches further back than may have been logically necessary.

The claim that a certain practice is intrinsically morally wrong has been used with some degree of success by those opposed to euthanasia and abortion. It has been argued that euthanasia and abortion are wrong because they violate the right to life — of the patient and fetus, respectively. The important feature of this type of objection is that it does not rely on the potential incidental (undesirable) consequences of the respective practices to justify their wrongness. This ensures that the debate concerning the moral status of euthanasia and abortion does not automatically focus on the possibility of appropriate safeguards to address incidental undesirable consequences stemming from the practices. Rather supporters of the practices are forced to first overcome the threshold issue of whether the practices are bad per se.

In the context of the eugenics debate, an argument along these lines seems less tenable. Although even genetic screening has been labelled as genocide against the disabled,[6] eugenics does not *necessarily* involve the infringement of any type of recognisable, let alone important, human right or interest. The parties directly involved in the process are the parents, the eugenicist, and sometimes the fetus—depending on whether conception has occurred. From the perspective of the first two parties, there is no question that neither of their interests are in any respect violated. They are simply consenting adults involved in what is essentially an information gathering process. Further, from the parents perspective involvement in the process allows them to make informed choices about the traits of their offspring, thereby increasing their level of autonomy.

The fetus may have a stronger ground for complaint, especially if the results are not favourable, in which case termination may be the outcome. At present, this only occurs in a small percentage of cases—for example, in some cases following a diagnosis of Down's syndrome. As genetic technology improves and tests are available for a larger number of diseases, it is likely that this type of 'family planning' will increase. However, even if eugenics leads to a higher abortion rate, this does not translate into an inherent moral drawback of the practice.

The decision to terminate is not a necessary by-product of an adverse genetic finding, merely a common outcome of such a finding. Parents who receive the bad news are not committed to aborting, instead they could use the information to take pre-emptive steps to try to minimise as far as possible the difficulties that may be faced by their child. Accordingly, the fact that increased genetic knowledge and screening will invariably lead to more abortions[7] must be placed in the bad consequences side of the argument.

Where the eugenics process relates not to screening for disease carrying genes, but rather to endowing the progeny with the 'strongest' possible genetic makeup, it would seem that there is even less cause for complaint by the child. The child is blessed with the strongest possible compliment of genes, thereby maximising his or her potential and giving the child every possible chance to succeed in life. Where enhancement objectives relate to subjective qualities, such as height and hair color, the child may have some cause for grievance—he or she may simply develop different tastes to his or her parents. But it is not clear that the child has any greater reason to complain in such circumstances than where the 'choices' are made as a result of the lottery of the birth process.

Thus, when one focuses directly on the intrinsic features of eugenics there is no basis for arguing that it is morally wrong. In order to establish that the practice is morally repugnant the only path left is to argue that it will lead to unacceptable side effects.

5.3 BAD CONSEQUENCES AND SLIPPERY SLOPE ARGUMENT

There are two ways in which such an argument can be developed. The first is that eugenics will cause undesirable social consequences. The second is that while eugenics, in at least some form, may be acceptable it will invariably lead to other practices which are morally unacceptable. This is commonly termed the slippery slope, the features are set out in chapter one. I consider the objections in that order.

5.3.1 Inequality

A common criticism of eugenics is that it will result in social inequality. Permitting parents input into the genetic makeup of their children it is feared will produce a 'super class', which has significant advantages over the rest of the community whose parents could not or would not utilise gene therapy.

Given the spiraling cost of health care, there is little question that genetic testing and the opportunity to participate in decisions relating to the genetic makeup of one's child will be confined to the rich—at least initially. This will mean that the benefits of eugenics will be confined to the elite wealthy section of the community, resulting in the children of the rich having better health and more talent and ability than those of the poor. Theoretically, this is unfair. This is so whether one ascribes to the needs or deserts notion of justice —the children of the rich being no more needy or deserving of the genetic advantages conferred on them. They were just pot lucky that they happened to have rich parents.

However, this type of head start is no different to the type of inequities that society currently condones. There are two main variables which determine the level of achievement that will be attained by an individual. The first is his or her genetic make up. The other is the environment in which the person is raised. So far as environment is concerned, the main variable is simply the amount of resources (or more crudely money) that one's parents have. This influence is so strong, that without knowing a single thing about the characteristics of the children in question, one can be relatively confident that the next child born to parents that have a million dollars in the bank will obtain a university education, not spend a single day unemployed or wanting for anything much. This compares to the next child born to a homeless couple who in all likelihood will not complete high school, have few employment opportunities and be fortunate not to serve a stint in prison.[8] There is no question that the single most important indicia concerning the level of achievement of a child is the net wealth of his or her parents. Once again this is simply pot luck.

This is a situation which we as a society could address, at least to some degree. For example, one way to mitigate economic unfair advantage is to introduce laws preventing inheritance. While such laws would not affect the advantage gained by children while their parents were alive, if drafted properly (thereby preventing avoidance techniques) they would cut very deeply every generation. Instead of property passing to one's next of kin, it could be appropriated by the government and redistributed among the poorer members of the community. A less drastic measure aimed at achieving the same result would be to introduce death taxes. However, death taxes no longer exist in most Western nations and there is no sign that they will be re-introduced.

Given the nature of the democratic systems in Western nations, the reluctance by governments to implement such measures and the lack of community pressure for them means that one can assume that there is at least a broad level of (tacit) community support for a taxation and fiscal system that condones enormous disparities in wealth and the consequent inequalities of opportunity. In a system that already tolerates so much inequality of opportunity, it seems indefensible to argue that the types of inequalities that may arise from eugenics are necessarily morally offensive. In terms of the net result, biological advantages stemming from eugenic procedures are not different in nature to economic advantages—at worst, biological advantages will merely serve to perpetuate existing unfairness. A community that was serious about the notion of equality of opportunity would take measures along the lines discussed above to redress fundamental imbalances arising out of our present social and political system.

A counter to this line of reasoning is that morality is normative not descriptive. As we saw in chapter one, an 'ought' cannot be derived from an 'is'. Hence the fact that we tolerate existing inequalities of opportunity does not entail that we *should*. This line of argument probably lays the strongest foundation from which to criticise the unfair advantages that will be bestowed on the eugenic super class. Ideally all people should have the same opportunity to maximise their potential, pursue their goals and to flourish. Although, it would take an enormous reversal of prevailing pragmatic community attitudes to achieve this, it can be argued that, we should continue striving for this ideal rather than surrendering meekly to accepting existing causes of inequality and condoning other practices which will perpetuate them.

However, proponents of the social equality argument are then confronted with the paradox that a true commitment to levelling the playing field of opportunity requires the elimination of *all factors* that contribute in a meaningful way to one's level of achievement—including, of course, genetic makeup. Even if the problems stemming from economic disadvantage could be eliminated, children who have the fortune to be dealt a good gene hand at birth will still have an enormous head start over those who have an inferior genetic makeup. Thus, a full commitment to equality in fact drives us towards eugenics —for all people. To this end, the splendour of eugenics is that unlike wealth which is a finite resource, good genes are not. Potentially everyone can share in them.

Thus, opponents of eugenics find themselves in a difficult dilemma if they wish to pursue the equality of opportunity argument. Approaching the issue from the perspective of conventional morality it would seem that the argument can be countered by the fact that society is in fact willing to tolerate the type of inequalities that will stem from the creation of super children. Changing tack to the 'in principle objection', is even less comforting since it commits them to the position that eugenics should be available to all. They are cornered into the position that the problem with eugenics is not that it may be practiced *at all*, but rather that it will not be practiced *enough*.

There is also the further point that it seems arbitrary that the moment of birth should mark the moment at which it is appropriate to commence implementing strategies to maximise a child's potential. Parents already engage aggressively in social engineering, by making education and lifestyle choices for their children which will indelibly shape their lives. There seems no reason that 'parenting' should commence only at birth: gene therapy 'may present choices, but it is the moral equivalent . . . of activities present in the context of parenthood'.[9] Given that parents spend enormous resources on nurturing and maximising the physical and mental capabilities of children after they are born and society as a whole devotes endless resources to the education and health of its citizens, it seems irrational to proscribe the pursuit of the same goals at the planning level—before a child is born or even at a point prior to conception. This is particularly so when one considers that as a result of biotechnological advances it will soon be the case that it is prior to conception that resources to these ends could be most effectively and efficiently deployed.[10] To leave pursuit of these objectives to a time after birth is inefficient and in many cases is simply to 'close the gate after the horse has bolted'.

5.3.2 Slippery Slope Argument

The slippery slope argument has been used widely in the context of the eugenics debate. In its logical form, the slippery slope argument is unconvincing in this context. The reasons advanced in favour of eugenics, such as the desire to eradicate disease and produce children that are more capable do not logically justify morally undesirable practices. In theory, these reasons can be used to distinguish between the process of attempting to improve the human race through the control of hereditary factors and other types of practices:

> The hope of using science and medicine to create children who get the best possible start in their lives is very different from the forced use of medical and scientific knowledge to solve society's perceived ills by creating biologically superior populations or simply killing those deemed inferior.[11]

In the context of the eugenics debate, the strongest support for the empirical version of the slippery slope argument is history.[12] Most notably the systematic process of the sterilization and killing of millions of Jews, Gypsies and Slavs in Nazi Germany which occurred against the backdrop of the desire to improve the genetic makeup of the German people and the fundamental belief that other races were inferior:

> Eugenics consumed the German medical, biological and social scientific communities in the decade before World War II. Many physicians and scientists were frantic about threats they saw to the genetic health of the nation posed by the presence of inferior populations such as Jews, Gypsies, Slavs and, to a lesser extent because the threat was more distant, African peoples. The steps they took to protect against the public health disaster of a 'polluted' racial stock were so awful, so immoral and so heinous that they have, rightly, shaped all subsequent discussion of the ethics of both human genetics and eugenics.[13]

It has been contended that this is an inevitable path to which eugenics leads:

> As was made abundantly clear under the nazi programme of mass genocide, a well-functioning eugenics operation is never satisfied for long with modest results. It is almost inevitable that whenever such policies are found "useful," increased activity of the same sort will be seen as "more useful."[14]

However, it has been pointed out that the motivations that resulted in the death of millions of innocent people at the hands of the Nazis differ significantly from those moving the present eugenics movement:

> There is no slope that leads inexorably from therapeutic . . . interventions intended to benefit future persons to the creation of eugenically-driven, genocidal social policies. Nazi eugenic policies were not aimed at benefiting individuals. The state of the Volk, not the individual, was the object of the Nazi eugenic policy. Public health not individual therapy was the driving force behind the Nazi medicalization of eugenics.[15]

As is adverted to above, *logically* there is a significant difference between eugenics in the form of consenting individuals seeking to utilise scientific knowledge in order to maximise the capabilities of their children and the genocidal practices employed in Germany in the middle part of the last century. However, it is at least tenable to argue that eugenics will promote (if not ingrain) a culture which sanctions a strong preference towards certain traits. The corollary of this is that such an attitude will engender a bias against individuals lacking the 'proper pedigree', resulting in less moral concern and respect being shown towards them. This may then diminish the sphere of protection accorded to such people.

Thus, the appalling consequences that resulted from one foray into eugenics, provides a compelling reason for at least treading very wearily before engaging in practices of a like nature lest they once again provide the catalyst for a like type of catastrophe.[16] The events in Nazi Germany were so horrendous that perhaps the eugenics movement should be put on hold until there is firm evidence that the values and beliefs which permitted such an evil regime to flourish have totally dissipated from the human psyche.

However, even if this level of caution is adopted, the considerable moral progress made by humankind in the past sixty years provides strong reasons for giving the green light to eugenics.

As noted in chapter one, modern society can view with a considerable degree of achievement and pride its preparedness to embrace and promulgate many fundamental moral norms. Following the Second World War, there has been a discernible increase in the level of awareness of the types of interests and protections which are a pre-condition to human flourishing. There is still a long way to go before something approaching a universal moral code can be declared, but there are promising signs that some degree of convergence is emerging regarding the scope and content of basic moral prescriptions.

Without question large scale human rights violations continue to occur. The recent mass killings in nations such as Uganda, the Democratic Republic of Congo, Afghanistan, Iraq and Rwanda unfortunately graphically illustrate this. Despite such events there is no question that the types of beliefs and values which underscored the practices in Nazi Germany have been largely, at least ostensibly, dispelled by most communities—at least in the Western World. Racism and elitism are not only morally offensive, but are also legally prohibited and have been replaced by a commitment (at least at the formal level) to accepting the equal moral worth of each person. Laws prohibiting discrimination on the grounds of race and sex are designed to facilitate such ends. Even if many members of the community merely pay lip service to such laws, the educative role of the law, one expects, will ensure that such beliefs will ultimately permeate the belief system of most members of the community.

Thus, there is solid evidence that eugenic ideals can lead to bad side effects by fuelling an attitude that individuals who lack the 'proper pedigree' are in some sense less worthy of moral concern. However, this is not a decisive reason for rejecting eugenics. Ultimately, eugenics is no different to many discoveries, such as splitting the atom[17]—it can be used for good or bad. The manner in which eugenics will be used depends on the moral and legal environment in which it is practiced. A strong level of disapprobation towards racism and elitism and a genuine commitment to the equal moral worth of each individual are the pre-conditions that ought to be satisfied before the next aggressive venture into eugenics is undertaken. Formally, at least in most Western countries, there is a commitment to promoting the notion of equality. Whether this has yet translated into a genuine belief in the equality of all persons is far more difficult to ascertain.

5.4 BALANCING ALL THE CONSIDERATIONS

On the plus side of the eugenics scales are the significant benefits of the practice in terms of improving the health and physical and mental capabilities of the population. On the other side of the scale is the fear that the practice will foster a culture whereby the interests and perhaps even the lives of many other citizens may be devalued. In terms of the importance of the competing interests, the scales are finely balanced—or at least there is no clear victor. It is simply not clear how an enormous improvement in the health and capabilities of one individual stacks up against a diminution in the concern shown to the welfare of another person. However, in balancing the scales the competing nature of the interests is only one variable.

The other important variable is the certainty or likelihood that the respective gains or risks will eventuate. Given the advances in gene therapy, there seems to be a very high level of probability that such technology can produce immense benefits in the form of eradicating disease and enhancing human capability. The load on the other side of the scales is far more speculative in nature. Hopefully, society is aware of the cost of devaluing any life. Changes to the moral and legal landscape since World War II indicate that this is the case. This is supported by the fact that genetic testing for a small range of diseases is already commonplace[18] and in some parts repositories already exist for storing gametes from men who have displayed scientific, athletic or entrepreneurial acumen.[19] Such, albeit relatively minor, forays into eugenics do not appear to have eroded the level of moral concern that generally exists in the community. Accordingly, it seems that the time is right again to give eugenics the green light.

NOTES

1. H Holmes, 'Choose Better Human Genes': http://health.upenn.edu/~bioethic/genetics/articles/10.holme.better.html. See also Hon Justice Michael Kirby, 'Legal Problems: Human Genome Project' (1993) 67 *ALJ* 894.

2. G McGee, 'Pragmatism and Genetic Engineering' (1994) at http://health.upenn.edu/~bioethic/genetics/articles/3.mcgee.pragmatism.html. There is of course a danger that the possibilities stemming from eugenics have been overstated: see T Caulfield, 'Underwhelmed: Hyperbole, Regulatory Policy, and the Genetic Revolution' (2000) 45 *McGill Law Journal* 437.

3. 'Testing Times', in *Economist.com*: http:// www.economist.com/displayStory.cfm?Story_ID=398173.

4. For a good overview of the difference between single gene disorders and polygenic disorders, see D Keays, 'The Legal Implications of Genetic Testing: Insurance, Employment and Privacy' (1999) 3 *JLM* 357, 358–59. There are already over 100 genetic conditions or predispositions that can be diagnosed using genetic testing.

5. The issue of whether there is a morally relevant difference between seeking to use genetics to cure disease as opposed to enhancement of non-disease traits is not directly addressed in this chapter. Logically, however, it seems difficult to identify a non-arbitrary distinction between the two objectives. On this issue, see for example, J Harris, 'Is Gene Therapy a Form of Eugenics' (1993) 7 *Bioethics* 178.

6. For example, see 'The Spectre of Eugenics' (1996) 86 *Living Marxism*: http://www.infominc.co.uk/LM/LM86/LM86_Eutures.htlm.

7. For example, see J Hunt, 'Perfecting Humankind: A Comparison of Progressive and Nazi Views on Eugenics, Sterilization and Abortion' (1999) 66 *Linacre Quarterly* 129.

8. For a discussion of the connection between social disadvantage and offending, see my comments in M Bagaric, 'Double Punishment and Punishing Character: The Unfairness of Prior Convictions' (2000) 19 *Criminal Justice Ethics* 10.

9. G McGee, 'Pragmatism and Genetic Engineering': http://www. health.upenn.edu/~bioethic/articles/3.mcgee.pragmatism.html.

10. 'The Spectre of Eugenics', above n 9. According to one study, in the United States biomedical advances, as well as lifestyle changes, are projected to result in the saving of billions of dollars in health costs by 2015, including $76 billion of costs avoided for Alzheimer's disease: see Malinowski, above n 13, 343—references at note 96.

11. A Caplan, 'If Gene Therapy is the Cure, What is the Disease': http://www.health.upenn.edu/~bioethic/articles/I.caplan.gene.therapy.htlm.

12. Ibid.

13. Ibid. For an overview of the eugenics movement in Germany and other countries, see A B Marks (ed), *The Wellborn Science: Eugenics Germany, France, Brazil and Russia* (New York, Oxford University Press, 1990). See also, K Bayertz,

GenEthics: Technological Intervention in Human Reproduction as a Philosophical Problem (Cambridge University press, Cambridge, 1994).

14. *Eugenics Watch*: http://www.africa2000.com/ENDX/endx.htm
15. Caplan, above n 11.
16. On this point, see P Gray, 'Cursed Issue' (1993) 153(1) *Time* 84.
17. The analogy between eugenics and splitting the atom is also made by J Glover, *What Sort of People Should There Be?* (Penguin, New York, 1984).
18. Newborns in many Western Countries are already routinely screened for cystic fibrosis, congenital hypothyroidism and phenylketonuria between three and five days of birth: see L Skene, 'Access to and Ownership of Blood Samples for Genetic Tests: Guthrie spots' (1997) 5 *JLM* 137.
19. A Caplan, above n 11.

Chapter Six

Stem Cell Research and Abortion

6.1 INTRODUCTION

Stem cell research, like eugenics, promises immense health benefits. Broadly there are two different forms of stem cell research. The first involves using stem cells obtained from embryos—either through (therapeutic) cloning or using surplus embryos from assisted reproductive technology (ART) programs. In each case this involves destroying the embryo. Therapeutic cloning (also known as somatic cell nuclear transfer) requires scientists to remove the nucleus from a donated egg and substitute it with a nucleus from a patient's cell. The stem cells from the embryo are then removed after a few days. This destroys the embryo. The stems cells are then normally used to grow tissue, including heart and nerve tissue that is identical to that of the patient's therefore minimising the risk of rejection by the immune system.

The second involves using stem cells obtained from adults. The advantage of adult stem cell research is that it does not involve the destruction of a fetus or any other entity. The disadvantage is that many scientists believe it has less curative benefits than embryonic stem cells. In most Western nations it is permissible to use excess embryonic stems from ART programs for research, but therapeutic cloning is prohibited. Adult stem cell research is also permitted.

The majority of scientists and ethicists agree that adult stem cell research is morally permissible, yet at this stage the science is unreliable and the potential of such research is unclear. The principal focus of this chapter is on embryonic stem cell research. Unless expressly indicated to the contrary, this is what I mean by stem cell research—I do not distinguish between cloned embryos and surplus ART embryos.

Stem cell research is a very extremely divisive issue. This is not surprising. It promises significant benefits to human health but arguably comes at the expense of violating the most fundamental moral virtue—the right to life. The debate has become increasingly emotive.

The Catholic Church has labelled stem cell research as cannibalism.[1] Sydney Catholic Archbishop George Pell has stated that therapeutic cloning was worse ethically than reproductive cloning, which would 'at least involve the intention to nurture the life of the human clone'.[2] Rev Ross Carter of the Uniting Church, added weight to this view when he said that 'we don't condone using human beings as a repair kit for others, no matter how tragic those lives are'.[3] Such remarks have led perhaps the world's most famous moral philosopher, Peter Singer, to label the Church, which has over a billion followers, as irrelevant.[4]

Prior to addressing the morality of stem cell research, I provide a brief overview of nature and potential benefits of stem cell research. The normative discussion of stem cell research is principally devoted to considering the arguments against the practice. I do not discuss at length the arguments in favour of the practice. This is for two reasons. First, as I detail in the following section, the possible good consequences are patently obvious. Secondly, and more importantly, as discussed in chapters one and two, liberty ranks highly in any moral code. This entails that all acts and practices should be presumed to be morally permissible unless sound reasons are provided to the contrary. The same point is made in the context of the cloning debate by Russell Blackford:

> In a modern liberal democracy . . . there is an onus, which should not be met easily, on those who wish to use the state's power to suppress particular activities, techniques or investigations, however unpopular. . . . [S]ome rationally compelling justification must always be given for the enactment of legislative prohibitions.[5]

I acknowledge that many believe that there are stronger arguments for using excess embryos produced for IVF than using embryos which are deliberately created for use in research.[6] This chapter does not, however, consider the persuasiveness of distinctions that can possibly be made between such practices. The principal issue in relation to all embryo experimentation is the point at which life commences. Logically, it is only once this issue is resolved that subordinate moral issues and distinctions should be tackled.

The moral status of abortion turns on many of the same issues which are at play in the stem cell debate. Once they are evaluated in the context of stem cells, the morality of abortion becomes relatively clear cut. This is discussed in the last part of this chapter.

6.2. THE POTENTIAL BENEFITS OF STEM CELL RESEARCH

The potential health benefits of embryonic stem cells stems from their 'pluripotentiality', meaning that they have the ability to develop from an undifferentiated cell mass into all or nearly all of the tissues in the human body. Scientists are presently trying to determine how to control the differentiation process so that embryonic stem cells can be used in the most therapeutically effective manner. Embryonic stem cells have the potential to cure a number of cell-based diseases (such as Parkinson's, Alzheimer's, diabetes and heart disease) through utilising stem cell lines derived from research. The use of insulin-secreting cells, for example, could be used for the treatment of diabetes, and nerve cells could be generated for the treatment of Parkinson's disease. Embryonic stem cells could also potentially be used to develop tissue that can be transplanted into patients to repair failing organs (such as the liver or kidney).

Furthermore, it is expected that human embryonic stem cell technology will be important for its practical application in the area of drug discovery (as the stem cells can be used to measure how specific cell types respond to being treated with chemicals), and will be important for undertaking study into early stages of human development.

Research on embryonic stem cells is still, however, at its preliminary stage, and much further work is still necessary to determine how to most effectively control the differentiation of stem cells, and to make sure that the use of stem cells for a range of scientific, medical and commercial applications will be both safe and reliable.

Research into adult stem cells is also considered to have medical promise, but the orthodox medical view has been that the benefits are not likely to be as dazzling as that from embryonic stem cells. The main difficulties with research on adult stem cells are considered to be that their ability to regenerate is limited, they are much harder to isolate compared to embryonic stem cells, and they are difficult to control in a laboratory (making it difficult to obtain clinically significant amounts for research purposes).

Recent findings, however, seem to indicate that the therapeutic promise of adult stem cell research may have been underestimated. As is noted in the Andrews Committee Report:

> There is growing understanding that adult stem cells may be more flexible than previously thought. Recent research has shown that adult stem cells can differentiate into developmentally unrelated cell types such as nerve and blood cells. ... 'Lineage defined progenitor cells [stem cells] in adult tissue may be more plastic than hitherto thought They might have the capacity to de-differentiate, or be reprogrammed becoming totipotent stem cells' (references omitted).[7]

In addition to this, there are also some possible advantages that adult stem cells may offer over embryonic stem cells. They could be harvested relatively simply and transformed in the laboratory and transferred back to the patient, thereby avoiding rejection problems.[8]

Michael Casanova, the Victorian president of the Australian Family Association, recently suggested that in fact adult stem cell research may prove more promising than embryonic stem cell experimentation:

> More than 60 different conditions have been treated, including leukaemia, breast cancer (and 20 other types of cancer); multiple sclerosis, Crohn's disease, rheumatoid and juvenile arthritis (and 10 other auto-immune diseases); heart attack and corneal damage; 10 blood conditions; three immunodeficiencies; six metabolic disorders; jaw bone replacement and three other wound or injury types; and, yes, Parkinson's disease, stroke damage and even spinal cord injury....
>
> The 65 stem cell applications are not mere dreams that might come true in 10 or 15 years, they have long passed the stage of successful animal trials, they're here already....
>
> All these successes have been achieved using stem cells from patients' own bodies, or from umbilical cord blood. The twist is that, to date, there have been no human success stories from stem cells taken from human embryos. Even in animals, the literature shows very little beyond a lot of dead rats. Why? Embryo stem cells are very potent, but also very unstable: they have a tendency to form teratomas, tumour-like masses that can include teeth, skin, hair and bone. That is not good for mouse brains or rats' knee joints. Beyond that, embryo stem cells have a tendency to accumulate mutations.
>
> And the problem of patients' bodies rejecting embryo stem cells is bigger than expected. Human cloning is seen as one way to overcome the problem, but the body can sometimes recognise the danger of these erratic embryo stem cells, even when there are practically no DNA differences.

6.3 THE MORAL STATUS OF STEM CELL RESEARCH

I now analyse the moral status of embryonic stem cell research.

6.3.1 Non-consequentialist Arguments against Stem Cell Research

The first line of attack available to those who oppose stem cell research is to argue that the practice necessarily violates some important norm—making it inherently morally wrong. There have been two principal criticisms made along this line. The first is that the practice is objectionable because it violates the right to life, which is the most fundamental human right. Destroying stem cells, it is argued, is no different in principle to killing developed human beings. This sentiment was echoed in the submission by Pro-Life Victoria to the House of Representatives Standing Committee on Legal and Constitutional Affairs during its recent inquiry into the regulation of human cloning and stem cell research in Australia:

> If human beings are created for the purpose of experimentation and then destruction, this creation is itself objectionable and shows flagrant disregard for human rights and the value of human life.[9]

In a similar vein, it has been argued that:

> All embryos that result from the union of male and female gametes are created with a potential to create life. That is the core of our being. To fertilise an ovum just for scientific manipulation and [with that destroy] the embryo's only possible fate, denies that very essence of our humanity.[10]

If this argument is valid, it would constitute a significant blow to stem cell research. As was adverted to above, the right to life is the most basic of rights. Logically, non-observance of the right to life would render all other human rights devoid of meaning. Recognition of this is found in the fact that the 'the intentional taking of human life is . . . the offence which society condemns most strongly'.[11] The House of Lords has declared that 'this principle, fundamental though it is, is not absolute'.[12] There are some well established exceptions to the right to life, such as self-defence and war, however, stem research cannot be analogised with such practices—in the case of war and self-defence there is at least a perception that the other party is a wrongdoer.

The other main non-consequentialist objection to stem cell research is that it violates Kant's categorical imperative, which is the view that people should always act as if every action were to become a universal law. From this, it follows that we should treat others as ends given that that is how we regard ourselves, and never simply as a means.

> Every human being has a legitimate claim in respect from his fellow human beings and is in turn bound to respect every other. Humanity itself is a dignity; for a human being cannot be used merely as a means by any human being but must always be used at the same time as an end.[13]

It is argued that to engage in stem cell research is to treat another person as a thing or tool (to promote the health of another person) and not as a moral agent. To engage in stem cell research involves 'treating a new human as a commodity like a drug or some other curative process . . . and as such offends against the inherent right to life of the new human being, ignoring his/her own individual personality'.[14] More emotively, as we have seen, this line of reasoning has lead to the charge of cannibalism—killing one person so that another can flourish.

6.3.2 Consequentialist Arguments against Stem Cell Research

The most direct consequentialist attack that could be levelled against stem cell research is that it results in net diminution in utility because the happiness to the (ultimate, sometimes distant) patient will be outweighed by the unhappiness caused to the stem cell. This argument is obviously flawed. Quite simply a stem cell is incapable of having any experiences, let alone happiness. A narrow consequentialist argument (that is, one that only considers the interests of the parties directly affected) could only be made if the notion of happiness is extended from actual happiness to potential happiness. This would require the balancing of the potential happiness of the embryo against that of the potential patient. Such a balancing exercise, however, does not appear to be plausible. There is simply no coherent manner in which one can calculate the potential happiness of entities that are not yet in existence—the notion is so indeterminate to be vacuous.

A consequentialist attack on stem cell research can, however, be mounted if one looks beyond the interests of the parties directly affected. In the context of the stem cell research debate, it could be argued that stem cell research might promote (if not ingrain) a culture whereby all life is devalued. If the stringency of the prohibition against ending human life in one context is relaxed (by permitting stem cell research) there is, arguably, the risk that it may result in a diminution in the importance accorded to the right to life across the board. Thus legalising stem cell research may encourage a culture which more readily tolerates killing human beings when it is convenient to do so. This would reduce the sense of security experienced by all members of the community. More narrowly, it has been suggested that allowing stem cell research may lead to cloning for reproductive purposes.

> Acceptance of such a process raises the ethical issues often referred to as 'slippery slope' issues (that is, that in the acceptance of research on human embryos in order to produce desired tissues and organs an irreversible step may be taken that will lead to scientific advances that in turn will make the cloning of human beings more likely to be accepted).[15]

6.3.3 The Importance of the Commencement of Life Issue

Accordingly, there are three principal moral objections to stem cell research. The key aspect to note about these objections is that their persuasiveness largely turns on one issue: when does life begin?

This issue has figured prominently in the abortion debate. But it arises even more acutely in the context of stem cell research. In the case of abortion, the issue could be feasibly circumvented by the fact that even if the fetus has a right to life this is not necessarily decisive of the moral status of the practice. There is a *clear* countervailing interest—that of the mother. The capacity of the fetus to exist and continue to develop is contingent upon a duty being imposed upon the woman to carry the fetus for nine months or so.[16] The uncertainty regarding the existence and scope of such a duty allowed, to some extent at least, the right to life issue to be diluted or circumvented.

The community does not have the same luxury in the case of stem cell research. The issue of when life begins is clearly the central issue in this debate.

This is a point noted by George W Bush, during a moment of enlightenment, in 2001:

> Research on embryonic stem cells raises profound ethical questions, because extracting the stem cell destroys the embryo, and thus destroys the potential for life... *At its core, the issue forces us to confront fundamental questions about the beginnings of life and the ends of science*. It lives at a difficult moral intersection, juxtaposing the need to protect life in all its phases with the prospect of saving and improving life in all other stages. As the discoveries of modern science create tremendous hope, they also lay vast ethical mine fields.[17]

In order for the debate on stem cell research to advance in a transparent, informed and honest fashion the issue regarding the point at which life begins must be tackled-head on. This is so irrespective of whether one adopts a deontological or consequentialist normative theory. As we saw earlier there are two key deontological arguments against stem cell research. The first is simply that it violates the right to life. A necessary (though, as discussed below, not necessarily sufficient) pre-condition for this is that the entity (in this case a stem cell) has a life. The Kantian objection also involves the same assumption—*people* (that is, entities in relation to which life has commenced) should not be used as means. Potential consequentialist attacks on embryonic stem cell research would also, as we saw above, be highly persuasive if in fact the practice involved the destruction of life.

6.4 THE CENTRAL ISSUE: WHEN DOES LIFE BEGIN?

There are several points at which it could be claimed that life exists. Three of the most common views are that life begins at birth, at some point during the (normal) gestation process or at conception.

The strongest argument in favour of birth is that this is the point where the being can to some extent enjoy an independent existence—at least insofar as it is no longer physically dependent upon its mother. This, however, does not seem to be a sound distinction. After birth, it is not assumed that people will lose their right to life if they are deprived of their capacity to live independently. For example, patients living with the assistance of respirators or other medical equipment do not have a diminished right to life.

There is no obvious point during the gestation process which can be used to signify when life commences. Gestation is an ongoing gradual process. At no point during the process does the fetus have relevantly different attributes to a point marginally earlier in time. Despite this, there have been some attempts to identify a distinctive point at which the line can be drawn. In this regard, perhaps the most popular view is that life commences when 'consciousness' begins. There appears, however, to be intractable problems with this proposal.

The first relates to identifying what exactly is meant by consciousness. Savulescu seems to equate it with the capacity to feel pain,[18] and notes that the structural development for this is not present in a fetus before 26 weeks.[19] Michael Tooley on the other hand sets the bar far higher. For Tooley, consciousness means that an agent is capable of desiring to continue existing as a subject of experiences and other mental states—a characteristic which is obviously not shared even by infants.[20] Thus, there are widely divergent views regarding the nature of consciousness, making it an inappropriate criterion for demarcating an event of such significance as the commencement of life.

Even if we accept Savulescu's minimum criterion for consciousness, it is not clear why the capacity to feel pain marks the point for the commencement of life. In all other circumstances the ability to feel pain is clearly not a *necessary* pre-condition for life. Plants and lower order animals do not feel pain, yet there is no question that they are alive. Further, human beings who have lost the capacity to feel pain through accident or illness are certainly not regarded as dead. It may be that the capacity to feel pain is a *sufficient* criterion for life, but this does not assist Savulescu—it still leaves unanswered the issue of what is the minimum condition necessary for life to exist. It seems that Savulescu makes the mistake of merging two not necessarily related issues: the point at which life commences and the criteria for a being to have a moral status.

Finally, it could be argued that life commences at conception. As is noted by Savulescu, this argument has been extended to include a totipotent stem cell produced by cloning.[21] An argument that conception is a non-arbitrary point can be made on the basis that from this moment onwards the make up of the entity is etched in stone. The entity is now unique, in that it differs from every other entity before it and after it. Some time must pass in order for this uniqueness to be *exhibited*, but it is submitted that lack of patent differentiation is not relevant to the moral status of a being. The fact that many baby boys look alike at birth, or that 'all grown pigs look the same', is not a basis for diminishing the moral status of such beings.

Savulescu attacks the view that life begins at conception on several grounds. First, he argues that it implies that some current practices are like murder. One example he uses is abortion. This, however, is not a persuasive criticism. Morality is normative, not descriptive. The mere fact that a practice or activity does occur, no matter how frequently and how widely it is accepted, does not mean that it should happen. As noted in chapter one, this is unequivocally demonstrated by human history concerning suppression of minority groups and women. Abortion might well be murder (or manslaughter). Further, in the case of abortion, as was indicated above, there is perhaps a countervailing principle that arguably overrides the right to life of the fetus — the right of the mother to bodily integrity.

Secondly, he argues that to destroy a zygote (prior to day 14) is akin to destroying an egg and a sperm that would have created an identifiable person. This is because of what he terms 'logical problems' with the view that we begin to exist at conception. He elaborates on this by using several practical examples. One is the phenomenon of twinning.

> What happens when a zygote A divides into identical B and B* at day 2? When did B begin to exist? Was B identical with A? Both B and B* cannot be identical with A, because this would imply that the twins B and B* are identical to each other — that is, that they are both the same thing. This implies that B and B* came into existence when A divided on day 2, not conception. Indeed Dame Mary Warnock said: 'the embryo hasn't decided how many people it is going to be'. Thus the Warnock Committee in the United Kingdom influentially concluded that embryo experimentation was justifiable until 14 days after conception.[22]

The process of twinning can, however, be coherently incorporated into the view that human existence commences at conception. The simple response is that B and B* both come into existence at conception. Whether or not twinning occurs will occur is simply a biological process which is, presumably, pre-determined at the point of conception. The reality of the situation should not be confused with the issues of evidence and substantiation. The fact that at this point in time scientific knowledge is not sufficiently advanced to determine whether a zygote will remain the one entity or divide into two entities does not seem morally relevant. Principle should not be trumped by the limits of current day scientific knowledge. This is especially the case where the exception being mooted (twinning) is extremely rare and is used in an effort to rebut a principle of wide application and considerable importance.

Quite simply, the twinning example invites us to make 'bad law on the basis of hard cases'.

Thus, the most coherent logical point at which life begins appears to be at conception. I do not deny that there are difficulties with this approach. The entity at this point obviously varies markedly from developed human beings. It has no consciousness (irrespective of how that term is defined), no organs, and no capacity to maintain an independent existence. What it does have, however, from this point onwards is individuality or uniqueness and the building blocks for the development of life as we normally view it. Further, on matters pertaining to life and death, it is better to err on the side of conservatism.

Thus, the issue of when life begins is a complex one due to the fact that from the point of conception development is a slow incremental process. Such processes do not readily avail themselves to the drawing of sharp lines. In light of this, the least arbitrary point at which life begins is conception. This should be a bedrock upon which many our moral decisions are reached.

6.5 RAMIFICATIONS FOR MORALITY OF STEM CELL RESEARCH

This analysis has significant ramifications for stem cell research. Devotees of a deontological view of morality must oppose the practice unless they can in some way circumvent or diminish the applicability of the right to life principle in the context of stem cells. This is not necessarily implausible. Perhaps it could be argued that the commencement of life and the right to life do not necessarily coincide. Eminent philosophers such as HLA Hart have argued that in order for an agent to enjoy a right not only must he or she be capable of enjoying the relevant entitlement, but also be in a position to elect whether or not to exercise the particular right in question.[23]. A similar point is made by Michael Tooley who argues that human life is not intrinsically valuable and that for a person to have a right to life he or she must be capable of desiring to continue existing as a subject of experiences and other mental states.[24] Alternatively, it might be argued that the right to life comes in different strengths: for example, being commensurate with a person's level of development. Previous attempts to advance such an argument have been unpersuasive. Given my reservations about a non-consequentialist account of morality, there is no merit in trying to develop such arguments in this forum. However, non-consequentialists have been put on notice regarding the path they must tread in order to justify embryonic stem cell research.

The moral status of embryonic stem cell research is not clear from a utilitarian perspective. The fact that a being is in existence is not a sufficient basis for attributing moral status to it. The ultimate criterion for extending moral standing to a being is its capacity to experience pleasure and pain.

Stem cells cannot experience pleasure and pain and hence their interests are not directly relevant to the utilitarian calculus. However, stem cells may obtain moral standing in a derivative manner because the taking of life in one context may cheapen the value of life all around- thereby leading to a net reduction in personal safety and sense of security. The amount of weight that this argument has on the utilitarian scales will turn on the clarity with which it is possible to distinguish between destroying stem cells to assist others and sacrificing humans in other circumstances when it is serves the interests of others. The key question then becomes whether we can compartmentalise taking life to the context of stem cell research. Or will giving the green light to stem cell research lead to a gradual erosion in the respect for life? The answer to this necessarily involves a large degree of speculation. It depends on untested human and societal traits.

The practice of abortion provides some support for the view that legalising the destruction of the fetus in one context will lead to adverse consequences. The number of abortions in the United States since the landmark decision of *Wade v Roe* in 1973, which authorised abortion in limited circumstances has grown enormously, to a point where according to the National Center for Health Statistics now more than one in five pregnancies ends in abortion. That correlates to about a million abortions annually in the United States — although in recent years there has been a slight decline. More than 40 percent of all women will end a pregnancy by abortion at some time in their reproductive lives.[25] In addition to this more than five percent of abortions occur after more than fifteen weeks gestation.[26]

In deciding whether a social experiment (controlled or otherwise) should be permitted, it is, however, important to look at both sides of scales. As noted above, embryonic stem cell research is highly promising. If it is tenable that the same benefits can be derived in a manner which does not threaten the high regard paid to human life, then the risk should not be taken. This requires a detailed and fully informed assessment of the likely benefits of adult stem cell research compared to the benefits of embryonic stem cell research. The scientific community is presently undecided on this.

In light of this, it is necessary to wait for further evidence before we go any further with embryonic stem cell research. Embryonic stem cell research should only be contemplated if persuasive evidence emerges that it is has far more health benefits than adult stem cell research. If such evidence emerges, embryonic stem cell experimentation should occur in a highly regulated environment (using the minimum number of stem cells possible) which pays due regard to the risks that are inherent in dealing with such precious material.

6.6 ABORTION

The incidence of abortion, the intentional destruction of the fetus normally in the first trimester of pregnancy, is on the rise in most nations. The United States is bucking this trend. The most recent data shows that in the United States the abortion rate is approximately 21 per 1,000 women aged between 15 to 44, down from a high of 29 per 1,000 women in that age group in 1981.

In many countries abortion is strictly only legal in a limited range of circumstances, such as where the fetus is deformed or the woman's physical or mental health is at risk if she continues with the pregnancy, however the reality is otherwise. However, the reality is that abortion is in fact available on demand due to the very liberal interpretation that has been given to the notion of mental health. Most abortions that are performed are done so to advance the woman's economic well-being.

In light of the above discussion relating to stem cells, a bit of clear thinking and priority sorting can provide a correct moral and legal outcome. The abortion issue involves balancing two main competing interests: the right to life versus the right to one's body.

As we saw above, there is no obvious point during the gestation process which can be used to signify when life commences. Gestation is an ongoing process. At no stage during the process does the fetus have relevantly different attributes to a point marginally earlier in time.

The least arbitrary point at which life begins is at conception. At this stage the embryo has individuality and uniqueness and the building blocks for the development of life. Further, on matters pertaining to life and death it is better to err on the side of conservatism.

Nevertheless the right to life is not absolute. The right to one's body means that we cannot force others to donate blood or a kidney to save another person. Thus, it has been argued that women cannot be forced to deliver unwanted children.

However, when the notion of personal responsibility is factored into the abortion benefits and burden calculus the baby's right to life trumps a woman's right to her body. More is expected of people who bring about a state of affairs. That is why if you cause an accident you must try to rescue injured people, while onlookers have no such obligation.

Thus, abortion is unethical. Its widespread acceptance does not change this. Rather it illustrates that our moral judgments continue to be unduly shaped by emotion as opposed to logic. The fact that we can actually see a being and hear it cry is no basis for conferring it enhanced moral status. Morality involves the development of universal standards; its reach is not exhausted by what we can sense and feel.

While abortion is morally unsound, pragmatically it is not feasible to suggest a blanket ban at this point in time. The genie is too far out of the bottle. Despite the drop in the abortion rate in the United States, there are still approximately 1.3 millions abortions annually—meaning that more than one in four pregnancies ends in abortion. Moreover, over 40 per cent of abortions are performed on women who had at least one previous abortion.

The only realistic way to stop abortions is to opt for a step wise approach—as we are doing with the banning of cigarettes.

The first step is to limit numbers. Each woman should be permitted to have one abortion during her lifetime. Thereafter the rights of the fetus prevail and the baby gets to live. That's the solution to the thorny abortion debate.

A one abortion policy would save thousands of lives. It would also still confer considerable 'family planning' flexibility to women, while at the same time forging a mindset that the practice is at best morally questionable.

At the minimum it will keep the abortion issue firmly on the ethical consideration list. If this is done logic will inevitably prevail over emotion and abortion will be made illegal in all circumstances except where the pregnancy arose out of forced sex or its continuation presents a real (as opposed to feigned) serious risk to the welfare of the woman. (This exception would also apply to allow women to have more than one abortion under the proposed one abortion policy).

While the right of women to their bodies should be given some weight, every right has its limits. This is clearly reached after the destruction of a single fetus.

This proposed solution to the abortion conundrum will no doubt be criticized for its simplicity. But complex responses in the nature of the existing policies have failed dismally—abortion of demand proofs that.

No doubt pro-choice groups will be opposed to this fetter on embryo and fetus destruction. They should reflect, however, on the fact that the only reason they get to voice this opposition is because they got lucky—their mother decided not to exercise her choice to destroy them. To the maximum extent possible we need to eliminate luck from considerations of life and death.

Finally, it is important to note that approximately half of the thousands of lives that will be saved if the above policy is adopted will be female. Allowing thousands of female bodies to continue to develop provides a perspective check to the inevitable counter-argument that my proposal interferes with the right of women to do as they wish with their bodies.

NOTES

1. See D Wroe, 'Human Cloning will be the Next Step: Churches, *The Age* (Melbourne), 6 April 2002.
2. *The Age* (Melbourne), 28 September 2005.
3. *The Herald Sun* (Melbourne), 1 October 2005.
4. P Singer, Why we should ignore the Catholic Church on stem cells', *The Age* (Melbourne), 29 March 2002. It is noteworthy that singer is hypocritical on this point. He argues that the position adopted by the Church is only relevant to those who *already* accept the moral and religious framework of the church. The same point equally applies to Singer's views. It will only strike a chord with those who *accept* a utilitarian position (ie, the theory adopted by Singer) or at least those who accept that moral judgments are the ultimate norms by which conduct is to evaluated. It has never been established, however, that people are logically committed to this view. Some people merely refuse to engage in moral dialogue. If this is the case, no reason or logic can compel them to do otherwise.
5. R. Blackford, 'Thinking about Cloning: A Reply to Judith Thomson' (2001) 9 *Journal of Law and Medicine* 238 at 239–40.
6. See, for example, the House of Representatives Australia, *Human Cloning: Scientific, Ethical and Regulatory Aspects of Human Cloning and Stem Cell Research* (2001) ('Andrews Committee Report'). This report cites other similar reports in the United Kingdom and United States.
7. Ibid, para 3.48.
8. Ibid, para 3.61.
9. Ibid, 109.
10. Editorial, 'Embryo Farms Should Be Put on Hold', *The Australian*, 13 July 2001.
11. House of Lords, *Report of the Select Committee on Medical Ethics* vol 1 (1994), at p. 13.
12. *Airedale NHS Trust v Bland* [1993] 2 W.L.R. 316 at 367 per Lord Goff.
13. I. Kant, *The Metaphysics of Morals* (M Gregor, trans, 1996), 209. According to Kant, in the key criterion for ascribing moral duties is rationality, not personhood. Stem cells obviously lack the characteristic of rationality, and hence do not have ethical duties, but there is no reason in principle that they cannot have moral standing if they are considered members of the human species.
14. NSW Right to Life submission to the Andrews Committee Report, above n 3, 113.
15. Australian Health Ethics Committee, *Scientific, Ethical, and Regulatory Considerations Relevant to Cloning of Human Beings* (1998), para 3.17. See also Andrews Committee Report, above n 3, 114–115.
16. See for example, J. Thomson, "A Defence of Abortion" in P Singer (ed) *Applied Ethics* (OUP, 1986) at p. 49, where she argues that a woman's right to do determine what happens with her body is the most relevant consideration in determining the morality of abortion.

17. Available on-line at: <http://www.whitehouse.gov/news/releases/2001/08/20010809-2.html.

18. Although he is somewhat cryptic on this point. See B. Tobin, 'Reply to Savulescu: Why we Should Maintain a Prohibition on Destructive Research on Human Embryos' (2000) 30 *Australia and New Zealand Journal of Medicine* 498.

19. Savulescu, 'The Ethics of Cloning and Creating Embryonic Stem Cells as a Source of Tissue for Transplantation' (2000) 30 *Australian and New Zealand Journal of Law and Medicine* 492, 504.

20. M Tooley, 'Abortion and Infanticide', in P Singer (ed), *Applied Ethics* (1991), 69.

21. Savulescu, above n 19, at 494.

22. See Savulescu, above n 19, 495. Savulescu also gives the example of two zygotes fusing after conception to form one enduring entity.

23. H L A. Hart, '*Are there any Natural Rights?*' (1955) LXIV *Philosophical Review Quarterly* 175.

24. M Tooley, 'Abortion and Infanticide', in P Singer (ed), *Applied Ethics* (1991), 69. This is discussed further in chapter 13.

25. *Abortion*: http://www.emedicinehealth.com/articles/38399-1.asp.

26. http://www.cdc.gov/mmwr/preview/mmwrhtml/ss5103a1.htm.

Chapter Seven

Euthanasia

7.1 OVERVIEW AND DEFINITIONAL ISSUES

Euthanasia raises one of the most striking paradoxes in western political and legal systems. Public opinion appears pointedly to favour euthanasia. Polls in Australia, the United Kingdom, Canada and the United States consistently show that about three quarters of the population are in favour of euthanasia.[1] The preponderance of academic commentary also favours the legalisation of euthanasia. Yet despite the strong democratic nature of the political systems in these countries, none of them have not gone down the path of legalalising euthanasia. Euthanasia is, however, lawful in the Netherlands and (more recently) Belgium. In Australia, the practice was legalised in the Northern Territory in the mid 1990s. The Federal Parliament quickly passed a law disallowing the Territory legislation.

In this chapter I consider the moral status of euthanasia. First, I attend to definitional matters. Euthanasia means to kill a person at his or her request. It is not confined to terminally ill patients, as often thought to be the case. To restrict euthanasia in such a way, at least at the definitional stage, is unduly narrow. It closes the door on a whole range of circumstances in which people may wish to die, unduly disregards one of the strongest arguments in favour of euthanasia (the argument from compassion which is obviously not confined to those with a terminal illness) and ignores the fact that in the Netherlands euthanasia is not confined to those with a terminal illness.

A related concept to euthanasia is 'mercy killing'. This has the same essential features except that it does not have the same clinical connotations of euthanasia. Mercy killing involves a friend or family member intentionally killing the victim out of pity.

There are several different types of euthanasia. Voluntary euthanasia is where the ill person has expressly manifested a desire to be killed. Active euthanasia refers to the taking of direct action, such as inflicting a lethal injection, to kill someone who has expressed a wish to die. It has been described by the British Medical Association as an active intervention by a doctor to end life.[2] A typical example is the use of a drug or lethal injection to kill the patient.

Passive euthanasia is to withhold or withdraw life sustaining medical treatment from a patient with the intention of accelerating the patient's death at the patient's request.

Whether the withdrawal of futile treatment amounts to passive euthanasia is controversial. Some argue that the withdrawal of 'ordinary' means of prolonging life amounts to euthanasia, whereas the cessation of 'extraordinary' means of sustaining life does not.[3] Others maintain that passive euthanasia is not an appropriate description for withholding or withdrawing treatment[4] and that it is proper medical practice to discontinue treatment in appropriate circumstances.

The distinction between active and passive euthanasia is the area where the opposing sides have dug their trenches very deeply. This is to be expected given the practical significance of the distinction. Ostensibly medical professions refrain from active euthanasia, however passive euthanasia is standard medical practice despite spirited charges that there is no relevant distinction between it and active euthanasia. The significance of the difference between active and passive euthanasia is thought to turn largely on the acts and omissions doctrine and the distinction between ordinary and extraordinary medical treatment.

Voluntary euthanasia is to be distinguished from non-voluntary and involuntary euthanasia. Non-voluntary euthanasia is killing someone where he or she is either not in a position to have or to express any views on whether he or she would wish to be killed, for example, a person in an irreversible coma. Involuntary euthanasia is killing against one's express wishes. Typically this relates to situations where it is felt that someone's future is likely to be so miserable that life cannot be worth continuing. Neither involuntary nor non-voluntary euthanasia can rely on many of the arguments which are customarily used to support voluntary euthanasia, such as respect for personal autonomy, and are almost universally condemned. Accordingly they will not be considered further. Throughout this chapter euthanasia refers to voluntary active euthanasia unless indicated to the contrary.

7.2 ARGUMENTS FAVOURING EUTHANASIA

We feel enormous sympathy for people contemplating euthanasia because the minimisation of pain and suffering ought to be the first priority of a civilised society. We also strongly value the notion of personal liberty and viewed from the perspective of the parties directly involved (the patient and health worker) euthanasia is not inherently objectionable. In the case of clear minded, rational people it will advance patient autonomy and in some cases relieve the person of considerable pain. These are strongest reasons in favour of euthanasia and are encapsulated in the euthanasia catch cry of the 'right to die'. The arguments from autonomy and compassion are now considered more closely.

7.2.1 The Argument from Autonomy

Historically, perhaps the most compelling argument in favour of euthanasia is the argument from liberty or autonomy, which in its simplest and most powerful form provides that it is an unjustifiable encroachment upon individual liberty[5] to prevent a competent terminally ill patient and a co-operative doctor from acting upon the patient's desire to end life. The right to autonomy has been the catalyst for perhaps the most emotive slogans in the debate, including: 'Whose life is it?', 'It is my life and no-one else's', 'Give me liberty and give me death'; and 'The right to die with dignity'.

On its face denying a patient the right to a die in the circumstances of his or her choosing impairs his or her autonomy. The claim that in any particular case we can never be certain that a patient is fully committed to dying has also been advanced in a bid to soften the argument from autonomy. Suicide is not unlawful in most Western countries, and there is little to stop those desiring to die and who have the physical capacity to implement the wish from ending their lives. It is only in rare cases that people lack the capacity to end their life. It is argued that those who have the capacity to suicide, but elect to display 'a vacillation about self-destruction which vitiates their stated desire for death'[6] makes them inappropriate candidates for euthanasia, which, at most, should be confined to the small number who lack the physical means to take their own life.

This argument has considerable intuitive appeal. Generally if you want something, and it is within your reach, you will attain it — unless of course you are not really committed to it. However, while this provides some support for questioning the conviction of some euthanasia candidates, it is not decisive. Failure to implement our intentions, does not always call into question the firmness of our convictions when to achieve our goals we must overcome a necessary, but daunting obstacle—intense fears are capable of trumping long term goals. The thought of being required to effect one's own end, in circumstances which may not be quick, painless and non-violent, may be so overwhelming that one is forced to cast aside his or her genuine commitment to dying.

The fact that a person is not prepared to jump in front of a train or off a bridge does not entail that he or she genuinely do not wish to die and the community should certainly be taking measures to discourage such desperate acts. Also patients who are denied assistance in dying often use inappropriate and unsuccessful means, which often lead to further distress and complications.[7] Accordingly, the fact that many euthanasia candidates have means to take their own lives, but elect not to is one further reason for questioning their conviction, but not for ignoring it.

It follows that although the argument from autonomy has probably been over-stated there is some appeal to the view that in some circumstances euthanasia promotes patient autonomy. However, in order to assert that euthanasia promotes autonomy to any meaningful extent, measures must be implemented to ameliorate the burdensome and potentially overwhelming conditions in which a choice to die is often made, otherwise in many cases only submission rather than consent can be claimed.

7.2.2 The Argument from Compassion

The argument from compassion or mercy has been described as 'a cornerstone of the case for the legalization of active voluntary euthanasia'.[8] The argument provides that it is cruel to deny people who are in great pain and whose death is inevitable a dignified exit when they request it: 'dying is an integral part of living . . . it follows that the right to die with dignity should be as well protected as is any other aspect of the right to life. State prohibitions that would force a dreadful, painful death on a rational but incapacitated terminally ill patient are an affront to human dignity'.[9] In a similar vein, it has been noted that 'proponents [of euthanasia] argue that to maintain the legal prohibition on active voluntary euthanasia amounts to cruel and degrading treatment and that cruelty is evil which must be avoided so far as possible'.[10]

Thus euthanasia is portrayed as the kind thing to do, and perhaps more than any other feature of the debate, the ability of the euthanasia lobby to win the 'kind vote' has resulted in its widespread appeal.

The empirical evidence, however, casts doubt on the strength of the argument from compassion. The standard of palliative care in Western countries is such that nowadays very few terminally ill patients suffer intolerable pain. In about 95 per cent of cases of terminal illness pain can be overcome, in the other five per cent it can be partly relieved[11] — though the highest level of palliative care is not available to all patients. The Remmelink Report into euthanasia in the Netherlands in 1992 stated that loss of dignity was the most common reason for requesting euthanasia; with fewer than five per cent of patients giving intolerable pain as the reason for the request.[12]

Further, studies have shown that the main reason that patients request euthanasia is not pain, but loss of independence and loneliness.[13] This is confirmed by data from Oregon which shows that the most frequently noted reasons for ending life across the first years of the operation of statute were loss of autonomy (2000, 93%; 1999, 78%; 1998, 75%); participation in activities that make life enjoyable (2000, 78%; 1999, 81%; 1998, 69%) and concern about becoming a burden to family or friends.[14]

In light of this the argument from compassion must be broken into two limbs. The first dealing with treatable suffering; the other with unavoidable suffering. There are two ways to alleviate physical preventable suffering. We can either permit euthanasia or extend palliative care. The latter seems to be the preferable choice. Certainly it is the one most consistent with societal norms. In all areas of human activity death is not viewed as a satisfactory solution for dealing with individuals who for one reason or another find themselves in extreme or difficult situations. No matter how pitiful, wasteful or precarious life seems vast public resources are devoted towards tackling the underlying problem.

Death is also an option for people with other 'difficulties', such as the insane, the orphaned, the poverty stricken, the chronically ill and those with a violent disposition. However, nowadays death is not considered a feasible way of dealing with such people. This is most readily explicable on the basis that the regard paid to human life, all human life, is too high.

All other avenues are normally exhausted before killing. Hence (apart from the exceptional situation in some parts of the United States — where capital punishment is still performed), society devotes immense resources towards housing even the most despicable and wretched of its citizens — serious violent criminals. While the prisoner analogy may be criticised, since most prisoners desire to live, the same principle, of death not been viewed as a solution, is invoked even in cases where the person him or herself places no value on life and wishes to die. Large resources are devoted to preventing suicide and dealing with the underlying problems of people with such inclinations, irrespective of whether the problems stem from lack of self-esteem, depression, unemployment, or so on. Similarly, it can be forcefully argued that to deal with preventable suffering we should extend care, not kill.[15] Accordingly, in the case of treatable suffering the argument from compassion is more emotive than substantive.

The case for legitimising euthanasia for those with untreatable suffering is stronger. However the significant feature here is the relative scarcity of such cases. To legislate on grounds pertaining to only a very small minority is generally unwise: hard cases make bad law.[15] This is because, as is discussed in the next section, it is often difficult to compartmentalise the effects of legislation to the targeted few and the overall result may be more harm than good. Whether this is the case is taken up below.

7.3 ARGUMENTS AGAINST EUTHANASIA

While considerations of autonomy and compassion favour the practice of euthanasia, in assessing the moral status of any act it is necessary to look beyond the rights of those immediately affected. It is at this point that the argument in favour of euthanasia falters.

The risks do not outweigh the potential benefits. The benefits of conferring a right to be killed to some will probably be outweighed by the diminishing right to life of the many more. In this regard there are several possible adverse side-effects of legalising euthanasia.

First, it has been suggested that it may result in pressure being brought to bear on some patients to 'consent' to an early death. The terminally ill are obviously at very vulnerable points in their lives and it is foreseeable that unscrupulous relatives or 'friend' may pressure patients to take the euthanasia 'option'. This is not, however, a knock down argument against legalisation— merely a reason to ensure that rigorous safeguards are put in place to prevent such abuse.

7.3.1 Voluntary Euthanasia Leads to Non-voluntary Euthanasia

The next reason is, however, more compelling. Legalising voluntary euthanasia carries the risk that health professionals will commit acts of non-voluntary euthanasia. Once again this can perhaps be addressed by stringent safeguards. The empirical evidence, however, suggests to the contrary.

7.3.1.1 *Dutch Studies*

The best evidence of the where euthanasia will lead us comes from an analysis of euthanasia practice in the Netherlands—the only location where it is openly practised for a significant period of time. In 1991 a government committee, headed by P J van der Maas,[17] reported that in 1990 approximately 1.7% of all deaths in the Netherlands were the result of voluntary euthanasia (defined as the administration of drugs with the explicit intention of ending the patient's life at the request of the patient) and 0.2% were the result of physician assisted suicide. This equated to 2300 cases of voluntary euthanasia and 400 cases of assisted suicide. The most troubling finding of the survey was that there were 1,000 cases (which amounted to 0.8% of all deaths) of non-voluntary euthanasia—death was caused by the administration of drugs with the intention of ending the patient's life, *without* the patient's request. This translated to 27% of doctors admitting to terminating lives without request.[18]

It has been suggested that these finding are somewhat ameliorated by the fact that 'in more half of [the 1,000 instances of non-voluntary euthanasia], this *possibility* had already been *discussed* with the patient, or the patient had expressed, in a *previous phase* of the disease a wish for *active voluntary euthanasia*, if his or her suffering became unbearable (emphasis added)'.[19] However, this is no cause for comfort. Merely canvassing a certain option with another party does not approach anything even resembling consent to that course of conduct. And a suggestion that a wish for voluntary euthanasia makes non-voluntary euthanasia in some way more acceptable does more to support than undermine the slippery slope argument.

The findings of the survey have been seized upon by opponents of euthanasia who have charged that the survey supports the contention that the practice of euthanasia has not resulted in greater patient autonomy, but in doctors 'acquiring even more power over the life and death of their patients',[20] and that within a relatively short period of time the Dutch have proceeded down the slippery slope from voluntary to non-involuntary euthanasia. 'This is partly because the underlying justification for euthanasia is not . . . self-determination, but rather acceptance of the principle that certain lives are not worth living and that it is right to terminate them'.[21]

A follow up study in the Netherlands in 1995, revealed similar results to those some four years earlier. There was a slight increase in the percentage of overall deaths stemming from active euthanasia (2.4%, compared to 1.7% in 1991). The number of deaths resulting from physician assisted suicide remained constant at 0.2%), but there was a slight decrease in the number of cases of non-voluntary euthanasia: from 1000 to 900 in 1995 (ie, a reduction from 0.8% to 0.7% of all deaths).[22] These results are somewhat equivocal in terms of establishing a general trend. Given the small drop in the number of cases of non-voluntary euthanasia it could be argued that this throws doubt on the slippery slope argument. This can be countered on the basis that the decrease in the incidence of non-voluntary euthanasia (10 per cent) over the four year period is not statistically significant and that the period of time between the surveys was insufficient for the further erosion of the views and ideals pertaining to the importance of human life. Given the relatively small period of time between the two studies and the close correlation of the relevant data, perhaps the most telling result from the 1995 study is that it confirms the accuracy of the previous survey.

The significance of the Dutch surveys has been questioned. The valid point has been made that in order to obtain meaningful information regarding the slippery slope dangers it is necessary to compare the level of abuse before and after voluntary euthanasia was introduced. For this reason it can be argued that a final verdict has not been reached.

This, however, should not prevent the forming of a prima facie view. The evidence, the *only* cogent evidence, shows that in a climate where voluntary euthanasia is openly practiced there are also a large number of cases of non-voluntary euthanasia. It may be that the rate of non-voluntary euthanasia in Holland was not increased by the decision to effectively give the green light to voluntary euthanasia. But given that we know that one state of affairs (ie where euthanasia is openly practised) *definitely* leads to undesirable consequences and are unsure about the situation in the alternative state of affairs (where euthanasia is prohibited), logically we ought to opt for the latter— speculative or possible dangers being accorded far less weight than certain ones.

Accordingly, the slippery slope argument was given significant impetus following the Dutch surveys and is probably the most widely endorsed argument against euthanasia. It has proved very influential with law reform bodies and the like. Five inquiries, some of which preceded the Dutch surveys, which have been conducted to inquire into the consequences of decriminalising euthanasia have all concluded that it should not be legalised largely due to unacceptable detrimental consequences which would ensue.[23] The sentiments expressed by the House of Lords Select Committee on Medical Ethics is typical of some of the dangers which are adverted to in the various reports. Concerned that vulnerable people may feel pressure to request an early death if euthanasia was legalised, it stated that:

> Issues of life and death do not lend themselves to clear definition, and without that it would be impossible to ensure that it would be possible to frame adequate safeguards against non-voluntary euthanasia were voluntary euthanasia to be legalised. It would be next to impossible to ensure that all acts of euthanasia were truly voluntary, and that liberalisation of the law was not abused.[24]

7.3.1.2 Australian Study—Does Not Distort Conclusions from Netherlands

The most persuasive counter to the above slippery slope argument are statistics from jurisdictions where euthanasia is prohibited which show that rate of non-voluntary euthanasia is these jurisdictions, namely Australia and Belgium (prior to its legalisation in Belgium), is even higher than in Netherlands.

The most widely publicised survey of this nature is a postal survey by Kuhse, Singer, Baume, Clark and Rickard of Australian doctors in July 1996 published in the Medical Journal of Australia in 1997 (the 'Kuhse-Singer survey').[25] The objectives of the Kuhse-Singer survey were to estimate the proportion of medical end-of-life decisions in Australia, describe the characteristics of such decisions and compare these data with medical end-of-life decisions in the Netherlands (where euthanasia is openly practised). The Kuhse-Singer survey used an English version of the questionnaire used by van der Maas et al and employed the same definitions of euthanasia and non-voluntary euthanasia used in the Dutch context. They revealed a higher rate of non-voluntary euthanasia in Australia than the Netherlands.

The findings of the Kuhse-Singer survey threaten to undermine the central premise of the slippery slope argument. Quite simply the survey shows that one of the central dangers warned of by slippery slope theorists (that voluntary euthanasia will lead to non-voluntary euthanasia) is as prevalent in Australia as in the Netherlands.

The findings of the survey lead the authors to conclude that:

> Our study undermines suggestions that the rate at which doctors intentionally end patients' lives without an explicit request is higher in a country where euthanasia is practised *openly* (the Netherlands) than in a comparable country which has not allowed euthanasia to be practised *openly*, such as Australia.

Elaborating on this, Margaret Otlowski states that:

> The Australian [Kuhse-Singer] study, involving a sample of 3,000 doctors from all Australian States and Territories, revealed a much higher incidence in Australia of unrequested active euthanasia than for active voluntary euthanasia (3.5% of all deaths compared with 1.8% for active voluntary euthanasia) and far in excess of the figure for the same category in the Netherlands (0.7% according to the 1995 study). This appears to be largely attributable to the illegality of the practice and the lack of openness on the issues with the consequence that doctors are often taking this decision upon themselves... The substantially higher incidence of non-requested euthanasia in Australia strongly suggests that there are greater risks inherent in the current laws which hold active euthanasia to be illegal, but which are in practice flouted, than exist when genuine attempts are made to control and regulate the practice as has occurred in the Netherlands.[26]

Thus, the Kuhse-Singer survey potentially undermines the slippery slope argument by showing that similar levels of non-voluntary euthanasia occur irrespective of whether euthanasia is legalised or not. This being so the implication that one is left with is that legalising euthanasia is not the *cause* of abuse by doctors in relation to end-of-life decisions. Accordingly, it can be argued, that there is no evidence to support the slippery slope argument and the best manner to minimise abuses is to legalise the practice, thus opening it up and implementing safeguards.

On its face this is a sound argument. If the type of abuse that slippery slope theorists fear are occurring both in an environment where euthanasia is legal and where it is prohibited then the cause for the abuses cannot be found in the different legal treatment of euthanasia.

However, the results of the survey, even taken at their highest, do not provide a foundation for comparing the level of abuse in a country where euthanasia is condoned to one where it is prohibited.

The authors of the survey are right to note that in Australia euthanasia is illegal. It consists of the intentional killing of another person. There are no defences available to doctors who kill in such circumstances. Hence, it amounts to murder. However the law, effectively, does not prosecute the intentional killing of patients by doctors. At the time of the survey (and still to this day) Australian doctors could practice euthanasia with impunity—there is no realistic possibility that they will be prosecuted for such conduct.

The results of the survey support this view. It is noted that in Australia there were 125,771 deaths from July 1994 to June 1995 (which is the time frame of the survey).[27] This means that in total there were approximately 6,700 cases of murder (voluntary and non-voluntary euthanasia: 1.8% and 3.5% of all deaths respectively)—*not one of which was prosecuted.*

It follows that in *substance* the law prohibiting euthanasia by doctors is not enforced and the legal situation at the time of the survey was not in any meaningful respect different to that in the Netherlands during the times of the relevant surveys.

Admittedly there was a formal difference between the legal situation in the Netherlands and that in Australia at the time of the respective surveys. However, there was no difference in a *relevant* sense. In both countries euthanasia was on its face illegal. In both countries there were no doctors prosecuted for euthanising patients. The only difference was the *reason* that no cases of euthanasia were prosecuted. In the Netherlands this was due to an open non-prosecution stance. In Australia it was due to the fact that there was no political, legislative or prosecutorial interest in prosecuting doctors who killed terminally ill patients with only days or weeks to live. Although in one nation the non-prosecution policy was open and in the other it was clandestine, the same situation existed in both jurisdictions. Quite simply doctors in Australia are not prosecuted for euthanasia. The next informed doctor who is contemplating euthanising a patient knows (as he or she did at the time of the survey) that the chances of him or her being prosecuted (let alone convicted) should he or she proceed are about zero.

The counter to this argument is that the level of prohibition in Australia at the time of the survey was much higher than in the Netherlands. At least in theory, doctors who euthanised patients could have been convicted of murder. If the law is an effective mechanism for regulating life and death decisions, surely this threat should have led to a reduction in euthanasia and associated abuses. After all, the argument continues, the risk of prosecution was still higher than that in the Netherlands at the time of the relevant surveys—where doctors where *formally* advised that they would not be prosecuted for euthanasia if they observed certain guidelines.

This counter implies that merely having a law on the statute books serves as an effective deterrent—especially where the possible penalty is serious. This is wrong. Simply prohibiting a form of behaviour is not likely to serve as a deterrent. This is so even when the penalties are very high. The theory of marginal general deterrence, which provides that *there is a linear relationship* between the incidence of a particular crime and the severity of the sentences which are imposed in respect of the crime has never been substantiated.[28]

As we shall see in chapter 8, empirical studies have shown that the most important consideration regarding deterrence is not the penalty, but rather the perceived likelihood of apprehension.

Thus, the mere fact that doctors in Australia *potentially* faced prosecution for euthanising patients is not a basis for assuming that they were operating in an environment which differed from that in the Netherlands. Australian doctors had no reason to fear prosecution and hence the mere formal legal prohibition of euthanasia at the time of the survey is not likely to have influenced their conduct—certainly no more than was the case with their Dutch counterparts.

By comparing the incidence of non-voluntary euthanasia in Australia to that in the Netherlands, it has been contended that the Kuhse-Singer survey undermines the slippery slope argument against euthanasia by showing that the dangers inherent in legalising euthanasia are just as pronounced in jurisdictions where euthanasia is prohibited. The survey does in fact show that non-voluntary euthanasia occurs even more frequently in Australia than in the Netherlands. However, despite the formal differences in the manner in which euthanasia is treated in the two jurisdictions, the critical point which has been overlooked is that in both jurisdictions euthanasia was in a de facto sense not proscribed—medical practitioners in both jurisdictions could euthanise patients with confidence that they would not be prosecuted, let alone convicted. Accordingly, the findings of the Kuhse-Singer survey give no reason to believe that the dangers postulated by slippery slope theorists are less likely to eventuate in jurisdictions where euthanasia is condoned and regulated. The Kuhse-Singer survey in fact supports the slippery slope argument. It provides another piece of evidence that in an environment where euthanasia is condoned, there is a significant level of abuse by doctors in relation to end-of-life decisions.

Thus, in the context of the euthanasia debate the slippery slope is persuasive. Unlike other situations in which the argument has failed (such as torture), there is credible empirical evidence that if euthanasia is condoned in one context it leads to other forms of euthanasia, which are unacceptable.

7.3.2 Loss of Respect for Life

There is one further undesirable risk stemming from legalising euthanasia: it carries the risk that it will foster or instill the notion that some lives (namely, the terminally and gravely ill) are less valuable than others. This sets an undesirable precedent. Followed to its logical conclusion it would leave the door ajar for similar arguments to be made in relation to all people whose capacity to flourish is for some reason (whether physical, mental or social) gravely impaired. There is no principled way to distinguish between qualitative and quantitative impairments. If reduced life expectancy is seen as being a basis for less value being attributed to life, then why not other handicaps or disadvantages.

The counter that pro-euthanasia arguments do not entail a lower level of lives being accorded to some lives is fictitious. This is evident from the fact that society does not regard deliberate killing as a solution to any (other) personal problems. We do not kill the miserable, depressed or evil. This is because of the supreme value placed on all human life. Problems are not cured by killing. So it should be in the case of euthanasia.

Perhaps adequate safeguards could be implemented to prevent voluntary euthanasia leading to non-voluntary euthanasia, and perhaps we could be adequately conditioned into accepting that deliberate killing in one context does not implicitly cheapen the value of all human life. However, as a community we should tread slowly before condoning practices which suggest that some lives are not as valuable as others.

7.4 OVERVIEW OF MORAL STATUS OF EUTHANASIA

When the ostensibly private practice of euthanasia is viewed in light of its broader implications for the community, the probable adverse consequences accompanying the practice are so dangerous that a decision to nevertheless decriminalise euthanasia would be misguided. In a nutshell, euthanasia should not be legalised because the benefits of conferring a right to be killed to some will be outweighed by the diminishing importance attributed to the right to life of many more.

Prohibiting euthanasia will seem insensitive to those desperately seeking a quiet and peaceful exit. However, morality requires that individuals sometimes compromise their interests for the common good. This is an indispensable part of living in a community.

We need to entrench a culture of life—not erode it. This will enhance all our lives. As indeed it enhanced the existence of those who unfortunately find themselves contemplating euthanasia.

Yet we cannot ignore the pleas of those in pain.

Following a review of *Washington v Glucksberg* and *Vacco v Quill*, Edward Larson and Darrel Amundsen conclude that the court offers Americans the opportunity to decide in what sort of community they want to live and die:

> Adequate pain management, effective procedures for patient control over life sustaining treatment and responsive treatment for depression are among the life affirming alternatives to physician assisted suicide and euthanasia that call for a new level of societal commitment to the dying.[29]

It is these ends that society should promote in order to deal with the euthanasia dilemma. People contemplating euthanasia should not be encouraged to do so. They should be told that their life continues to have immense meaning and it would be a tragedy if it was deliberately cut short.

NOTES

1. M. Charlesworth 'Dying and the Law' (1995) 4 (2) *Res Publica* 12, 15. This result is consistent with the submissions to Australia's Northern Territory Select Committee on Euthanasia where 72 per cent of the total submissions (1126) favoured euthanasia: Legislative Assembly of the Northern Territory, *Report of the Inquiry by the Select Committee on Euthanasia: The Right of the Individual or the Common Good?* (1995) vol 1, 31 (henceforth this report is referred to as Report of the Northern Territory Select Committee on Euthanasia). A poll published in the *Australian* on 15 February 1995 showed that 81 per cent of people favoured euthanasia. This figure is in line with international trends. Polls in the United Kingdom, the United States and Canada show approval rates for euthanasia of 78 per cent, 68 per cent, and 78 per cent respectively (Report of the Northern Territory Select Committee on Euthanasia 50-1). The results of a comprehensive range of surveys on euthanasia are detailed in the Report of the Senate Legal and Constitutional

Legislation Committee, Parliament of Australia, *Euthanasia Laws Bill 1996* (Canberra, 1997) 81–92.

2. BMA Working Party Report, *Euthanasia* (London, 1988) 3.

3. T O'Donnell, ' Review of The Physician's Responsibility Toward Hopelessly Ill Patients' (1984) 51 *Linacre Q* 351; D.Louisell, 'Euthanasia and Biathanasia: On Dying and Killing' (1973) *Catholic UL Rev.* 723, 730.

4. R Weir, 'Abating Treatment with Critically Ill Patients' (New York, 1989) 302; E.Keyserlingk, *Sanctity of Life or Quality of Life in the Context of Ethics, Medicine and Law* (Ottawa, 1979) 120–3.

5. The terms autonomy and liberty are used interchangeably in the following discussion. As is discussed below, the right to autonomy is in essence the right to exercise one's personal liberty free from arbitrary or otherwise unjustified interference. If one's liberty is respected, then so is one's autonomy- thus to some extent the right to autonomy is derivative from the right to liberty. For the purposes of this discussion, however, the distinction is not important. In keeping with the terminology normally used in the context of the euthanasia we will principally base the discussion in the context of the right to autonomy.

6. P E Mullen, 'Euthanasia: An Impoverished Construction of Life and Death' (1995) 3 *JLM* 121, 125.

7. J Pugliese, 'Don't Ask—Don't Tell, The Secret Practice of Physician Assisted Suicide' (1993) *Hastings Law Journal* 1291, 1307.

8. M Otlowski, Voluntary Euthanasia and the Common Law (1997), 203.

9. *Rodriguez v A-G British Columbia* [1994] 85 CCC (3d) 15, Cory J.

10. Otlowski, above n 8, 203.

11. D Doyle et al., (eds.), *Oxford Textbook of Palliative Medicine* (Oxford University Press, 1993).

12. The Remmelink Report, *Health Policy* (Special Issue) 22 (1992) 1.

13. C Seale and J Addington-Hall, 'Euthanasia: Why People Want to Die Earlier' (1994) 39(5) *Social Sciences and Medicine* 647.

14. http://www.ohd.hr.state.or.us.

15. It is true that pain is more than physical. It also stems from the impending depravation of faculties, the prospect of total reliance on others and the loss of what some may regard as a dignified existence: I. Freckelton, Editorial (1995) 3 *JLM* 99–100. However, such mental anguish is also often treatable, sometimes by altering the attitudes of those around the dying person. To this end, it has been contended that what is needed is 'a greater realisation of what can be done to alleviate physical and mental suffering, and determination on behalf of health care professionals and society to do it': Submission by National Council for Hospices and Specialist Palliative Care Services to the House of Lords Select Committee on Medical Ethics, vol. II of the Report of the House of Lords Select Committee on Euthanasia 202, 210.

16. It is for the same reason that one cannot be influenced by the possibility of miracle cures as an argument against euthanasia.

17. P J van der Maas et al., *Euthanasia and other Medical Decisions Concerning the End of Life* (Elsevier, 1992). For a summary of these findings see J Keown, 'Some Reflections on Euthanasia in The Netherlands' and 'Further reflections on Euthanasia

in the Netherlands in the Light of the Remmelink Report and The van der Maas Survey', (ed.) L Gormally, *Euthanasia, Clinical Practice and The Law*, (Linacre Centre, 1994) 193, 219.

18. J Keown, 'The Law and Practice of Euthanasia in the Netherlands' (1992) 108 *Law Quarterly Review* 51.

19. Otlowski, above n 8, 430–1.

20. A M J. Henk & V M Velie, "Euthanasia: Normal Medical Practice?" (1992) 22(2) *Hastings Centre Report* 34, 38.

21. J Keown, 'Further reflections on Euthanasia in the Netherlands in the Light of the Remmelink Report and The van der Mass Survey', (ed) L. Gormally, *Euthanasia, Clinical Practice and The Law* (Linacre Centre, 1994), 219, 239.

22. The results of the 1995 study are summarised in the Report of the Senate Legal and Constitutional Legislation Committee, The Parliament of Australia, *Euthanasia Laws Bill 1996* (Canberra, 1997) 101–6.

23. These inquires were: Law Reform Commission of Canada, *Euthanasia, Assisting Suicide and the Cessation of Treatment* (1982); Social Development Committee of the Parliament of Victoria, *Inquiry Into the Options for Dying With Dignity* (1987); House of Lords Select Committee on Medical Ethics (1994); New York Task Force on Life and the Law, *When Death is Sought* (1994); and Special Committee on Assisted Suicide and Euthanasia of the Senate of Canada, *Of Life and Death* (1995); Senate Legal and Constitutional Legislation Committee, *Euthanasia Laws Bill 1996* (1997) . Only the Report by the Northern Territory Select Committee on Euthanasia failed to be decisively swayed by the dangers of legalising euthanasia.

24. Report of the House of Lords Select Committee on Medical Ethics (1994), 49.

25. H Kuhse et al, 'End of Life Decisions in Australian Medical Practice' (1997) 166 *MJA* 191–196. For a similar comparison with Belgium, see L Deliens et al, 'End-of Life Decisions in Medical Practice in Flanders, Belgium: A Nationwide Survey' (2000) 356 *The Lancet* 1806.

26. Ibid, xiii–xiv.

27. Kuhse, et al, above n 25.

28. The recent empirical evidence concerning the failure of marginal general deterrence is summarised in M Bagaric, *Punishment and Sentencing; A Rational Approach* (Cavendish Publishing, London, 2001) ch 5. See also chapter 8 below.

29. "The Road Home—Caring not Killing" in 'A Different Death' (inter Varsity Press, Illinois, 1998) 244 at 252.

Part D

DEALING WITH WRONGDOERS

Chapter Eight

Punishment and Sentencing

8.1 INTRODUCTION

Approximately 30 years ago, United States federal judge Marvin Frankel described sentencing law as a wasteland in the law.[1] This comment reflected the fact that sentencing law was devoid of an overarching rationale, it was purposeless, lacked principle and judges pretty much did what seemed appropriate at the time, resulting in a large amount of inconsistency and unfairness. As a result of the widespread use of fixed penalties, things have changed considerably in the United States over the past three decades.[2]

The specific framework adopted in the United States is flawed. This is not because of the broad approach (which builds policy into sentencing) but because it flies in the face of empirical evidence of what can be achieved through sentencing. Ultimately, sentencing in the United States is too heavy-handed. As far as the general approach to sentencing is concerned, things have not changed much in many other Western jurisdictions, especially Australia and the United Kingdom. Sentencing is still in the embryonic stage — bereft of a verifiable justification and guided by unreflective intuition. It is not surprising that it has been labelled the 'high point in anti-jurisprudence'.[3]

The most fundamental failing of sentencing law and practice in many parts of the world is that the objectives of sentencing law and practice are based on *assumptions* concerning what can and ought to be achieved through a process of state imposed punishment, as opposed to being founded on empirical evidence concerning the pursuits that can be achieved through sentencing and normative analysis regarding the goals that the community should pursue by punishing criminals.

Moreover, the discharge of the judicial task of sentencing is remarkably 'at large', due to the 'instinctive synthesis' approach to sentencing,[4] which provides that sentencing is largely an intuitive process and therefore it is unnecessary for sentencers to detail the exact reasoning process by which they reach their decisions.

This chapter provides a blueprint for a more coherent and justifiable system of sentencing.

8.2 PICK A THEORY OF PUNISHMENT

The first step in the process is to decide which theory of punishment will underpin sentencing practice.[5] Punishment is the study of the connection between wrongdoing and state imposed sanctions. The main issue raised by the concept of punishment is the basis upon which the evils administered by the state to offenders can be justified. Thus, sentencing and punishment are inextricably linked, with punishment being the logically prior inquiry. In order to properly decide how, and how much, to punish, it must first be established on what basis punishment is justified and why we are punishing.

There are two main theories of punishment that have been advanced. Utilitarianism is the view that punishment is inherently bad due to the pain it causes the wrongdoer, but is ultimately justified because this is outweighed by the good consequences stemming from it. These are traditionally thought to come in the form of incapacitation, deterrence and rehabilitation. The competing theory, and the one which enjoys the most contemporary support, is retributivism. While retributive theories of punishment are not clearly delineated; they share the common view that the justification for punishment does not turn on the likely achievement of consequentialist goals: it is justified even when 'we are practically certain that attempts [to attain conseqentialist goals, such as deterrence and rehabilitation] will fail'.[6] Thus, is it often said that retributive theories are backward looking, merely focusing on past events in order to determine whether punishment is justified in contrast to utilitarianism which is concerned only with the likely future consequences of imposing punishment.

Most commentators have claimed that radically different sentencing goals stem from the particular theory of punishment endorsed. However, in reality on *either* a retributive or utilitarian account of punishment, as is discussed below, general deterrence is the goal which justifies punishing wrongdoers, while the principle of proportionality fixes the amount of punishment). The key at this point is simply to note that *a* (tenable) theory of punishment must be adopted—the corollary being that it is impermissible to pick, choose and swap a theory at whim, which happens to support one's intuitive predisposition.

The theory that is chosen must, however, provide a justification for punishing criminals. Not all practices or types of behaviour call for a moral justification. We do not need to justify playing sport, visiting friends or dancing. However, punishment requires a moral justification because it involves the intentional infliction of some type of harm and hence infringes upon an important concern or interest. As such, it is not dissimilar to activities such as slavery, abortion and euthanasia. Zimmring and Hawkins note that:

> The need to justify punishment is reflected in moral logic as well as history. Since penal practices are by definition unpleasant, the world is a poorer place for their presence unless the positive functions achieved by them outweigh the negative elements inherent in the policies.[7]

If it was established that a state imposed system of punishment was clearly morally repugnant, as a community we would be (morally) obliged to abolish such a system. We may of course decide on pragmatic grounds to ignore this mandate. However, this is no minor matter. Invariably, while there is no end of evil in the world, individuals and societies do not expressly accept (or at least acknowledge) that are they engaging in immoral behaviour, no matter how repugnant their activities may seem to be. The reason for this stems from the fact that morality is, as we saw in chapter one, the ultimate set of principles by which we should live. Thus, the normative dimension is important in setting a framework for a sentencing law and practice.

Moral theory also plays an important role in setting the amount and type of punishment that is permissible within a properly developed system of sentencing. In particular, it acts as a side constraint to prevent certain forms of treatment, such as exemplary punishment, sacrificing the innocent and vicariously punishing family members of offenders.[8]

Thus, while moral theory does not exhaust the range of considerations that properly inform the development of a state imposed system of punishment, moral considerations cannot be ignored in this process. It is on other considerations that the remainder of this chapter focuses.

8.3 IGNORE PUBLIC OPINION

The next step in developing a coherent sentencing system is to accept that sentencing is a purposive social endeavour which must be guided by rational inquiry, not raw impulse. It is legal commentators, practitioners and other experts (namely, criminologists, penologists, sociologists, moral philosophers and econometricians) who should be educating the public about how to frame a sentencing system—not the other way around. Seeking public views on sentencing is analogous to doctors basing treatment decisions on what the community thinks is appropriate or engineers building cars, not in accordance with the rules of physics, but on the basis of what lay members of the community 'reckon' seems about right. Sentencing is an intellectual social discipline. It should have underlying principles which govern the way it ought to be administered. These are ascertained through a process of inductive and deductive logic and analysing the relevant empirical evidence to determine what objectives are and are not achievable through a system of state imposed punishment. Guidance on sentencing matters should be sought from experts in the field not the uninformed.

8.4 IDENTIFY THE OBJECTIVES OF SENTENCING— INCAPACITATION, DETERRENCE AND REHABILITATION?

The third step involves working out what can be achieved through a process of state imposed punishment of wrongdoers. This is essential because it is pointless striving for aims which are not attainable. The sentencing system should purse only those objectives that empirical evidence shows are attainable through a system of punishing wrongdoers.

Broadly, it has been suggested that there are three positive *benefits* that may be secured through a system of State imposed punishment: incapacitation, deterrence (both general and specific) and rehabilitation. However, current empirical evidence provides no basis for confidence that punishment is capable of achieving most of these goals.[9] Incapacitation is flawed, since we are very poor at predicting which offenders are likely to commit serious offences in the future.[10] There is nothing to suggest that offenders who have been subjected to harsh punishment are less likely to re-offend, thus there is no basis for pursuing the goal of specific deterrence.[11] Rehabilitation fares no better. There are no far reaching rehabilitative techniques which have proven to be successful at producing positive internal attitudinal change in offenders.[12]

However, experience shows that absent the threat of punishment for criminal conduct, the social fabric of society would readily dissipate. Crime would escalate and overwhelmingly frustrate the capacity of people to lead happy and fulfilled lives. Natural social experiments concerning the effects of police strikes (and the like) reveal that without the threat of criminal punishment a far greater number of people would commit criminal offences.[13] Thus, general deterrence works in the *absolute* sense—there is *a* connection between criminal sanctions and criminal conduct.

However, there is insufficient evidence to support the theory of marginal deterrence, which provides that there is a direct correlation between higher penalties and the crime rate. As is noted by Zimring and Hawkins:

> Studies of different areas with different penalties, and studies focusing on the same jurisdiction before and after a change in punishment level takes place, show rather clearly that the level of punishment is not the major reason why crime rates vary. In regard to particular penalties, such as capital punishment as a marginal deterrent to homicide, the studies go further and suggest no discernible relationship between the presence of the death penalty and homicide rates.[14]

It follows that *marginal* deterrence should be disregarded as a sentencing objective—at least unless and until there is proof that it works.

The above conclusions summarise the current state of play concerning what can be achieved through sentencing. A genuine commitment to smart sentencing involves a continual monitoring of the relevant literature to ascertain if the evidence changes in terms of what goals can be achieved through sentencing.

8.5 MAKE THE PUNISHMENT FIT THE CRIME

The failure of marginal general deterrence means that (absolute general) deterrence justifies inflicting *some* punishment on offenders, but it is of little relevance in fixing the *amount* of punishment. Likewise with the goals of incapacitation and rehabilitation—sanctions should not be either increased or reduced on the basis of these goals.

In terms of fixing the amount of punishment, the cardinal determinant is the principle of proportionality, which prescribes that the punishment should fit the crime.[15] Despite this, sentences for similar offences vary widely from jurisdiction to jurisdiction and from court to court.[16] There are two reasons for this. The first is that legislatures and the courts have not developed a workable way to match the two limbs of the principle. The second is that the principle of proportionality is seriously distorted by the notion of aggravating and mitigating factors.[17] The manner in which these should be dealt with is discussed below.

At this point I discuss how legislatures can go about matching the two limbs of the proportionality principle. This, admittedly, is no easy task. How many years of imprisonment correlates to the pain endured by a rape victim? The main difficulty here is that the two currencies are different. The interests typically violated by criminal offences are physical integrity and property rights. At the upper end of criminal sanctions the currency is (deprivation of) freedom. The only conceivable way to give content to the proportionality principle is to adopt a uniform standard for measuring the offence gravity and punishment severity. Previous criteria that have been suggested included public perceptions of offence seriousness and statuted penalties.[18] In my view, both of these are inappropriate. They have no relation to *actual* offence seriousness.

A more appropriate measure is happiness and pain. Thus, the amount of unhappiness caused by the punishment should be commensurate with the seriousness of the offence. The reason that I select pain or suffering as the ultimate criterion is that it is capable of being felt by all; and desired to be avoided *most* by all. The desire to avoid suffering is the sentiment felt most strongly by all people at all points in history and across all cultures. As we saw in chapter two, there is a large amount of empirical data indicating the conditions in which human flourish best and social scientists are adept at making assessments of subjective well-being and happiness. Moreover, while noting the diversity in the range of activities through which people choose to express themselves the studies show that at the base we are not that different after all. We can now confidently identify the things that are conducive or inimical to happiness (and its converse, pain or suffering).

To complete this step requires surveys to be conducted that evaluate the subjective well-being of victims of crime. These should be compared to studies that analyse the degree of pain that actually stems from criminal sanctions. Well-being in relation to both aspects of the study will be measured by the extent to which a person's interests are adversely affected as a result of being either a victim of crime or subjected to a criminal sanction.

8.6 AGGRAVATING AND MITIGATING FACTORS—SCRUTINISE EACH OF THEM

The second last step in developing a sophisticated sentencing model involves addressing the issue of so-called aggravating and mitigating sentencing variables. There are between 200 and 300 factors that are relevant to sentencing.[19] Common aggravating factors are breach of trust, and offending while on bail or parole. Mitigating considerations include such things as co-operation with authorities and previous good character.

The relevance of most, if not all, of these considerations is questionable. The starting point is that all of these considerations should be ignored unless a cogent justification is given for them. To justify the existence of a sentencing practice or rule one must (i) state the sentencing aim(s) that is being invoked; and (ii) show how the consideration will assist in promoting the aim(s). Thus for example, if the objective of sentencing is to impose proportionate sentences, then a consideration like remorse should be excluded from the sentencing calculus. It might 'feel' right to punish the regretful criminal less than the defiant one, but feelings of regret will not mend the victim's broken bones, nor compensate for the stolen property. Contrition after the event also does not affect the accused person's level of blameworthiness at the time he or she committed the offence. It might be suggested, for example, that remorse diminishes the relevance of specific deterrence, but if this has been excluded as a relevant variable in step four then it cannot justify its retention as a sentencing consideration.

This analysis makes for a vastly different sentencing system to that at present. While general deterrence determines the type of punishment, legislatures should then look to the principle of proportionality to guide them on how much to punish. The most obvious change to sentencing that would follow from this is that the reliance on imprisonment would be significantly diminished: 'old favourites', such as specific deterrence, incapacitation and prior criminality could no longer be invoked to 'justify' incarceration.

The main rationales underlying the move towards harsher penalties are incapacitation and (marginal) general deterrence. Given that these objectives are flawed, it follows that what we should be doing is watering down the severity of punishment. At the same time, we should be striving for a lower crime rate. This may seem overly ambitious, but it is not unattainable. Any intuitive unease that lowering imprisonment rates would inevitably lead to increased crime rates is to a large extent allayed by a comparison of sentencing practice in jurisdictions such as Finland where sentencing premiums are not attached to pursue the aims of incapacitation or deterrence and the main determinant in setting criminal sanctions is the principle of proportionality.[20] The prison rate in Finland is about half of that in Australia and a fraction of that in the United Kingdom and the United States and when offenders are sent to prison in Finland they do not stay very long—prison sentences exceeding 5 years are rare.[21] Moreover, the crime rate in Finland is at least 35 per cent less than in the UK, the US and Australia.

Each of the main sentencing variables need to be critically evaluated regarding whether they are justified as being legitimate sentencing objectives.

8.7 ON-GOING REFORM

The last step is an on-going one. No system, be it health or education is beyond improvement. Whatever sentencing system is adopted will not be perfect; rather, it will necessarily be provisional—subject to new evidence regarding what can be achieved by punishing wrongdoers. The system proposed by the above model relies heavily on what research shows can be achieved through sentencing. I am skeptical, for example, about the efficacy of sentencing to achieve the goals of rehabilitation or incapacitation. However, the evidence is not conclusive in relation to this—more testing is needed. More sophisticated psychiatric techniques may make it possible to distinguish offenders who are likely to re-commit serious offenders from those who no longer present a danger to the community, thereby giving renewed impetus to an incapacitative sentencing regime. Likewise, better designed educational programs may make it possible to re-shape the value systems of criminals, which would make rehabilitation an attainable objective. We should not give up readily on the pursuit of such desirable outcomes. Thus, there is an on-going need for experimental controlled sentencing programs to see if they can achieve where other past programs have failed.

Given the crude manner in which sentencing has evolved in the Western World, there is room for considerable doubt concerning whether in the foreseeable future it would emerge from the dark ages and evolve into something akin to a social institution underpinned by a body of empirical and normative knowledge. Application of the above process provides the greatest prospect that this process can be considerably accelerated.

NOTES

1. M Frankel, *Criminal Sentences: Law Without Order* (Hill & Wang, 1972).

2. See M Bagaric, Double Punishment and Punishing Character—The Unfairness of Prior Convictions (2000) 19 *Criminal Justice Ethics* 10.

3. J Smith, 'Clothing the Emperor: Towards a Jurisprudence of Sentencing' (1997) 30 *Australian and New Zealand Journal of Criminology* 168.

4. See *Wong* (2001) 76 ALJR 79.

5. This of course, assumes that as a threshold consideration it is morally defensible to deliberately inflict punishment of wrongdoers. For comments on that, see M Bagaric and R Edney, 'What's instinct go to do with it? A blueprint for a coherent approach to punishing criminals' (2003) 27 *CLJ* 119–141.

6. R A Duff, *Trials and Punishments* (1985) 7.

7. Ibid, 5.

8. None of these prohibitions are, however, absolute: M Bagaric and K Amarasekara, 'The Errors of Retributivism (2000) 24 *Melbourne University Law Review* 124–189.

9. See M Bagaric, *Punishment and Sentencing: A Rational Approach* (Cavendish Publishing, London, 2001).

10. See F E Zimring and G Hawkins, *Incapacitation* (OUP, New York, 1995) 3
11. See Bagaric, above n 9.
12. See A von Hirsch and L Maher, 'Should Penal Rehabilitation be Revived' in A von Hirsch and A Ashworth (eds), *Principled Sentencing* (Hart Publishing, Oxford, 1998) 121, 122–3.
13. For discussion regarding the widespread civil disobedience which occurred following the police strike in Melbourne in 1923, see K L Milte and T A Weber, *Police in Australia* (Butterworths, Melbourne, 1977) 287–292. Similar civil disobedience followed the police strike in Liverpool in 1919 and the internment of the Danish police force in 1944.
14. F E Zimring and G J Hawkins, *Deterrence: The Legal Threat in Crime Control* (University of Chicago Press, Chicago, 1973) 43–4. For a more recent analysis of the relevant empirical evidence, see M Bagaric, above n 9, ch 6.
15. See *Ryan* (2001) 75 ALJR 815.
16. M Bagaric, What Sort of Fixed Penalties Should we Have? (2002) 23 *Adelaide University Law Review* 113.
17. Aggravating factors, such as prior criminality and breach of trust, and mitigating factors, such as age and remorse, divert the inquiry from the harm caused by the offence and the unpleasantness stemming from the sanction.
18. See C Anderson, 'Development of a national Offence Index for the Ranking of Offences' (2003) *AIC/ABS Conference—Evaluation in Crime and Justice: Trends and Methods*.
19. See J Shapland, *Between Conviction and Sentence* (Routledge & Kegan Paul, London,1981) 55; R Douglas, in *Guilty Your Worship* (LaTrobe University, Melbourne, 1980).
20. For an overview of the Finish system, see T Lappi-Seppala, 'Regulating the Prison Population: Experiences from a Long-Term Policy in Finland' (1998), part II, para 3: paper delivered at the *Back to Beyond Prisons Symposium* (Canada).
21. A von Hirsch, *Censure and Sanctions* (Clarendon Press, Oxford, 1993) 43.

Chapter Nine

Terrorism

9.1 TERRORISM: WHAT IS IT?

Terrorism is generally understood as an act involving the deliberate use of violence against civilians with the intent to induce a general atmosphere of fear, usually for political ends.[1] In a similar vein, it has been contended that terrorism is the 'the threat or use of violence in order to create extreme fear and anxiety in a target group so as to coerce them to meet political [or quasi political] objectives of the perpetrators'.[2]

Terrorism is perceived as the biggest threat to peace and security in many parts of the world—especially the West. At the international law level there is no accepted definition of terrorism. This is despite the fact that the matter has been debated in the United Nations for several decades. There are several reasons for this. Antonio Cassese notes that some developing countries remained steadfast in their view that the definition of terrorism must not include violence perpetrated by 'freedom fighters', ie groups that legitimately pursue self-determination. Also, these countries have insisted that a treaty proscribing terrorism could not be adopted unless the (historical, economic, social and political) causes underlying the violence are first examined and evaluated.[3] It cannot be said however that the complexity with defining terrorism stems from the fact that it leaves no room for 'freedom fighters'.

The lack of definitional convergence associated with terrorism resulted in the drafters of the Rome Statute, which established the International Criminal Court in 2002, refraining from including it as a crime within that Court's jurisdiction. It was also felt that including terrorism would have risked politicizing the Court and that terrorism should more effectively be addressed at the domestic level.[4]

This means that terrorism per se is not an international criminal offence. A recent definition of terrorism that has been advanced is that contained in Article 2(1)(b) of the 1999 International Convention for the Suppression of the Financing of Terrorism. It provides that terrorism is:

> Any other act intended to cause death or serious bodily injury to a civilian, or to any other person not taking an active part in the hostilities in a situation of armed conflict, when the purpose of such act, by its nature or context, is to intimidate a population, or to compel a government or an international organization to abstain from doing any act.

This definition is similar to that adopted by the European Parliament in its 1996 Resolution on Combating Terrorism in the European Union, where terrorism is defined as

> Any act committed by individuals or groups, involving the use or threat of violence, against a country, its institutions or people in general or specific individuals, which is intended to create a state of terror among official agencies, certain individuals or groups in society or the general public, the motives lying in separatism, extremist ideology, religious fanaticism or subjective irrational factors.[5]

Cassese argues that there is sufficient consensus in relation to this definition to constitute crime at international law, not only as a treaty obligation, but also as a matter of customary international law. According to Cassese terrorism at international law has three elements:

(i) The act must constitute a criminal offence under most national legal systems (such as assault, murder, torture, arson etc. . . .);
(ii) The act must be aimed at spreading terror (that is, fear and intimidation) by means of violent action or the threat thereof against the State, the public or particular groups of persons; and
(iii) The act must be politically, religiously, or otherwise ideology motivated, and not motivated for the pursuit of private ends.[6]

Irrespective of the context in which it is committed, terrorism can be committed by state agents or individuals.[7] Further, Cassese contends that terrorism only amounts to an international crime when the manner in which the act is carried out is with the support or acquiescence of a state, the act is very serious or otherwise is of concern for the whole international community, and is a threat to peace. Cassese contends that these features were underscored by the UN Security Council Resolution 1368 on 12 September 2001 which condemned the terrorist attacks in New York, Washington DC and Pennsylvania, and which regarded these acts 'like any act of international terrorism, as a threat to international peace and security' and called upon all states to work together to bring to justice the perpetrators of the acts.[8] However, in reality it does not seem that terrorism is currently an international crime. This is the only conclusion that can be adopted given that there is no settled definition of the concept and no prosecutions have occurred in relation to it.

The definitional issue can be clarified by looking at the distinguishing features of terrorism from other intentionally harmful conduct. There is an infinite number of ways in which people can and do harm each other, and the motivations for such conduct are also diverse, including rage, revenge, jealously and greed. In most jurisdictions, such behaviour where it is intentional is a criminal offence. The most serious criminal offence in most jurisdictions is murder—the intentional killing of another person. The circumstances in which murder can be committed range from the killing of another person in anger to the calculated serial killing of numbers of strangers. None of these acts constitute terrorism. Inherent in the concept of terrorism is a threat along the lines of 'do X or you will be subject to more conduct like this'. Serial killing can and often does strike fear into the minds of a community, but it does not amount to terrorism because it is not purposive beyond the immediate motivations for the attack; it is not designed to force the government or some group in the community to change its policies or practices in a manner which advances the interests of the wrongdoer.

With terrorism, the threat may be express, but is often merely implied. Thus, the attacks of September 11; the Bali bombings on 12 October 2002 and the London attacks on 7 July 2005 were labelled terrorist acts well before any group took responsibility for them. The threat is implied where the act is so harmful and untargeted (so far as the specific victims are concerned) that the motivation behind it is not apparently explicable by the normal range of misguided motivations that underpin criminal behaviour, and instead appears to be explicable only by reference to a motivation, which normally connotes some type of deeper ideological commitment.

Thus, broken down to its core elements, terrorism occurs where an agent performs an act that results in death or serious injury and the act aims to put pressure on a state or another group to change its policies or practices as a result of fear of further similar acts.[9] Unlike Cassese I do not accept that terrorism can be exemplified by acts which are of lesser gravity than those involving the loss of life or the infliction of serious injury. Harm below this threshold will almost certainly be ineffectual at agitating for a change of policy and will rarely spread fear. The requirement that the act should otherwise be an offence is otiose. Acts of terrorism are often seemingly random and it is for this reason that they can generate widespread fear—the community never knows who might be struck next. However, this is not an essential feature of terrorism. A bombing campaign against a certain group, such as politicians or judges, could also be defined as terrorism.

The above definition certainly captures attacks by freedom fighters, groups such as Al Qaeda and military incursions by states. Given the subjective evaluation involved in distinguishing between just and unjust ideological causes the starting point must be that all harmful acts are unjust. To the maximum extent possible, considerations relating to the objectives of the actors must be excluded from the definition: 'whether one terms a particular group of activists, terrorists or freedom fighters depends on one's political standpoint'.[10]

It also necessary to start with the assumption that violence is undesirable— rarely does the end (demonstrably) justify the means and hence exceptions to the proposed definition must be narrow. Where the agent is the state the only exceptions to my proposed definition are those relating to the international use of force. Where the agent is an individual or group not aligned to a state, self-defence and necessity should be the only exceptions. This gives little scope for states or individuals to engage in conduct which results in death or serious injury and which is aimed to put pressure on a state or another group to change its policies or practices as a result of fear or further similar acts.

9.2 RESPONSES TO TERRORISM—SECURITY VERSUS LIBERTY

Due to the threat of terrorism, many governments have introduced tough anti-terrorism laws. These laws often involve allowing security officials to detain for extended periods terrorist suspects without the normal judicial safeguards and curtail the right of proponents of certain ideologies to propound their views. In some jurisdictions terrorist suspects can be placed on 'control orders', whereby their movements are constantly monitored and often their right to silence is abolished and hence they must answer police questions.

I now assess the appropriate response to terrorism. Unlike other issues discussed in this book, the morality of terrorism is not in question. Taking innocent lives for questionable causes is unethical. The only issue in relation to terrorism is the measures that are proportionate to the threat.

The counter terrorism laws introduced in many Western countries have resulted in a fierce debate between civil rights activists and human rights crusaders on the one hand and government officials and representatives on the other. Tighter anti-terrorism laws have been criticised by civil libertarians who have managed to hold a straight face and charge that the laws are self-defeating, 'anti-democratic' and undercut the very values of freedom and due process that terrorists are attempting to damage.

Ultimately such criticisms are unsound. They are indicative of minds that are lacking in imagination or experience regarding the carnage that is caused by bombs going off in crowded places. The critics are also oblivious to the reality about the decisions made by democratic societies when they are confronted with a threat to their collective security.

There is nothing new about sacrificing the interests of individuals for the collective good of the community. When, as a community, we find ourselves between a rock and hard place and have to make a choice between individual interests and the collective good, we always (rightly) favour the collective good and make decisions which cause the least amount of suffering.

Thus, in relation to 'garden variety' crimes all legal systems condone detaining without trial those suspected of committing serious crimes who supposedly present a danger to our safety. These people are often ultimately found not guilty of any offence and when they are released from custody do not even get compensation.

It is easy to multiply examples of our willingness to sacrifice the individual for the common good. As we saw in chapter one, in times of war, we conscript young healthy men, under threat of imprisonment, to risk their lives for us. As we saw in the previous chapter, the fundamental principle of sentencing known as general deterrence, prescribes that it is permissible to increase the sentence of offender beyond their level of wrongdoing to make an example of them and hopefully discourage others from engaging in similar conduct. Incredibly, the legal system continues to condone this principle even though empirical evidence suggests that there is no link between longer sentences and lower crime. This practice should be abolished and presumably will be once legislatures are convinced of the flawed assumptions underlying the theory of marginal general deterrence. The fact that such information seems to fall on deaf political ears demonstrates, however, just how strong is the commitment to the common good over individual interests when there is even a perceived clash.

Thus, there is hardly anything new about a society sacrificing the interests of an individual for the good of the whole. History shows that it is the manner in which communities always react. And it is a good thing that they do. Ultimately, human lives and tangible interests must always trump grand, but empty, notions such as 'individual rights'. As noted in chapter one, lost lives hurt a lot more than bent 'principles'. The only true principle that exists is that there are no absolute principles and the closest thing to an absolute principle is that we must always act to maximise the common good and each person's life counts equally in this assessment.

A moral code which elevates individual rights and worships abstract notions above the common good is bankrupt and has no scope for application beyond the realm of fairy tales, where important rights never clash. The reality is that sometimes rights do clash. When they do, the least horrible thing to do is that which causes the least amount of harm.

This perspective needs to be firmly kept in mind when evaluating the response to the risk of terrorism. Of course it is undesirable to detain people without charge. It is even worse to do so without the involvement of the judicial process. Individual liberty and the process of fair trial are important ideals. But they are not as important as the right to life. Absent a strong commitment to the right to life, all other rights are meaningless. There is no freedom in the grave. Thus, interests such as liberty, privacy and due process must yield to collective safety and security.

This is lost on human rights activists because rights are innately individualistic and unrealistic. The reason that human rights 'theories' are just that—theories—is that they seek to atomise people. Human rights theories focus on the individuals, but as a species we don't live as individuals. We form communities—it is part of the way that humans are wired. We can't change that.

A society that confers greater powers to its security officials in times of risk does not undermine its commitment to important human ideals. To the contrary, such a response reflects a mature and sophisticated understanding of the ranking of human interests.

The extent to which individual interest can be curtailed for the common good is contingent on the level of risk faced by a community. So where in this risk spectrum are many Western countries currently placed? Certainly we are not in a war, but just as obvious is that we are not in a normal risk pattern. Since S11, Al-Qaeda has committed about 20 bombings, killing over 800 people. Depending on who you ask, the risk is put anywhere between remote to near certainty. If we split the difference it is a sure bet that there is a real risk (in the order of 50 per cent) that terrorists will launch an attack on another Western nation in the foreseeable future. If this attack is not thwarted many innocent people will be killed or seriously injured.

It is against such a context that the merits of the anti-terrorism laws should be debated.

Human rights crusaders will no doubt come to see this. But for them it will take a terrorist attack. Hindsight is a wonderful thing but foresight is bliss. Let's not rely on hindsight. Instead we should now confine the ramblings of human rights activists to the realms of fiction—a good read, but out of touch with what really matters.

9.3 THE TYPES OF RESTRICTIVE LAWS THAT ARE PERMISSIBLE

Thus, it is time for the human rights crusaders to remove their blinkers and extend their moral horizons and stop peddling a policy that threatens all our civil liberties. The picture is certainly far clearer a few steps up the moral mountain, above the fog that envelops the type of human rights discourse that permeates mainstream moral thinking.

Once the haze clears it becomes readily apparent that the right to not be questioned or searched or have one's fingerprints taken or iris scanned is meaningless if the right to life is not protected. The catalogue of so called other 'rights' is threatened even if people have the perception that their life is at risk. That's the reason that many Londoners stayed away from the underground following the bombings on 7/7 and that the airline industry was shut down following 9/11.

The best way to preserve our rights is to have a ranking of interests and to make sure that the interests at the top of the tree are not trumped by low order aspirations. Human rights advocates get muddled because they have no hierarchy of rights.

In order for people to flourish, the right balance must be struck between the powers we give to our security officials and our right not to live free from governmental interference. So what types of security intrusions are appropriate to try to avert such a risk?

Security officials should be able to demand that people provide an explanation for their activities. The right to silence is the preserve of those that have something to hide. If a person is detected taking photographs of the transport system or studying the plans of landmark buildings they need to explain their motive. Until they do, the best place for them is jail.

Security officials also need to have ample powers to install surveillance devices in relation to people suspected of criminal activities. We do not lose much by foregoing the right to privacy—not if we have nothing to hide. Random searches, of the type now to undertaken of people on the New York subway, of people in areas that are likely to be targeted should also become commonplace.

These measures will not shackle us. The will liberate us. We must all be prepared to give a little for the common good. Life matters too much to start whingeing about a few minor inconveniences.

A society that confers greater powers to its security officials in times of risk does not undermine its commitment to human rights. To the contrary, this is a humanistic response which underpins the commitment of a society to entrenching and protecting the interests that matter most to us.

9.4 THE RIGHT TO FREE SPEECH IS UNTRAMMELED—IT IS A WEAPON AGAINST TERRORISM

There is, however, one form of restriction that governments should be slow to impose in response to the terrorism threat. Several nations have passed, or are contemplating, laws banning communications that foment terrorism. These laws include criminal penalties for speech that justifies or glorifies terrorism.

The proposed laws will result in people that 'talk up' terrorism or keep a straight face while saying that Osama bin Laden is a good bloke being pinged and possibly slotted in jail.

While governments are right to introduce tough new measures that specifically target people that imperil our safety, the free speech limits are misguided. They are too crude to be effective and are likely to be self-defeating. This is not because the right to free speech is an absolute right. Not even close. Like all rights it must yield to the weight of producing good outcomes. There are many legitimate exceptions to the right to say whatever you want. Thus, we can't shout fire in a crowded cinema or spread lies which defame people and cause them harm. It is also wrong to say things that incite violence.

What is being considered by many governments goes beyond this. The proposed anti-terrorism speech laws would include a ban on words that 'indirectly' incite hatred or violence.

If we want to minimise the terrorist threat, we in fact need to be doing the opposite. We need ensure that we continue living a society which oxygenates, rather than stifles, the promulgation of all views, no matter how silly.

This is because such views will invariably be disseminated in any event. History shows that laws which prevent the expression of ideas, especially those which relate to activities or beliefs through which people define themselves are ineffective—it only drives those ideas underground.

Laws prohibiting the expression of political or religious views have been tried on countless occasions throughout the ages, normally by despotic and totalitarian regimes. They have never fully succeeded, no matter how severe the punishment.

Forcing these views underground increases the risk that they will in fact be adopted, and acted upon, by others. This is because in such an environment they are not subject to counter analysis.

The proposed laws would prevent communities from invoking one of the most effective repellants to silly views, which is that they can be contradicted. The sillier they are, the easier they are to rebut. But to do this, we first need to be aware of them. Thus, the best way to neutralise misguided and extreme views is to douse them with copious amounts of realism, to the point where they are consigned to the realms of delusional fiction.

An excellent example of this process was the recent public condemnation that Islamic teacher Abu Bakr received recently for his comments in Australia that Islam does not tolerate other religions and supports Muslims joining the jihad in Iraq. He also claimed that Osama was a good bloke.

Following these comments, the President of the Australian Federation of Islamic Councils, Ameer Ali, stated that the views of Mr Bakr are incorrect and noted that they do not represent the vast majority of Muslims in Australia. The Prime Minister also weighed in heavily against Mr Bakr.

The result: no more loopy statements by Mr Bakr. Moreover, people who may otherwise have been persuaded by his views have had the benefit of hearing the knock down arguments to the contrary—from leaders of all persuasions.

In the late nineteenth century famous English philosopher J S Mill stated:

> The peculiar evil of silencing the expression of an opinion is that it is robbing the human race... If the opinion is right, they are deprived of the opportunity of exchanging error for truth: if wrong, they lose, what is almost as great a benefit, the clearer perception and livelier impression of truth, produced by its collision with error.

It is important to not lose sight of this truth when it comes to dealing with extremists. The best way to neutralise them is not to command their silence but create an environment where they state their views loudly so that the breathtaking error of their ways can be made manifest.

Moreover, anti-terrorist speech laws are too vague and value ridden to work. Extolling the virtues of Osama in downtown Melbourne, London or New York sounds warped to most of us, but to the citizens living in the 'axis of evil' it would seem no less odious than talking up George W.

In the end, human flourishing is enhanced by more talk. It is the most effective way to unlock the truth in Iran, Syria, North Korea, as well as in Western Countries.

9.5 BROADER SOLUTIONS TO TERRORISM

There are several other points that need to be borne in mind when framing anti-terrorism laws and responses. First, like all crimes terrorism has a cause—misguided though it is—and a perpetrator. Given that we will not give terrorists what they want, it is necessary to focus on the potential perpetrators.

It is a world-wide phenomenon that people from poor and disadvantaged backgrounds are convicted of more criminal offences than the well-to-do. The reason for the link between social disadvantage and criminal behaviour is unclear. It has been suggested that social disadvantage not only prompts rebellion, but people from such groups have less to lose from being subjected to criminal sanctions.

What keeps most of us in check from committing crime is not that we fear jail. Rather it is the potential humiliation that we would suffer in the eyes of our family and friends, the risk of losing our job and being ostracised by the rest of the community. If we are stripped of these social bonds and live in a community that does not have any concern for us and deprives us of opportunities, we are far more likely to commit crime—including serious crime.

This means that Western nations with significant Muslim communities need to continue to show tolerance and understanding to their Muslim populations and share their considerable resources and wealth with all people within their border.

Extremism begets extremism. The best defence nations have against extremism within their orders is acceptance that the recent acts of terrorism are the deeds of a small number of aberrant fanatical people, whose ideologies have no semblance to those held by the growing number of Muslims that continue to enrich their nations.

Logically and morally it would be a grave mistake to stereotype and ostracise Muslim communities. Strategically it can only further imperil the safety of the entire community. People are far less likely to engage in appalling behaviour if they continue to be given a 'fair go'. The Muslim community is probably the best ally of the West in thwarting a terrorist attack, not a component of the risk.

At the transnational level, the risk of terrorism is not likely to be minimised by killing people in so called terrorist source countries or indeed by invading and conquering these countries. This is graphically demonstrated by the most recent incursion into Iraq, where terrorist attacks have increased almost exponentially since Saddam Hussein was overthrown. To the contrary, the answer to abating the terrorist threat lies in assisting impoverished nations to overcome the enormous amount of preventable suffering within their borders and providing for closer links and greater understanding by all the people in the world. This requires Western nations to increase their level of aid to the developing world and to loosen border controls. These matters are considered at length in the next two chapters in the context of discussing world poverty and the restrictive migration controls that exist in most Western countries.

Before to turning to these issues, it is useful to summarise the response that I believe is appropriate to the terrorist threat. It is three pronged. First at the domestic level, we need more stringent security and surveillance laws so that we increase the chances of detecting terrorism activities. These restrictions, however, should not be extended to curtailing free speech unless the communication directly incites violence. At the same time we need to continue to embrace local Muslim communities, who are a strong ally in warding off terrorism. The third prong involves dealing with terrorist producing countries. The solution is not to attempt to dominate, intimate or conquer these nations. Instead it is important to ensure that individuals growing up in these countries have the opportunity to flourish and hence are not attracted by desperate and extremist ideologies. People who have something to live for rarely behave in drastic ways. The 'home grown' bombers that were responsible for the 7 July 2005 London bombings seem to rebut this proposition, but in my view history will show that such conduct from individuals situated in such a manner is an aberration, rather than the norm.

NOTES

1. J F Murphy, 'Defining International Terrorism: A Way Out of the Quagmire', (1989) 19 *Israel Y B Human Rights* 13, 14.
2. O Schachter, *International Law in Theory and Practice* (1991) 163.
3. A Cassese, 'International Criminal Law', in Malcolm D Evans (ed), *International Law* (2003) 721, 750.
4. Cassese, ibid, 751.
5. For example, see the Resolution on Combating Terrorism in the European Union, OJ C 55/27, 24/02/1997.
6. Cassese, above n 3, 752.
7. Cassese, above n 3, 752.
8. Ibid.
9. Note that this definition of terrorism might embrace not only the September 11 attacks and similar outrages, but also, the violent overthrow of a government by foreign forces whether acting alone or in a 'Coalition of the Willing'. Bombing a country in order to force a change of government differs from terrorism, it might be said, in several ways of which some are subtle while others are not. It is the doctrinal difficulty involved with linking together a form of generalised words that can distinguish between such cases that has resulted in the stalemate over a definition of terrorism.
10. M Shaw, *International Law* (4th ed, 1997) 803.

Part E

DEALING WITH 'OTHER' PEOPLE AND ANIMALS

Chapter Ten

World Poverty

10.1 THE ENORMITY OF WORLD SUFFERING

Much of the humanity lives in conditions of unthinkable (by Western standards) deprivation. More than two billion people live on less than $2 a day. The most recent annual United Nations Food and Agriculture Organisation report notes that present levels of hunger cause the death of more than five million children a year. In more comprehensible figures, this equates to more than 13,000 daily deaths from hunger.

The situation is not improving. The number of chronically hungry people has hardly changed since the $800 million or so recorded approximately a decade ago. The British Prime Minister, Tony Blair, was correct when several days after the tsunami in South Asia that killed over 225,000 people on 26 December 2004, stated that there is a tsunami scale tragedy in Africa every week.

The response by Western nations to this on-going international crisis, depending on what one believes is appropriate, ranges from woefully inadequate to modest. There is a relatively well established international Convention that richer countries will contribute a portion of their wealth to poorer countries. The target which has been set by the United Nations is 0.7% of gross national income. This target is currently met (and in some cases exceeded) by several countries: Sweden, the Netherlands, Norway, Denmark and Luxembourg. It is not accidental that across a range of other social measures these countries are the most progressive in the world. Other nations punch well below their weight division in this domain. Australia, for example, gives a measly 0.28% of its per capita gross national income to the developing, and largely hungry, world. Still, Australians are not as stingy as the United States which contributes 0.14%.

The 'landmark' one off decision by the Group of Eight industrialized nations to forgive approximately $50 billion of debt from the 18 poorest countries announced on 11 June 2005 is a good start. In relative terms, however, the sum is trifling compared to the $2.6 billion spent *daily* on military activities.

The central question that ethicists in generations to come will come to ask of our community how is it that most of the citizens of the Western World have been so spectacularly successful at ignoring the desperate hungry cries from the developing world. What are the moral defects that accounted for this?

Before addressing this question it is important to point out that I conclude this chapter by making the rather obvious point that the answer to improving the living conditions of the developing world is more First World generosity. This is a point that has been made by many other commentators. The purpose of this chapter is to highlight what it is about the human condition that allows us to continue to ignore the pleas of other starving humans. This, I believe, is an essential step to forging a genuine commitment to eradicating world hunger.

There are in fact three fundamental failings that are imbedded in the moral thinking of the Western World that make it easy for us to effectively ignore the plight of approximately one billion hungry people. As noted above, these are so destructive that future generations will regard our moral code as more akin to a localised etiquette that is invoked by those with loud voices — namely, the rich and influential. We need to eradicate these failings from our moral psyche in order to develop a justifiable approach to preventable human suffering. Before we do this, we first need to be aware of the nature and content of these fallacies. It is to this that I now turn.

10.2 THE EXPLANATION FOR THE INADEQUATE RESPONSE

10.2.1 Acts and Omissions and The Maxim of Positive Duty

The principal normative rationale relied upon by first world nations to justify their lack of assistance is the *acts and omissions doctrine*—one is only responsible for one's positive acts, as opposed to events that one has failed to prevent (omissions).

The acts and omissions doctrine maintains that there is a relevant distinction between performing an act that has a certain consequence, and omitting to do something that has exactly the same outcome. Essentially, it is the view that provided we do not *do* anything contrary to accepted norms or rules we cannot be wrong. As a result, the state that stands by as another state is ravaged by hunger is beyond criticism whereas the state that summarily executes some of its citizens is morally culpable.

The acts and omissions doctrine is well entrenched in most western legal systems. However, this does not necessarily entail that there are sound normative reasons supporting the doctrine. Distinguishing between acts and omissions provides a simple method for demarcating lawful and unlawful conduct. This makes it easier to adhere to the rule of law virtues of consistency, uniformity and certainty. Adhering to these virtues is important if laws are to be effective in guiding conduct. Laws are framed in terms of *rules* (which are precise guides to certain actions, and apply conclusively to resolve an issue) rather than in terms of *principles* (which are general considerations that carry a degree of persuasion and form the underpinnings of the rules).

In light of the need for certainty the common law has shown a bias towards individual liberty. Hence we can do as we wish unless it is clearly wrong. The acts and omissions doctrine is simple and readily comprehensible and accordingly provides a basis for guiding conduct. As a general rule omissions are not unlawful, even if motivated by harmful intent, if no pre-established duty is owed to the other person. Adherence to the acts and omissions doctrine no doubt allows some reprehensible behaviour to go unpunished. However, it is felt that the ground lost here is more than made up in terms of the certainty that the doctrine provides and the harm which would arise if criminal sanctions were imposed on the basis of rules formed retrospectively.

Despite this, there are some circumstances where people are legally liable for their omissions. Thus parents have a duty towards their children and a positive duty to act has also been imposed upon those employed in areas having implications for public safety, such as police officers.

The acts and omissions doctrine has won widespread appeal largely due to the claim that it prevents our lives being intolerably burdened by demarcating the extent to which we must help others. It is the reason, so the argument runs, that we do not feel obliged to devote more resources to assisting people who are worse off than us, and why we feel *less* responsible for the deaths and tragedies we *fail to prevent* than for those we *directly cause*. The doctrine is one source of justification for why failing to feed the starving people in other nations is not on a par to shooting our neighbour.[1]

Despite its intuitive appeal, it is unclear whether the doctrine withstands close scrutiny. The first criticism of the doctrine that we explore is that as a general rule, there is no morally relevant difference between acts and omissions—sometimes morality requires us to perform a positive act.

As noted in chapter one, morality makes very few positive demands of us. It is essentially a set of negatively framed rules proscribing certain behaviour. However, it is premature to conclude that so long as we do not violate these negative rules we have discharged our moral obligations. There are occasions when acting morally requires us to do more than merely refraining from certain behaviour; where we must actually *do* something. Morality defined exhaustively as a set of negative proscriptions fails to explain why it is morally repugnant for Bill Gates to refuse to give his loose change to the starving peasant whose path he crosses, or why it is wrong to decline to save the child drowning in a puddle in order to avoid getting our shoes wet, or to refuse to throw a life rope to the person drowning beside the pier.

While the situations in which morality demands performance of a positive action are infrequent, when they do arise the obligations can be so clear, pronounced and unwavering that it would be implausible to postulate an account of morality which is not consistent with and explicable of such observations. As is discussed below in addition to the negative postulates of morality is one very important positive one: we must assist others in serious trouble, *when assistance would immensely help them at no or little inconvenience to ourselves* — the maxim of positive duty.

The acts and omissions doctrine is incapable of explaining why we are un-understandably appalled on becoming aware of clear breaches of this maxim. The public loathing directed at the witnesses of the Kitty Genovese murder is a practical illustration of the operation of the maxim. Kitty was beaten and stabbed by her assailant in Kew Gardens, Queens, New York City, over a 35 minute period in front of 38 'normal' law abiding citizens who did nothing to assist her; not even call the police, or yell at the offender. When finally a 70 year old woman called the police it took them only two minutes to arrive, but by this time Kitty was already dead.[2] Whether harm ensues as a result of an act or omission is in itself irrelevant to the moral appraisal of an action. The critical issue is whether one is responsible for the harm, where responsibility is assessed from the perspective of *all* of the norms and rules of morality including the maxim of positive duty.

James Rachels provides the following example which, with a slight alteration, illustrates the operation of the maxim of positive duty and the incongruity of the acts and omissions doctrine.[3] Smith stands to gain financially if his six year old cousin dies. One evening Smith sneaks into the bathroom and drowns his cousin and makes it look like an accident. In another case, Jones also stands to gain if his six year old cousin dies. One evening as the child is about to take his bath, he slips in front of Jones and falls face down in the bath and drowns in front of Jones who watches greedily. If the acts and omissions doctrine was tenable there would be some basis for differentiating between the culpability of Smith and Jones. However, morally the actions of Jones appear to be every bit as reprehensible as those of Smith. When assessed from the perspective of the maxim of positive duty we are left in no doubt as to why Jones is just as culpable as Smith—he, Jones, has grossly failed to discharge his moral obligation pursuant to the maxim.

Arguably, the principle of positive duty provides a far more accurate and coherent basis upon which we can reject intolerable demands on our time and resources than the acts and omissions doctrine. The doctrine is not necessary to explain why we should not work solely to assist others, since there is simply no pre-existing moral obligation to help everyone we possibly can. As is adverted to above, morality is essentially a set of negative constraints plus the maxim of positive duty. The proviso to the maxim, *when there is little or no inconvenience to oneself*, readily explains why our duty to assist others is extremely limited.

Thus, at the conceptual level the acts and omissions doctrine is unsound and cannot be used to justify the distinction between not helping and causing a situation of distress. For this reason, the doctrine should be rejected as a basis for withholding aid from needy people.

Another notion that inhibits a proper response to preventable suffering is the concept that proximate suffering matters more than anonymous distant suffering (the door-step principle). Like the acts and omissions doctrine, this is a distinction without moral significance.

10.2.2 The Door Step Principle

The second basis upon which the first world is reluctant to help third world nations is not a normative principle, but rather an aspect of how humans seem to be built. We are moved far more by immediate events rather than remote ones. As people, we are driven to far greater lengths to assist those whose suffering we are directly confronted with than those whom we can choose to ignore. Immediate lives weigh far more heavily on the sympathy scale than distant ones. As an empirical fact, we seem to be built in such a way that when an identifiable individual is experiencing pain and suffering (or is in need of help) this impacts on us much more heavily than when it is experienced by faceless strangers. Thus in 1995 the Australian Government spent $5.8 million rescuing French sailor Isabelle Autissier who was stranded while on a solo frolic around the world, when the same money could have saved thousands of starving people around the world. It is not putting the point too strongly to suggest that every adult in the first world is aware that every minute of the day people are dying in distant parts of the world due to readily preventable causes. The fleeting glimpse of starving children on the evening news evokes some sense of sympathy or guilt or responsibility. Unfortunately we are too good at escaping these feelings—we need to be educated that we should hold onto them. The limits of personal and state responsibility are not exhausted by our capacity to successfully block out 'distant' human suffering.

There is no basis for acting in this way. Each person ranks equally in any moral hierarchy. There is simply no logical basis for ranking one person's happiness more highly than that of the next person. Further, an attempt to do otherwise would be futile. The efficacy of morality is contingent on *widespread support*. People seem to have a strong tendency to act on the basis of reciprocity. People who have their interests disregarded or undervalued are less likely to observe the interests of others. If the happiness of certain individuals or a group is put above the rest of the community, there simply will not be enough participants in the moral game to attain individual happiness.

In order for human rights law to advance and have the opportunity to realise its aims, it is necessary to debunk the door-step principle and the acts and omissions doctrine. This would require action to be taken to disabuse world leaders of these unsound beliefs and to replace them with an acceptance of the maxim of positive duty. It is only after this occurs that genuine moral pressure can be placed on world leaders. The first world will then be given a stark choice: feed the hungry or accept moral culpability.

10.2.3 The Individualising Nature of Rights

The last explanation for the inadequate level of assistance provided by the First World to impoverished countries has been alluded to in chapter one. As we have seen, contemporary moral discourse is framed in the language of rights. We like rights. They are individualising claims and give us a protective sphere. But they limit our moral horizons to ourselves and sometimes to the person immediately before us. But rights are nonsense. They are simply an illustration of the fact that as a species we seem to be more greedy than smart or kind.

It is time to re-think rights, with consequences as our building blocks. What matters most is maximizing flourishing, not adding to the ever increasing catalogue of rights, which can only be enjoyed by most of the world at the conversation level.

10.3 CONCLUSION

Regrettably there is only a limited appetite for such generosity and self-serving aspects of our psyche and moral code allow us to ward off person blame for the plight of starving people in other parts of the world. A commitment to assisting the poor requires the doorstep principle and the acts and omissions distinctions to be abandoned. Although debunking these grounds will not necessarily increase the aid given to poor countries, it will neutralise the main grounds upon which Western nations deflect blame for the plight of people in the developing world and hence allow these countries to place considerable moral pressure on the West to provide more assistance.

Ultimately, the main cure for preventable mass Third World suffering is a massive injection of aid by the First World. There is no moral justification for prosperous nations such as Australia, the United Kingdom and the United States not meeting their 0.7% gross national income aid target.

Wealthy individuals should also be encouraged to contribute to the plight of the needy in other parts of the world. There will always be a degree of arbitrariness attached to what this equates to in a pragmatic terms. I suggest that individuals who derive more than $A200,000 ($US150,000) per year should donate in the order of approximately 5% of their income. An annual income of $A200,000 is so large that it is unlikely that anyone could argue, while maintaining a straight face, that 'it is not enough'. Five per cent is sufficiently large to be meaningful, yet small enough to not discourage people from continuing to work hard and innovation.

Apart from increasing foreign aid, another important reform that should be implemented in order to alleviate world poverty is to significantly loosen border controls, allowing much of the world's poor to immigrate to locations where resources are plentiful. This proposal is detailed further in the next chapter.

NOTES

1. H Kuhse, 'Euthanasia' in Peter Singer (ed), *A Companion to Ethics* (1991) 297, 310.

2. L P Pojman, *Ethics: Discovering Right and Wrong* (1990) 1-2.

3. J Rachels, 'Active and passive Euthanasia' (1975) *The New England Journal of Medicine* 78.

Chapter Eleven

Migrants: Opening up our Border

11.1 INTRODUCTION AND AN OVERVIEW OF ARGUMENTS AGAINST STRICT MIGRATION CONTROLS

A defining aspect of national sovereignty is that nation states have the right to determine which people are permitted to enter within their geographical borders. Many States exercise this power by placing restrictions on who can enter and remain within their borders. As a result, many people in the world are forced to live in States not of their choice. This often diminishes their opportunities and level of flourishing. In some cases, it is the difference between life and death. In many cases, the stakes are not that high, but nevertheless the stakes are high enough to force people to leave their place of origin and ultimately become 'displaced persons': people that nobody wants, at least not enough. At any point in time over the past decade or so there have been somewhere between roughly 12 to 18 million displaced people worldwide.[1]

This problem could be almost *eradicated* if countries abandoned migration controls. Arguably, some controls remain necessary in the interests of national security, but the problem would still be *significantly alleviated* if countries greatly increased immigration numbers. Problems of world-wide hunger and millions of people dying from readily preventable causes would also abate—one assumes that people in such desperate straits would go in search of greener pastures. Not all would have the energy and resources to succeed, but no doubt many would.

This chapter challenges existing immigration policies. It contends that unless we radically loosen migration controls we must accept that we are endorsing a racist policy. This diminishes the force of criticism levelled by States that implement such policies at other States which have internal laws that discriminate against their citizens.

At the international level, there is little momentum for reducing migration controls. The European Union 'experiment' aside, many States are tightening migration controls. Even in Europe, increased freedom of movement is limited to the already privileged—Western Europeans. Tighter migration controls will exacerbate the problems relating to 'forced State confinement'. This reality of States imposing strict migration controls is undeniable and is likely to continue into the foreseeable future. But it is not one that we should accept without question or at least reflection.

This issue has received scant philosophical or social commentary. As noted by Rainer Baubock:

> Until recently, with a few significant exceptions, political and moral philosophers had little to say about migration. It was mostly taken for granted that state sovereignty implied the right to control movements of persons across borders (and quite often within borders). Free internal movement and choice of residence within a state and the freedom to leave any state have become accepted only since the Second World War (see article 13 of the 1948 Declaration of Human Rights). That there is, or ought to be, an equivalent right of free immigration is generally denied by scholars of international law but has become a controversial issue in . . . normative political theory.[2]

In the end, the practice of imposing migration controls is discriminatory. It is the ultimate form of discrimination: 'super-discrimination'. I argue that there is no logical or moral reason why non-nationals of a State should not have the same opportunities and freedoms as nationals in that State. The decision to confer opportunities and privileges only on citizens represents an unjustified preference for those like oneself—the paradigm of discrimination. The result of this is of course a tragic irony given the considerable efforts that many Western States make to stamp out discrimination at the domestic level and the vast array of international anti-discrimination instruments, sponsored and loudly trumpeted by Western nations. For it is these very States that typically impose the strictest controls on immigration. I argue that the substratum upon which international law is built, with sovereign States at the cornerstone, is inherently discriminatory and is probably responsible for more harm caused by discrimination than the cumulative effect of all the domestic discrimination practices with which so many States are preoccupied.

Absent strict migration controls it is likely that people would spontaneously migrate so that there would eventuate a loose equilibrium between resources, such as food and water, and human need. We would at least correct the current, obscene situation in which much of the Western World is gorging itself to ill-health on super-size meals, while much of Africa continues to starve.

Critics will argue that there are sound pragmatic reasons for tight border controls. Appeals will be made to 'national security'. To this it may be pointed out that most States are far more liberal with admitting tourists (whose dollars they happily extract) than new permanent residents (who might be a drain on community resources at some future point), even though security concerns would apply equally if not more to tourists. Indeed if the sense of 'security' is widened to include crime in general, it is the tourist who often poses the greatest threat to the host community particularly in relation to sexual exploitation. While security considerations undoubtedly justify some vetting of immigrants, they do not justify the scale of current migration controls.

The most persuasive argument in favour of strict migration controls is expressed by the view that 'we made it and own it and don't want it ruined by others'. The absence of migration controls, arguably, could diminish the willingness of people to work collectively to create common amenities and resources. This is similar to the argument advanced in favour of the right to own private property—that people will not work if they cannot keep the fruits of their labour. This argument, while not trivial, ultimately does not justify the current strict levels of migration control.

In the next section of this chapter, I briefly detail the nature of sovereignty and the history of migration controls. Surprisingly, strict migration controls are a recent advent in the course of human history. I argue that open borders do not present a risk to state sovereignty. In section three of this chapter, I set out the advantages of liberalising immigration policy. In the process, I speculate on the likely effects. It seems that it would not be that drastic after all. Economic prosperity is only one of the many reasons that drive people-movement. Africa will not empty overnight if border controls in the Western World are lifted (although the argument could be made that this would not necessarily be undesirable). In section four of this chapter, I analyse the arguments in favour of the status quo. After concluding that they are unsound we propose an alternative migration control model in the final section of this chapter.

11.2 SOVEREIGNTY AND THE HISTORY OF MIGRATION CONTROLS

11.2.1 Territory and Sovereignty

The interrelated notions of 'territory' and 'sovereignty' underpin migration controls that restrict the movement of people. I provide a brief account and explanation of each to better understand the options for migration reform and to emphasise the point that reduced migration controls do not necessarily present a threat to national sovereignty.

International law as currently constituted depends crucially on the so-called 'Westphalian' unit of the sovereign State. To this end, the sovereignty norm now affirms the territorial integrity of the State and the rule of non-intervention.[3] Although the State constitutes the principal entity that is the subject of international law, the State system has a surprisingly short history. In the middle ages there was no concept of sovereignty.

> Humanity found its 'oneness' not in human rulers or the geographic reaches of their power but rather in the Respublica Christianity, the pervasive unity of God . . . Sovereignty in the sense of an ultimate territorial organ which knows no superior, was to the middle ages an unthinkable thing.[4]

The notion of a singular Respublica Christianitya was destroyed by the Reformation and replaced by the notion of State supremacy. In time, the sovereignty of the king came to be thought of as absolute, and this sovereignty became equated with the sovereignty of the State.[5]

The State system commenced in Europe in the seventeenth century and was originally confined to European States, 'the badge of entry being that the putative State satisfied the "standard of civilization", essentially that it was a Christian State'.[6] The expansion of the State system began in the nineteenth century and gained considerable momentum with the process of colonial self-determination during the period 1945 to 1990 when the number of States worldwide more than doubled.[7]

Statehood as the basis for sovereignty is defined by international law. An essential criterion is a defined territory. The boundaries of State territory are the 'imaginary lines on the surface of the earth which separate the territory of one State from that of another, or from unappropriated territory, or from the open sea'.[8] International law does not require the structure of a State to follow any particular pattern.

Apart from the need for a defined boundary, there are several other aspects that are essential for the existence of a State. Article 1 of the Montevideo Convention on the Rights and Duties of States 1933 sets out the most widely accepted formulation of the criteria of statehood. It provides that a State should posses the following four criteria: (i) a permanent population; (ii) a defined territory; (iii) government; and (iv) capacity to enter into relations with other States.

The right to self-determination is also central to statehood, either as an aspect of the need for government or an independent requirement. This requires the existence of a relatively stable and effective form of government. Self-determination is thought of as legitimating and empowering groups of people to implement norms and rules that reflect and are adapted to their distinctive expectations and desires. This supposedly facilitates global human flourishing. This position however relies on there being distinct sets of political needs, correlated with ethnicity: a formula that in its manifestations in previous centuries has been labeled racism.

According to Joan Fitzpatrick, three basic principles can be derived from the United Nations Charter version of the post-Westphalian form of sovereignty:

> (i) exclusive authority within a define territory; (ii) non-interference by states in the domestic jurisdiction of other states; and (iii) equality among states.[9]

Sovereignty refers to the ultimate legal authority within a national legal system (internal sovereignty) and the power to conduct relations with other States. Another name for internal sovereignty is jurisdictional sovereignty. This means that States may legislate as they choose on any matter whatsoever. A basal aspect of state sovereignty is that states can pass laws of any nature, subject to the constitution of the state (which itself can be changed, albeit with varying degrees of procedural difficulty). Thus in the Australian context, for example, it is widely agreed that a law prescribing that blue-eyed babies must be killed would be a valid, if deplorable, exercise of law making power. Jurisdictional sovereignty allows states to pass immigration laws. In fact migration control is the quintessential act of the sovereign State. 'Since the development of the modern state from the fifteenth century onward, governments have regarded control over their borders as the core of sovereignty. It is axiomatic that states decide which people to admit, how many, and from where'.[10]

11.2.2 Migration Controls

As noted above, jurisdiction sovereignty enables States to make migration laws of whatever nature they wish. This includes a total prohibition on entry into the State, however short the intended visit and for whatever reason. The opposite also applies: States may adopt an open border policy, enabling any person to come and live within their borders.

Mass migration is not a new phenomenon.[11] It was a notable feature of the ancient world. However, it is has only been relatively well documented since the start of the sixteenth century. Three distinct phases of mass migration since that time have been identified. The first relates to the European colonial regimes which from the sixteenth century developed expansionist programs and colonial ventures. This resulted in large numbers of

Europeans been transferred to administer colonies in order to create new markets and to 'spread civilization'. The main routes for migration were between Western Europe, the west coast of Africa and the Americas. This formed the infamous transnational triangle: the transfer of Western goods to Africa, of African slaves to the Americas and the produce from the Americas back to Europe. During the period of colonisation, migration was mainly coercive, driven by economic and social imperatives of Western Europe. Between 1500 to 1850 approximately 10 million slaves were transported from Africa to the Americas.

The second phase of migration involved millions of Europeans electing to leave their homeland to settle in the New World. This is refereed to the 'classical period' of migration. From 1825 to 1925 over 25 million people left Britain, mainly for the colonies or ex-colonies, such as Australia, South Africa, Canada and especially the United States. By the end of the nineteenth century the United States had already become the greatest industrialised nation in the world. The industrialization in urban areas occurred along with the 'de-peasantization' of rural societies. The rural population abandoned its links with the land to move to urban centres, although it did not always remain there. It is estimated that at the end of the nineteenth century 47 per cent of migrants who went to the United States from Europe returned home. Both migration and immigration allowed industrialization to take the rapid course that it did during this period.

From the late nineteenth century and into the twentieth century large numbers of migrants were being lured to foreign places, not by imperial dictates, but by the suggestions of their own family members, as a means to enhance their quality of living. 'During the nineteenth century, the idea of migration became a craze. Migration had entered the popular imagination as the cure to all ills. . . . Emigration represented the possibility of rebirth and salvation elsewhere'.[12]

The third phase of migration is post Second World War, and was driven by the need of employers to supplement national labour resources. This was in many respects the reverse of the colonial phase of migration. Most migrants were arriving in Europe from the colonies. Thus, Britain recruited workers from Ireland, the West Indies, India and Pakistan. France reached out to North Africa. Throughout this period, migrant movements were generally seen to be constituted by people who moved freely, for their own economic benefit.

However, the period of liberal migration movement changed with the advent of contract labour. The United States, Western Europe, Australia, Canada, Japan and more recently the Gulf States introduced contract labour schemes, which systematically recruited labour from abroad in order to perform specific tasks. This employment tended to be for limited duration on specific projects such as infrastructure, disentitling workers from the right to legal settlement. These schemes ended in the mid-1970s in the United States, Australia and Western Europe, at least in part due to the emergence of the very migratory flows and patterns of settlement that the governments had intended to prevent. Despite formal restrictions on settlement, migrants often found ways to bring their families and co-workers in to the new State, thus sowing the seeds of permanent social change, quite at odds with governmental policy.

The striking feature of the above, albeit cursory, account of migration is that most of the migration that has occurred during the expanse of human history has been unregulated. From the second phase onward it has been individual driven, not State controlled. This is in stark contrast to the present state of migration. Many countries, especially in the First World—where demand for space is the highest—have highly regulated and controlled migration intakes. Migration policy is dictated by what individuals can offer to the State in question. The principal objective in framing immigration policy has been to allow in people who will contribute something tangible to the receiving State. Individuals rich in money or skills, but not too rich in years of age, are in demand. Nations wish to attract people who will help to make the community richer or smarter. Beyond these parameters immigration is increasingly difficult.[13]

This, the present situation, is the fourth stage of mass people migration, so far as entry into the First World is concerned. It is in fact the 'anti-migration' stage.

> Western Europe has effectively frozen all formal programs of mass migration. Although the European Union has relaxed laws for the movement of citizens between member states, and while North America moves toward the creation of a free-trade zone, the borders of the regions have been increasingly tightened. Etienne Balibar's wry observation of relocation of the barriers between Europe and its other returns our attention to the linkage between racism and the crisis in Europe's identity problem. The future 'iron curtain' and the future 'wall' threaten to pass somewhere in the Mediterranean, or somewhere to the south-east of the Mediterranean, and they will not be easier to bring down than their predecessors.[14]

Multicultural western states like Australia, Canada and the United States have also developed more restrictive policies for labour migration and have tightened the opportunities for family reunification.[15]

For the sake of completeness a snapshot of international migration is as follows. All told, fewer than 7 percent of the world population are migrants (defined as people who live permanently or for long periods outside their countries of origin).[16] There are 56 million migrants in Europe, 50 million in Asia, 41 million in North America and 16 million in Africa. Australia has approximately 5 million migrants.[17] The proportion of migrants varies considerably from region to region. In Germany it is high at 9 percent and very low in Italy and Spain at 2 percent. Two-thirds of 'foreigners' in Europe are from other European states.[18] Almost one in ten persons in a more developed region is a migrant[19] and nearly one in 70 persons in a developing country is a migrant. People do not often choose to live in poor places.

It is important to emphasise that the age of 'anti-migration', while an emerging trend, is not a worldwide phenomenon.[20] In 1976 only some 7 per cent of UN members had restrictive immigration policies. This rose to 40 per cent in the early part of the 21st century. Advanced economies are at the forefront of this development.[21]

The above analysis highlights one important aspect of migration controls. They are not inevitable, even in a world where the principal entity is the sovereign State. Open borders do not necessarily present a risk to state sovereignty —no matter how liberal. Strict migration controls have a relatively recent advent, and history has shown that nations can flourish in times of relatively open borders without a loss of identity or risk to their existence. Sovereignty can co-exist with an open border regime. States can still pass any law they desire, it is simply that the subjects to whom those laws apply may be more transient than is presently the case—more denizens than citizens. The rest of this paper is an attempt to consign the current trend of increasing border controls to a small (unfortunate) place in human history.

11.3 ARGUMENTS IN FAVOUR OF REDUCED MIGRATION CONTROLS

11.3.1 The Right to Freedom of Movement and The Interests of Justice

There are several arguments that can be made in favour of removing or reducing migration controls. The most obvious is that it can be asserted that people have a right to freedom of movement, and that this is a 'fundamental human right' akin to the right to internal movement (ie within a State), and the right to exit one's State, enshrined in the Declaration of Human Rights.

As noted by Baubock there are several other possible sources of such a right. In the eighteenth century Immanuel Kant proposed that individuals have a right to free movement which is grounded in mankind's common ownership of the earth. Originally no person has a greater right to be in any place than anybody else, and the finite space on the earth makes it impossible for humankind to avoid trans-societal contact simply by dispersing further over the earth. Thus, all people have a right to offer themselves for social contact with inhabitants in any territory. However, this does not, according to Kant, provide a fully blown right to immigrate, only a right to right to travel and undertake peaceful trade.

Much more recently, Bruce Ackerman goes further than Kant and contends that people have a right (at least in the prima facie sense) of immigration. People can only be excluded from a certain resource where this can be justified on the basis of neutral criteria. This of course excludes claims of individual moral superiority. Ackerman contends that the only reason for restricting immigration is to protect the 'ongoing liberal conversation itself'. He suggests that once immigration exceeds a certain threshold, this may provoke a certain backlash of anxiety among the 'native' population, leading to the prospect of fascists seizing power.[22]

Some commentators have also argued the fundamental interests of justice mandate uncontrolled immigration. This would seem to follow from Rawls' theory of justice. As noted by Baubock,

> Behind a global veil of ignorance about their own societal position representatives of the original position would vote for a right to free movement both because it extends the overall system of liberties and because it seems to follow from the 'difference principle', namely that social inequalities should be arranged so that the least disadvantaged benefit the most.[23]

There is considerable merit in the above arguments. However, they do not represent the strongest path to justifying transnational freedom of movement. The strongest argument to this end does not require resort to esoteric or under-developed notions of justice and rights. The universally accepted and highly developed notion of discrimination provides the strongest logical and normative as well as emotive argument in favor of liberalising worldwide people movement.

11.3.2 Migration Control as Inherently Discriminatory

Precluding people from a good, service or resource is prima facie discriminatory. Discrimination appears to be a universal concept. It has rich history and nowadays has a powerful pejorative connotation. It is strongly proscribed at the international law level. This is evidenced by the large number of international instruments prohibiting discrimination. As noted by Rhona Smith, 'virtually every human rights instrument includes a non-discrimination clause'.[24]

A prohibition on discrimination requires that like cases should be treated alike and unlike cases should be treated differently. That is, to discriminate is to treat someone differently without a *relevant basis* for the difference.

Thus, excluding non-nationals from one's borders is discriminatory unless there is a relevant basis for the exclusion. One of the most common forms of discrimination is race—treating a person differently simply, in many cases, because of their place of birth. This is one of the starkest and most repugnant forms of discrimination because the location where a person is born is of course merely a happy or unhappy circumstance over which the individual has no control. An accident of birth should not qualify a person for extra privileges or opportunities. The world is a fairer place if to the maximum extent possible luck is taken out of the process for allocating benefits and burdens—which, arguably should be distributed on the basis of merit and desert.

The discrimination card can be readily played in the context of migration controls. In fact on its face migration controls are the purest form of racial discrimination. The only ostensible difference between a baby born a minute ago in Sydney and in the Niger is the location and consequently (in most cases) their racial identity. Their race cannot be changed, but location can—if we let this occur. History shows that we are unlikely to do so. We will embrace the baby born in Sydney into our community and shun the child from Niger. Our refusal to allow the baby from Niger to migrate to Australia is likely to have a devastating effect on its life. Studies indicate that the Sydney baby is likely to live to the age 80 and have the opportunity to participate in University education and perhaps acquire enormous sums of money. The child from Niger will probably die by the age of 46, spending much his or her time trying to gather food to ward off starvation. The prospect of any form of formal education is close to zero.

The policy of not permitting non-nationals into one's country will not be discriminatory if there is a valid reason, ie a relevant basis, for such an approach. This is examined further below. For now, I examine in greater detail the advantages for a world with more porous borders.

11.3.3 Reduction in Hunger and Preventable Deaths

The concept of breaking down national borders has several pragmatic benefits. First, it would enhance the liberty of all people and lead to a more just distribution of resources—not only food, medicine and clothing but also education and employment.

There are sufficient resources currently available in the world to ensure that all citizens enjoy some degree of flourishing. Despite this, as noted in the previous chapter millions of people, especially in Africa, find it difficult to subsist beyond the most basic of means. Tens of millions of people dies each year of malnutrition and readily preventable diseases.

This reality of a malnourished continent constitutes a stark contrast with the gluttony of much of the First World, where many of us are eating ourselves out of a healthy and long life. The increased incidence of obesity and the health risks associated with it are spelt out in the case of *Pelman v McDonalds*[25] where the plaintiffs sued the fast-food company McDonalds, claiming that as result of consuming McDonalds food they became overweight and developed diabetes, coronary heart disease, high blood pressure, elevated cholesterol intake, and/or other detrimental and adverse health effects. In summarily dismissing the cause of action, Sweet DJ of the New York District Court[26] stated:

> Today there are nearly twice as many overweight children and almost three times as many overweight adolescents as there were in 1980. In 1999, an estimated 61 percent of U.S. adults were overweight or obese and 13 percent of children aged 6 to 11 years and 14 percent of adolescents aged 12 to 19 years were overweight. In 1980, those figures for children were 7 percent for children aged 6 to 11 years and 5 percent for adolescents aged 12 to 19 years.
>
> Obese individuals have a 50 to 100 percent increased risk of premature death from all causes. Approximately 300,000 deaths a year in the United States are currently associated with overweight and obesity. As indicated in the U.S. Surgeon General's 2001 Report on Overweight and Obesity, 'left unabated, overweight and obesity may soon cause as much preventable disease and death as cigarette smoking.'
>
> Obesity and overweight classification are associated with increased risk for coronary heart disease; type 2 diabetes; endometrial, colon, postmenopausal breast and other cancers; and certain musculoskeletal disorders, such as knee osteoarthritis.
>
> Studies have shown that both modest and large weight gains are associated with significantly increased risk of diseases. For example, a weight gain of 11 to 18 pounds increases a person's risk of developing type 2 diabetes to twice that of individuals who have not gained weight, while those who gain 44 pounds or more have four times the risk of coronary heart disease (nonfatal myocardial infarction and death) of 1.25 times in women and 1.6 times in men. A gain of 22 pounds in men and 44 pounds in women result in an increased coronary heart disease risk of 1.75 and 2.65, respectively.
>
> In certain obese women, the risk of developing endometrial cancer is increased by more than six times. Overweight and obesity are also known to exacerbate many chronic conditions such as hypertension and elevated cholesterol and such individuals may also suffer from social stigmatization, discrimination and poor body image.

In 1995, the total estimated costs attributable to obesity amounted to an estimated $99 billion. In 2000, the cost of obesity was estimated to be $117 billion. Most of the costs associated with obesity arise form type 2 diabetes, coronary heart disease and hypertension.[27]

While this relates to United States data, the situation in many other parts of the First World, in terms of the escalating nature of the problem and the adverse health consequences associated with obesity, is similar. For example, it has been forecast that in Australia, obesity will overtake smoking as the biggest health problem of the decade. In particular, it has been noted that a quarter of the population will be suffering from weight-related diabetes by 2013.[28] The cost to the tax payer is considerable. It is estimated that health problems linked to weight cost taxpayers at least $3 billion a year.[29] In absolute terms, it has been reported that 'average weight of Australian adults has increased five per cent in the past decade, to 74.3kg. According to a recent Australian Bureau of Statistics report, more than half of all men (58 per cent) and 42 per cent of women are overweight'.[30]

Thus, at issue is not the capacity of the world to sustain itself in a comfortable fashion: 'there is enough grain alone produced to provide every human being on the planet with 3500 calories a day—enough to make most people fat'.[31] The problem is merely one of distribution of resources. Left to their own devices people would presumably gravitate to life sustaining resources. This includes not only food, but would probably extend to vital resources, such as shelter, clothing and security. Thus, it is likely that liberalising migration would result in a fairer distribution of resources.

This is not to assert that all of the hungry and destitute will migrate to richer lands. Many people are in fact so destitute that they do not have the resources, energy or capacity to travel significant distances. However, human ingenuity and will, as shown by the lengths to which groups of displaced people have managed to go with negligible resources in order to flee the scourges of war, famine and natural disaster, indicates that hungry and under resourced people may be able to successful migrate.

It is important to emphasise that population flows stemming from relaxed border restrictions may not be as great as might initially be felt. While there would seem to be a significant prospect that the First World would become considerably more populated with people from less well off countries leaving their country of origin in search of greater economic opportunities, this risk may not be as pronounced as might first appear. For example, during the 1950s numerous inhabitants of British Commonwealth states far from England were entitled (until legislation restricted the process)[32] to immigrate into the UK.[33] In the early 1960s it was estimated that one quarter of the world's population were legally entitled (on post-colonial and related grounds) to enter Britain.[34] While Commonwealth immigration was undoubtedly substantial and accelerating by the early 1960s, legal access to Britain had not given rise to mass re-locations of population—the West Indies had not emptied. What had happened was that (among other factors) the statutory restriction of West Indian immigration into the US[35] had diverted many people in the transatlantic direction. If Britain was not 'swamped' by its immigration obligations to three quarters of the global population in the 1950s, then it need perhaps not be feared that the rest of the First World would be swamped by recognising similar obligations to the entire global population.

Mass movements of populations, like the relocations of individuals, take place for complex reasons among which the opening of borders and economic considerations are but two. A number of theoretical models have been advanced to explain migration patterns.[36] The voluntarist perspective is best illustrated by the 'push-pull' model. On this view, migration is caused by twin forces. The crudest model asserts that people are pushed out of stagnant economies and pulled towards industrial urban centres. This regards economic opportunity as the main cause of migration. More sophisticated models also factor in other variables, including repressive political regimes, population growth and cultural considerations. A contrary theory is the structural perspective which places greater emphasis on more wide-ranging factors, such as state regulation, including forms of social segregation, industrial development and notions of social capital. Thus, it is not likely that under our proposal all of Africa would pack its bags and move to New York. Economic reasons are strong but are not decisive motivators when it comes to deciding where one should live. Affluence, while a motivation for migration, conversely often serves to exclude people from settling in wealthy areas. Affluence builds invisible, but effective, barriers to inroads by the poor. Thus, under present circumstances, the entire citizenry of the US has not moved to downtown Manhattan, despite the unfettered freedom enjoyed by them so to do. Nevertheless it may be that the prospect that many Third World citizens would immigrate to the First World and enjoy the copious resources and wealth available there may so terrorise the citizens of the First World as to provide the strongest possible incentive for them to feed the hungry in distant parts of the world.

11.3.4 The Strongest Possible Incentive for The West to Give Proper Aid to The Third World

Self-interest and misplaced group pride dictates that the First World will not be enthusiastic about the prospect of having 'their' land swamped with new arrivals. The reluctance of nations to share their economic resources with people less well-off is demonstrated by the current tightening of border controls. Ironically, this is also evidenced by the European Union model, which ostensibly centres on alleviating travel restrictions by providing reciprocal rights for freedom of movement and employment between states. One notable aspect of the formation of the EU is that membership was initially limited to states with well developed and highly successful economic systems. Subsequent membership is tied to states improving their economic productivity (and sometimes their human rights compliance). While this pattern is not unwavering, it is a relatively accurate statement of the development of the EU. Thus the richest states in Europe, such as France, Germany and Italy were foundational members. The poorest, such as Albania and Croatia will be among the last to gain membership.

Thus an indirect benefit that is likely to occur from removing migration restrictions is that the threat of hunger-motivated mass migration would provide the First World the strongest possible incentive to properly aid Third World nations. As noted in chapter ten, the First World has only paid lip service to this commitment. However, the thought that food-deprived Africa would empty into the cities of the United States, Australia and Europe would provided the strongest possible stimulus for these nations to properly add to the resource base of the Third World.

11.4 ARGUMENTS IN FAVOUR OF STRICT MIGRATION CONTROLS

Despite the good reasons for relaxing immigration restrictions, the presence of such rules is not discriminatory if there is a relevant reason for preventing transnational migration. This raises for consideration the notion of 'relevant difference'. The notion of what constitutes a relevant difference has not been directly addressed, let alone settled, by the courts, legal commentators or philosophers. At best, there is something approaching consensus on what is not a relevant difference.

A relatively uncontroversial aspect of the notion of a relevant difference is that there must be a 'universal' reason for any permissible discrimination. Wider moral theory informs us regarding what such a reason would be.[37] According to FA Hayek:

> The requirement that the rules of true law be general does not mean that sometimes special rules may not apply to different classes of people if they refer to properties that only some people possess. Such distinctions will not be arbitrary, will not subject one group to the will of others, if they are recognised as justified by those inside and those outside the group. . . . This does not mean that

there must be unanimity as to the desirability of the distinction, but merely that individual views will not depend on whether the individual is in the group or not. So long as, for instance, the distinction is favoured by the majority both inside and outside the group, there is a strong presumption that it serves the ends of both. When, however, only those inside the group favour the distinction, it is clearly privilege; while if only those outside favour it, it is discrimination.[38]

As a crude guide to what constitutes a relevant distinction, Hayek's test has considerable merit. The most appealing aspects of it are that majority status (both *within and outside* a group) is generally relatively easy to measure; and that it is consistent with out intuitions. To this end, there is no question that the process of excluding non-nationals from the borders of a State does not constitute a relevant difference. Those outside the borders obviously do not concur with the exclusionary policy. This is evidenced by the enormous mass of people frustrated at the inability to come to the First World—millions of whom are presently displaced persons, living in destitution.

However, 'majoritism' cannot serve as the ultimate standard regarding the soundness of a relevant difference. People are not always good judges regarding whether an activity or proposal is in their self-interest, and morality is ultimately not a popularity contest. The ultimate test of what constitutes a legitimate interest must be informed by whatever moral theory is most applicable. As noted in chapter one, the most sound theory of morality is utilitarianism. It would follow, that in relation to conferring benefits and burdens, a legitimate relevant difference is one that will serve to best promote net happiness. Rights based theorists would argue, no doubt, that a relevant difference is one that serves to promote the recognition of human rights. Irrespective of how the concept of relevant difference is defined, the important point to note for the purposes of this discussion is that the concept is universalisable and must be informed by the moral theory to which one subscribes.

Given the large degree of overlap between rights based theories and utilitarianism, in terms of the ultimate interests which are accorded to people, it is doubtful whether the application of the relevant difference test from the respective perspectives would yield meaningfully different outcomes. The ultimate question in this context is whether rights or happiness are maximised by disentitling people from certain privileges and opportunities on the basis of geographical birth origin. I now examine the reasons that could be advanced in support of such a policy.

Prior to doing so, it is important to emphasise that in searching for a difference in relation to a practice that is on its face discriminatory, the onus is on the party advocating the practice to establish that there is a relevant basis for the different treatment. This is the case in relation to violations of all moral norms. Lying, stealing and killing are all undesirable but the prohibition against all of these practices is not absolute. Thus, for example, it is permissible to kill in self defence. However, the act of killing itself calls for an explanation. There is a prima facie ban on such conduct. So too in the case of discrimination. It may be permissible to treat people differently, but where this is done, an obligation arises to justify the conduct.

11.4.1 'National Security'

National security is an argument that is commonly used to justify the strict vetting of migrants. The need to control who crosses national borders has a significant basis in fear and anxiety about the composition of a State. Personal security is important to all individuals and communities, and no State wishes to have this threatened by admitting 'dangerous' people into its borders. Thus it is commonplace for new arrivals to be carefully screened in relation to their prior criminality and their antecedent lifestyle, including their associates and any connection with undesirable organisations.

This practice is generally unexceptionable, on the same basis as bio-safety checks of foodstuffs or animal matter at the border. It does not, however, justify a highly restrictive immigration policy—only a policy of strict security checks. This is a matter at least tacitly accepted by governments. Western nations accept a far greater number of tourists than migrants. In some cases the difference is vast. For example, in 2004 Australia had approximately 4.8 million tourists and only approximately 130,000 new migrants (of which only about 13,000 were part of the humanitarian program). Tourists have ample opportunity to commit crime and engage in acts of serious civil disobedience. We are more relaxed about tourists because we derive a net positive economic advantage from them. It is not so clear that the sums work out in our favor with permanent arrivals, and hence we exclude most people who want to settle in our land.

A net economic sum in our favour does not appear to constitute a permissible relevant difference. Morality, unlike economic evaluation, is not one-sided. There is no tenable moral theory that allows the interests of one person to count for more than those of another, and no place for notions of individual inferiority in any moral theory. It might also be said that net economic detriment to the citizens of a state, must mean a net economic benefit to potential migrants. Thus, the revenue base is ultimately neutral and therefore morally irrelevant.

11.4.2 'We Built It and We Own it'

The most powerful justification for tight border controls is linked to the right to property. If a nation cannot control people traffic, the populace may be less motivated to invest in social capital and build up a stock of resources in the form of hospitals, police, schools and roads. People should not be permitted, so the argument runs, to reap the rewards of that to which they have not contributed. Community amenities are owned by those who built them and, arguably, should not be made available to those who had no input into them. Thus, an argument in favour of restrictive migration controls could be made by drawing an analogy with the right to own property. Quite simply, people would not nation-build if they cannot control who can enter the nation.

The right to private property is not controversial in Western, market driven, democracies. Moreover, philosophical legitimation can be found. Robert Nozick claims that the right to ownership of property and resources is derived from the fact that the person we each own is not just the tangible body parts, but also consists of certain abilities which permit us to utilise resources in the world—which we will only do if we are permitted to enjoy the benefits of our talents.[39] Without the opportunity or possibility of appropriating and enjoying the products of our input, our talents would not be exercised and hence we would effectively be denied the full exercise of the rights to our person.

It is notable that such a right transcends many current provisions of the law. In particular, it may be noted that intellectual property principles vest ownership in the agent whose labour brought about the design, invention or resource. The right to reap the fruits of our labour is assumed to be so strong that it forms the foundation upon which pharmaceutical companies can control the provision of life-saving drugs to millions of poor people around the world. The principle also arguably applies to communities represented by nation states. Property rights allow us to exclude unwanted individuals from our houses, why do not they not allow us to exclude foreigners from our State?

The persuasiveness of this argument is eroded by the fact that contribution to an asset (in this case represented by facilities and amenities) is not in fact a pre-condition to enjoying that asset. Simply being born within a state's geographical boundaries nearly always confers citizenship rights in that state. This is despite the fact that the newborn has not contributed anything to the collective resources of the society and may in fact never do so. The parents of the newborn may well have contributed to the capital resources of the State, but each person is autonomous and must (on this logic) be assessed on the basis of his or her merit and desert. The decision to allow offspring to enjoy the benefits of nation building is ultimately driven by emotion—not by logical or moral imperatives. It would seem that migration controls are, likewise, first and foremost emotion-based—a concession to a group pride phenomenon that appears to inhere in most people but which is difficult to justify.[40]

Moreover, the right to exclude others from the benefits of our labour assumes that we started with something approaching a moderately level playing field. This is not the case with potential migrants. They obviously have not had the opportunity to add to the social capital of States where they have not lived, and given the poverty of their homeland are generally not in a position to make a cash injection on their arrival.

11.4.3 'Our Quality of Life Would Be Diminished'

An argument commonly used in favour on controlling immigration numbers is that unlimited immigration would diminish our quality of life. The community resources would be stretched further meaning that we each have less. It is not clear that this argument is valid. Each new person that arrives in a country requires more resources in the form of food, clothing education and so on. Thus, they add to the demand side of the economic equation. Their labor also adds to the supply side. How the numbers ultimately pan out is unclear.

There is no clear answer regarding the likely effects of free migration. Buabock summarises the research as follows:

Research shows a rather ambiguous pattern of benefits and burdens [from free migration]. Sending countries might benefit during an initial period from remittances but will often suffer long-term costs as a result of losing the most active members of their populations. Instead of leading to a flow of resources towards the sending states, free labour immigration mostly opens up inequalities within the receiving countries. Overall, consumers would gain modestly from free immigration because of cheaper labour costs. Employers of immigrant labour will clearly profit and native workers competing within the same economic sector will lose while the distribution of benefits will be inverse to other sectors of the economy. Immigrants themselves will benefit in economic terms, but at the same time the system of social security might be eroded by an abundant supply of additional labour.[41]

More recent research suggests that immigrants have a net positive effect on prosperity and little or no effect on wages and job prospects of locals. This also goes for their contribution to sustaining pension schemes in the context of ageing populations.[42]

In any event, a slight diminution in the living standard of Western countries is a small price to pay in order to reduce global hunger and poverty. As noted above, in order to determine whether a more relaxed approach to migration is justifiable, one cannot start by looking at the situation only (or even principally) from the perspective of the locals. In the moral sphere the preferences and interests of each individual count identically.

11.5 REFORM PROPOSALS AND CONCLUSION

The above analysis envisions a vastly different world. It entails that people ought to be able to travel and settle in any country of their choice so long as they do not present a security threat. In this regard, as a rule of thumb, the right to migrate should be no more limited than visiting a nation as a tourist. This goes against the practice of heavily restricted and controlled migration which is so entrenched in Western nations. In this regard, we endorse the sentiments of Baubock that:

> All immigrants who have not shown by their personal misdeeds that they are hostile to a liberal democratic order must be attributed the capacity to become citizens of a liberal state, independently of their racial or cultural origins.[43]

Security interests aside, the only consideration possibly justifying exclusion of non-nationals is where this will adversely affect the maintenance of a comprehensive system of democratic and civil rights. At what point, if ever, this is reached is unclear. However, demonstrable evidence of this would be required. If this point is reached more resources would then need to be administered to addressing the root causes of the demand for immigration such as hunger, poverty and civil unrest in the sending countries.

Many readers will no doubt find this reform proposal counter-intuitive and even jarring. However, in assessing the merits of the proposal it is necessary to go beyond one's reflexive intuitions and to examine whether as a matter of principle there is a sound basis for excluding non-nationals from one's borders. On considering the potential justifications, I argue that the answer is no.

This logically calls for a fundamental revision to the migration policies and practices of most States, greatly liberalising the ability of the world community to settle and live wherever they want to in the world. Is this likely to happen in the foreseeable future? I fear not. Patriotism and the preference to associate with those 'like ourselves' is so strong that no amount of logical persuasion is likely to significantly reverse existing migration policies. We may, at least, share our dream of a new kind of 'promised land'.

NOTES

1. Figures from the United States Committee for Refugees show that the number of refugees and asylum seekers from 1992 to 2003 is as follows: 1992: 17,600,000; 1993: 16,300,000; 1994: 16,300,00; 1995: 15,300,000; 1996: 14,500,000; 1997: 13,600,000; 1998: 13,500,00; 1999: 14,100,000; 2000: 14,500,000; 2001: 14,900,000; 2002: 13,000,000; 2003: 11,900,000: *US Committee for Refugees, World*

Refugee Survey 2004 (2004) 4. The main reason for the reduction in refugee numbers is not due to increasing generosity on behalf of receiving countries. Rather it is due to an unprecedented level of voluntary repatriation over the past two years, with some 3.5 million refugees going home, most of them Afghans from Pakistan and Iran: UN High Commissioner for Refugees UNHCR, *Sharp decline in refugees, others of concern in 20 UN High Commissioner for Refugees,* 17 June 2004.

2. R Baubock, 'Ethical problems of Immigration and Control and Citizenship' in R Cohen (ed), *The Cambridge Survey of World Migration* (1995) 551.

3. W Aceves, 'Relative Normativity: Challenging the Sovereign Norm Through Human Rights Litigation' (2002) 25 *Hastings International and Comparative Law Review* 261.

4. R A Brand, 'Sovereignty: The States, the individual, and the first international legal system in the twenty first century' (2002) 25 *Hastings International and Comparative Law Review* 279, 281.

5. Ibid, 281–82.

6. C Warbrick, 'States and Recognition in International Law' in M E Evans (ed), *International Law* (2003) 205, 205.

7. Ibid.

8. R Jennings and A Watts, *Oppenheim's International law* (9th ed, 1992) 661.

9. Sovereignty, Territoriality and the Rule of Law' (2002) 25 *Hastings International and Comparative Law Review* 303, 311.

9. Ibid, 281–82.

10. M Weiner, 'The Global Migration Crisis', in W Gungwu (ed), *Global History and Migrations* (1997) 95, 103.

11. The brief summary of migration in the section is derived from N Papastergiadis, *TheTturbulence of Migration* (2000) ch 1.

12. Ibid, 29.

13. Refugee law is the main exception to this principle. It focuses on what we as a community can do for a person fleeing serious harm, rather than what he or she has to offer us as a nation. Refugees make a significant contribution to the country, but this is an incidental outcome of refugee policy. see J Vrachnas, K Boyd, M Bagaric, P Dimopoulos, *Migration and Refugee Law: Practice and Policy in Australia* ch 18 (2005). Worldwide about 9 percent of migrants are refugees.

14. Papastergiadis, above n 11.

15. Ibid.

16. J Lorentzen, 'Keep Out! Protectionism, Migration Control, and Globalization' in R Tiersky (ed) *Europe Today: National Politics, European Integration and European Security* (2nd ed, 2004) 145, 153.

17. United Nations, *International Migration Report* (2002) 3.

18. Ibid.

19. Ibid.

20. Migrants are now mainly travelling to Arab states under tightly regulated labour recruitment schemes and to industrial projects in the Third World: Papastergiadis, supra n 11.

21. Lorentzen, above n 16, 154-55.

22. B Ackerman, *Social Injustice in the Liberal State* 1980).
23. Baubock, above n 2, 553.
24. R Smith, *International Human Rights* (2003) 184.
25. *Pelman v. McDonald's Corp.*, 237 F.Supp.2d 512 (S.D.N.Y. Jan 22, 2003) paras 13-14.
26. The plaintiffs were given leave to replead all claims, but the amended complaint was also later dismissed: *Pelman v McDonalds Corporation* (2003) US Dist LEXIS 1502.
27. *Pelman v. McDonald's Corp.*, 237 F.Supp.2d 512 (S.D.N.Y. Jan 22, 2003) paras 34-39.
28. Katrina Creer, Simon Kearney and Mandi Zonneveldt, 'Half our nation is now overweight Ministers plan to trim the fat health crisis', *The Sunday Telegraph* (June 8, 2003).
29. Ibid.
30. Ibid.
31. P Bone, 'We can be what we eat' *The Age* Melbourne), 12 March 2005, 12. The problem is also one of democracy. As noted by Amartya Sen, 'No democratic country with a free press has suffered a famine. Governments that can be thrown out by the people have a vested interest in making sure the people can eat'.
32. Commonwealth Immigration Act (UK) 1962: Alan Sked and Chris Cook, *Postwar Britain: A Political History* (2nd ed, 1984) 179.
33. In fact the British government did not impose restrictions of entry and residence in Britain until the mid-nineteenth century, well after it selected convicts for transportation to Australia and introduced assistance programs for people it wished to encourage to move to Australia.: J Vrachnas et al, supra n ch 1.
34. Sked and Cook, supra n 32, 178.
35. Ibid.
36. See Papastergiadis, supra n 11, ch 2.
37. See, J Waldron, *The Law* (1997) 43—44.
38. Constitution of Liberty (1960) 154.
39. Robert Nozick, *Anarchy, State and Utopia* (1974).
40. See D Myers, *The Pursuit of Happiness* (1991).
41. Baubock, supra n 2, 552; citing P van Parijis, 'Commentary: Citizenship Exploitation, Unequal Exchange and the Breakdown of Popular Sovereignty' in Barry and R Goodin (eds) *Free Movement: Ethical Issues in the Transnational Migration of People and Money* (1992).
42. Lorentzen, supra n 16, 160.
43. Baubock, supra n 2, 552.

Chapter Twelve

The Environment: Giving Content to Our Environmental Moral Obligations to Future Generations

12.1 INTRODUCTION

The environment is a popular concern. Despite this, it is surprisingly difficult to identify a concrete moral basis for giving weight to environmental issues. Environmental interventions generally require the present population to compromise their standard of living to advance the interests of future, and sometimes distant, generations. Why should we indulge less now so that future people can live better? It is questionable whether the notion of deferred well-being or happiness is viable at the individual level, let alone at the interpersonal or cross-generational level. In this chapter I examine the source and scope of the environmental duty. I place this in the context of the Kyoto Protocol. I argue that an environmental duty stems from the maxim of positive duty. Despite this, there is no moral imperative to implement the Kyoto Protocol. The benefits of the Protocol are too speculative when weighed against the certain disadvantages.

12.2 GROWING INTEREST IN ENVIRONMENTAL LAW—LIP SERVICE ONLY?

Interest in the environment and environmental law has grown significantly over the past two decades or so. Despite this, there remains an underlying suspicion that the commitment of most individuals and nation states to the environment is somewhere between patchy and tokenistic. In *principle* most people are committed to the environment and it is undoubtedly a popular concern, but it is questionable whether many of us are prepared to make meaningful sacrifices for the sake of the environment. This is underscored at the international level by the reluctance of many states, including Australia and the United States, to ratify the Kyoto Protocol to the United Nations Framework Convention on Climate Change (Kyoto Protocol) on global warning.

12.2.1 Alarmist Views Cause Some Desensitization

This equivocation towards a commitment to environmentally sound practices is understandable for two reasons. The first is that the science concerning just how much abuse the earth can handle before the climatic and atmospheric conditions change to a point where human existence is threatened or made more oppressive is unclear. Additionally, there is considerable evidence suggesting that predictions of impending catastrophes in the next hundred years or so, arising from the greenhouse effect and the ozone layer have been overstated. The most balanced projections at this point seem to indicate that current levels of carbon dioxide omissions will cause some damage to the environment, but nothing that is unmanageable. The world may be slightly warmer in decades to come, necessitating some lifestyle changes but hardly of the magnitude that will stretch the human capacity to adapt and improvise. Earlier alarmist predictions, now largely discredited, may have had a desensitizing effect on many people to the extent that they view the expression of any environmental concerns as mere hype.

12.2.2 Why Should We Care about Distant, Faceless and Future People?

The other reason that many people are ambivalent about a commitment to the environment is that the source of a duty to care for it has not been established. Why *should* individuals or states care about the environment? Sure it is possible to coerce people to engage in environmentally friendly activities (such as recycling and using less plastic bags) by the use of legal measures but in order to move people and nation states to implement more environmentally sound domestic laws it is important to source the imperative in a clear normative principle. Empirical studies have revealed that normative issues are closely linked with compliance with the law. People do not merely obey the law because it is in their self-interest to do so, but also because they believe it is morally proper to do so.[1]

The issue as to why people ought to care about the environment, despite the significant advances in environmental law, remains unresolved. To this end, I note that virtually all legal commentaries on the environment have as their *starting* point that we have a duty to care for the environment. This is a matter that needs to be established, not merely asserted. Ultimately, environmentally friendly behavior requires us to indulge less now so that other people (often faceless strangers in other parts of the world) and people that will exist in the future can live better. But why should we do this? Why do we owe any obligations to people in other parts of the world or those that are yet to be born? What is the source of the imperative by which people not yet born can impose constraints on our behavior? Moreover, what is the content of this obligation?

12.2.3 Extinction of Human Species Is Not an Indefensible Moral Position

A sound argument can be made that we do not owe an obligation to people in distant parts of the world or future generations. Conferring lifestyle advantages on those people through prudent environmental practices involves diminishing our quality of life. All normative theories place a high premium on individual liberty. This permits people to engage in any practices they wish that do not directly and demonstrably harm *others*. At the individual level, it is rare that environmentally imprudent behaviour will tangibly harm another individual. More typically, it is the collective effect of generations of unsound practices, such as driving motor vehicles, which lessens the quality of life of future generations. Thus, individuals can assert, as a causal reality, that it was not their behaviour that created the problem.

Moreover, it is not clear that 'others' in the moral equation includes faceless people in distant parts of the world or unidentifiable people not yet born. Surely, so the argument runs, the sphere of one's moral concern must have some boundaries—and better to care for our neighbour by letting him or her utilise copious amounts of (albeit environmentally harmful) resources rather than trying to factor distant and future people into our moral reasoning. Our lifestyles and quality of life should not be curtailed by distant others. As a community we had no choice but to 'take the world as we found it' and so too should other people and generations. Arguably, the concept of a cross-generational obligation has never previously been seriously touted in human existence and there is no sound basis for it now.

The incongruity of establishing an obligation to non-neighbours is illustrated by the difficulty in trying to balance the needs of people in other states against future generations. Much preventable suffering could be eradicated if increased resources were applied to current generations by for example, even using greater levels of fossil fuels to increase food production, provide more heating and cooling and increase the availability of therapeutic drugs. The increased energy consumption required to do this could, however, have detrimental environmental effects by depleting various stocks of natural resources thereby diminishing the quality of our children's lives. Whose interests rate more highly in this conflict?

There is no clear answer on whether we should choose to alleviate the misery of the living at the expense of the interests of future people. Moreover, there is not even a coherent framework by which this tension can be resolved. This shows the vacuousness, it can be argued, of the notion that we owe a duty to non-neighbours.

12.2.4 Outline of Chapter

In this paper I examine whether we are morally obliged to act in an environmentally sound manner. I argue that there is such a duty. The most persuasive argument in favour of an environmental duty stems from the maxim of positive duty, which was discussed in detail in the context of world poverty in chapter 10. This is the principle that people have a positive moral duty to act where it would cause them little inconvenience but constitute a significant benefit to another person. In this regard, 'other people' include strangers and those not yet born. While at the normative level a case can be made for an environmental duty, there is a psychological obstacle to this duty being actioned. As we also saw in chapter ten, it is a pervasive aspect of human nature that we are more inclined to cure suffering that is proximate to us than anonymous distant (or potential) suffering. In order to overcome this it is necessary to take positive steps to eradicate it from our individual and collective psyches. These issues are examined below.

In the next section I argue that there is a need to ground a commitment to the environment in an express moral principle. Despite its contemporary popularity, a commitment to the environment is not self-evident. In part four of the paper I apply the principles propounded in part three to the Kyoto Protocol and examine whether, as a community, we are morally committed to implementing the treaty. I conclude that no such obligation exists. The benefits to be derived from the Protocol are too speculative and do not outweigh the certain drawbacks of the Protocol.

12.3 A MORAL ENVIRONMENTAL DUTY IS NOT SELF-EVIDENT

12.3.1 A. Extinction of Human Species Is Not an Indefensible Moral Position

The obvious counter to the threshold issue raised in this paper (whether we do in fact have a moral environmental obligation) is that it is *obvious* that such an obligation exists. In other words, it is self-evident that we have an obligation to care for the environment either for its own sake or for the benefit of future generations. It can be argued that pragmatically, if not logically or morally, we must accept as a starting point that maintenance of the environment is important. This is apparent, so the argument runs, from the fact that denial of such an obligation would have catastrophic and unthinkable consequences. Followed to its logical conclusion, a denial of the existence of an environmental ethic could ultimately mean the destruction of the world, or at least the extinction of the human species. Thus it could be asserted that a commitment to the environment is obvious from the fact that the price of indifference—the possible extinction of the human species—is simply untenable.

However, this reality does not as a normative matter necessarily commit one to growing an environmental sympathy gland. Mere membership in a particular species (homo sapiens) does not entitle an agent or group to special rights, such as the right to ongoing survival. Difference in species is not of itself a patently obvious morally relevant difference. There is no logical or moral incongruity associated with the sentiment that it does not matter if the human species, as a result of its glutinous lifestyle, consumes itself out of existence. 'Tis not contrary to reason to prefer the destruction of the whole world to the scratching of my finger.'[2] Thousands of plant and animal species become extinct each year. We are prepared to stand by and accept this, thereby tacitly (at least) endorsing that extinction is a tolerable phenomenon.

On one level, it can be argued that it matters even less if the human species becomes extinct. We are the only species that is aware of the risks involved in engaging in environmentally destructive practices and hence we are culpable for our demise, should it occur.

In order to possess superior rights or special interests, it is necessary to identify what in particular it is about humans that make us so special. Other animals have many features in common with humans: they live, think, feel, and so on, and some animals even have higher cognitive functions than seriously disabled or young people. *Something more* than mere membership in the privileged class is necessary morally to justify the special position we enjoy. Without identifying this *something* more, the bias towards homo sapiens appears to be arbitrary, in the same way as it is arbitrary to discriminate between different groups, such as black and white people, within the same race. Philosophers have attempted throughout the ages to give a higher ranking to humans in the 'ethical food chain' by resorting to qualities such as dignity, which are supposedly possessed only by humans. Such attempts have met with little success, as we saw in chapter one.

12.3.2 Humans as Special—Is a Self-Serving Belief

As individuals, empirical evidence shows that we tend to overrate our sense of worth.[3] The claim that human beings are special could simply be the ultimate self-serving 'beat-up', which continues to be uncritically perpetuated simply because those who have an interest to speak against it (i.e. non-humans) have no voice. In this regard there are two salient points which need to be mentioned. First, saying something (no matter how frequently) does not make it so. The wildly held belief that the world was flat did not result in the flattening of the spherical earth, and dogmatism, regarding the existence of witches and unicorns, has not led to confirmed sightings of such creatures—at least not yet. Secondly, dogs, pigs and most other animals seem to prefer their own company and, if polled, would probably also assert their species' *specialness*.

One should not, it can be argued, lament if in the end the collective outcome of human gluttony is that we gorge ourselves out of existence. This is especially true, given that we have the intelligence that allows us to foresee the likely consequences of our glutinous existence. The notion of personal responsibility plays an important role irrespective of which of the mainstream normative ethical theory one subscribes to. Collectively, we cannot avoid the application of this concept. Moreover, as a general rule, we endorse the view that creatures which cause environmental damage should be exterminated. There is of course no greater environmental vandal than the human race.

Thus, an environmental duty must be established, not merely asserted. It is to this that I now turn.

12.4 GROUNDING A MORAL ENVIRONMENT DUTY

12.4.1 Sometimes We Have a Duty to Assist Others

As noted above, despite its popular appeal, there is no ready rationale which places the environment on the ethical radar. However, there is one principle which pervades most moral theories and, when fully explored, can at least ground a modest environmental obligation. This is the maxim of positive duty, which was examined in chapter ten. The flip side of this maxim is that we should not engage in conduct which will have seriously set back the interests of others where this will only confer a minor benefit on ourselves. This maxim ties in neatly with environmental ethics. It explains why we are required to make some sacrifices for other people, even in distant parts of the world, but need not be 'slaves' to them by depriving ourselves of an adequate quality of life. It is important to note that, as is discussed below, our non-neighbours are included in this principle by virtue of the fact that there is no logical or normative basis for ranking the interests of one person higher than another.

Thus, we should not engage in activities which damage the environment where this will have a disproportionate adverse affect on others, no matter where they are located. It is, however, not so easy to make a case for caring about the interests of people not yet born. The problems of justifying an obligation to future generations has bemused philosophers over the ages.[4]

Future people do not have the capacity to feel pain; they have no interests; and arguably should be ignored in our moral calculations. In a similar vein, Richard T. De George has noted that only existing entities have rights because what is non-existent cannot be the subject or bearer of anything. 'Just as non-existent entities have no rights so it makes no sense to speak about anyone's correlative duty towards non-existent entities'.[5]

Also, as noted earlier, there is no intrinsic harm stemming from the extinction of the human species. The species is simply an aggregation of the interests of each individual and as I have noted, future people have 'zero' interests — a billion times zero is still zero. This analysis would make for a very limited form of environmental obligation, whereby our concern ended at about the anticipated expiry of our lives.

12.4.2 Generational Layering Grounding a Concern for the Environment

While there is no intrinsic worth in promulgating the existence of the human species, future people can secure some moral concern in a derivative manner by way of the constant layering of generations. To speak of particular generations of people as occupying the earth at any one time is simplistic to the point of being misleading. At any point in time the cross-section of ages of people occupying the earth ranges from the new born to centurians. It is never the case that one generation dies off and is immediately replaced by another. There is a constant layering of generations. It is this layering phenomenon that provides the key to a commitment to people who will live beyond the date of one's death.

As individuals we have rights and broader interests (including that stemming from the operation of maxim of positive duty) that we can assert against other individuals and society as a whole. While the content of these rights is of course highly controversial, and none are absolute, at the core there are certain non-controversial rights and interests. These include the right to life and liberty. These rights impose correlative duties on others, that is, not to kill and imprison us, and we in turn assume these duties to others. These duties and responsibilities are assumed by each of us toward *all* other individuals, no matter where they are situated and irrespective of their age (subject to the exception that minors do not have moral duties). Thus, the maxim of positive duty locks in the twenty year old vis-a-vis the eighty year old, in the same way as it does the ninety year old vis-a-vis the new born.

Given that the life span of each new born may tenably be 80–100 years and that each new born has interests, and these minimally include a desire to live a 'full' life and enjoy some semblance of human flourishing, we should not engage in environmentally destructive practices which are likely to impair other people realizing these goals. However, individuals do not have a duty to refrain from engaging in activities that may result in environmental damage beyond the expected life span of those with whom they share the earth. Thus, the scope of our environmental duty (on the basis of current human longevity expectations) is capped at about 100 years. This of course will not cease in 2105. It will continue into perpetuity, but only 100 years at a time.

Against this background, I evaluate the desirability of ratifying the Kyoto Protocol. But before doing so, I first discuss the leading pragmatic obstacle to the global community adopting a serious commitment to the maxim of positive duty and the environment.

12.4.3 We Take Far More Interest in Those Immediately Before Us

In order for the maxim of positive duty to have a practical effect it is necessary to address and discard the 'door step phenomenon', discussed at length in chapter 10.

In order for environmental ethics to advance and have the opportunity to realize its aims, it is necessary to debunk the door-step principle and to adopt the maxim of positive duty. It is only after this occurs that genuine moral pressure can be placed on individuals and nation states to engage in constructive and principled environmental planning and behaviour. Eliminating the door step principle from our collective psyche is admittedly not likely to be an easy matter. However, as with any reform the first step to progress is identification of a problem. The next is raising awareness followed by education.

12.5 PRACTICAL APPLICATION: SHOULD WE RATIFY THE KYOTO PROTOCOL

12.5.1 Overview of the Kyoto Treaty

The Kyoto Protocol to the 1992 United Nations Framework Convention on Climate Change (UNFCCC) was adopted in December 1997 as an international instrument for reducing greenhouse gas emissions. The Protocol requires developed countries to reduce emissions of greenhouse gases by an average of 5.2% below 1990 levels by 2012. Flexible mechanisms, including emissions trading, can be used to reach these targets. Developing countries are excluded from the targets as a concession to their developing status and minimal contribution to greenhouse gas emissions in the past.

In order for the Protocol to enter into force, two conditions must be met. First, not less than 55 countries must ratify the treaty. Secondly, the parties which ratify the Protocol need to incorporate states which cumulatively account for at least 55% of the total carbon dioxide emissions.

The first requirement was readily satisfied. However, for several years implementation stalled at the second hurdle. Most of the 120 plus nations that readily ratified the Protocol were developing nations with low levels of carbon dioxide emissions, which accounted for approximately 40% of the total carbon dioxide emissions.

The Protocol finally entered into force on February 16, 2005, following its ratification by Russia on 18 November 2004. At the time of writing this paper, over 150 countries had ratified the Protocol. Key abstainers from the Protocol remain the United States and Australia.

12.5.2 Adverse Economic Effects

The opposition to the Protocol expressed by the United States is particularly disabling, given that it is the largest producer of greenhouse gases in the world, accounting for nearly 25%. In 1997 the US Senate unanimously passed a resolution that affirmed that it would not ratify any global climate treaty that would harm the United States economy.[6] A report by the American Council for Capital Formation Center states that loss of productivity in the United States following implementation of the Protocol would be between US$120 billion to $400 billion in the time from 2001 to 2010. Gross domestic product per household would reduce between US$1,950 to $3,750. There would also be considerable job losses—somewhere in the range of 2.4 million. The cost of electricity could increase by up to 85%. Gas prices could rise up to 55%, while natural gas would increase by over 120% and living standards would drop by 15%.[7]

12.5.3 Questionable Science

More relevant, for the purpose of this chapter, is the US objection that the science underpinning the Protocol was flawed. As mentioned earlier, the principal aim of the Kyoto Protocol is to reduce global warming, which it is feared will occur if positive steps are not taken to curtail the burning of fossil fuels. The science behind this supposed link between burning fossil fuels and global warning is complex. In brief, burning fossil fuels has caused a large increase in the amount of greenhouse gases in the atmosphere. The surface of the earth is warmed by heat from the sun. Normally about 70% of this heat is reflected back into space. Increased greenhouse gases result in more heat being retained in the atmosphere and hence a rise in global temperatures. So the theory goes.

This obviously raises a number of issues. Even if the unfettered use of fossil fuels will raise world temperatures, why should we care? World temperatures have always fluctuated from year to year and human flourishing has not been seriously retarded, let alone threatened. Where is the evidence that the current world temperature levels are optimal?

Environmental scientists have forecast impending catastrophes if carbon dioxide emissions are not curtailed. Typical of these forecasts are reports by the United Nations' Intergovernmental Panel on Climate Change (IPCC). Its 2001 report predicted a range of catastrophes, ranging from coastal floods, increased droughts, more crop failures and a higher rate of mosquito-borne diseases if global warning was not halted. In its 1995 assessment report the IPCC stated that temperature increases by the year 2100 could range from less than two degrees Fahrenheit to more than six degrees Fahrenheit.

> For the United States the National Climatic Data Center has calculated that the average national temperature for November 2001 [through] January 2002 was 39.94 degrees Fahrenheit, 4.3 degrees above the 1895–2002 average. Globally, the World Meteorological Organization calculated that 2001 was the second warmest year on Earth since 1860, when systematic record-keeping began. Nine of the ten warmest years have occurred since 1990, the warmest being 1998. The next two warmest were 2001 and 1997, respectively. More ominously, recent events in the polar south have clearly indicated major disruptions in the local environment. In March 2002, a 3,250 square kilometer area of ice estimated to weigh 500 billion tonnes broke off the Antarctic continent's Larsen B ice shelf. This collapse is believed to have dumped into the Southern Ocean more ice than all the other icebergs since 1950 combined. Moreover, a second monster iceberg has been detected as being in the process of breaking off the Southern Admunsen Sea. Iceberg B22, as it is called, is more than 64 kilometers (40 miles) wide and 85 kilometers (53 miles) long, and covers an area approximating 5,500 square kilometers. The belief by scientists is that such ice retreats are attributed to global warming in the region, particularly around the Antarctic Peninsula. As the circumpolar waters warm, the ice sheets fracture, and collapse. As the ice shelves collapse, and the ice melts, sea levels will rise. Of greatest concern is the Western Antarctic Ice Sheet, which is grounded on muddy ocean floor, not a

solid subglacial continental rock foundation. Should the entire West Antarctic Ice Sheet melt, sea levels worldwide could rise five to six meters. In the past, sea level rise attributed to global warming has been more theoretical speculation than scientific fact. The recent collapse of these ice shelves in Antarctica clearly suggests that greenhouse-induced global warming may be taking a real toll in the first years of the twenty-first century.[8]

However, considerable doubt has been cast over the credibility of global warning, let alone the doomsday predictions associated with this.[9]

Professor S F Singer notes that the Kyoto Protocol has caused the polarization: 'Many on the right have called it economic madness, while for many on the left it is an ecological article of faith. There seems to be no position in between'.[10] He highlights potential serious deficiencies with the protocol:

> The requirement imposed by Kyoto . . . does nothing to stabilize the atmospheric concentration of greenhouse gases. At best, Kyoto would merely slow down somewhat the rate of rise, which by the year 2020 will be largely determined by emissions from major developing countries like China, India, Brazil, and Mexico —none of which are covered by the accord.
>
> The Kyoto Protocol's main emphasis is on carbon dioxide produced by burning fossil fuels. By contrast, the powerful greenhouse gas methane is barely mentioned—perhaps because its main sources, while human-related, are "natural": rice agriculture and cattle-raising. Furthermore, the Protocol does not mention other factors that affect the climate, such as sulfate aerosols from coal-fired power plants, soot from diesel engines, and smoke from the burning of biomass (mostly in developing countries).[11]

A large number of other independent reviews have also been critical of the IPCC report. The Director of the Environmental Program at the Reason Public Policy Institute, Dr. Kenneth Green, for example, claims the report to be flawed on the basis that it presents what is mere speculation as fact. He argues that the report makes predictions based on simple models that fail to take into account observed, current or historical climate phenomena and processes, and that it projects an 'appearance' of certainty not supported by tested evidence.[12] According to Green, the report fails to distinguish between causative factors that are anthropocentric in origin and those that are not. He claims that by failing to distinguish between predictions based on human and non-human factors, the report does not contain the sort of verifiable information on the basis of which informed policy decisions about possible future climate change can be made. Green also criticizes the report for containing predictions based on a number of overly pessimistic and unsubstantiated assumptions. Green concludes that until a consensus based on sound science can be reached, it would be irresponsible for the U.S. government to agree to mandatory emissions reductions.[13]

12.5.4 Maxim of Positive Duty Applied to Kyoto Treaty

The overwhelming point to emerge from the, albeit brief, discussion above is the high level of uncertainty associated with even the fundamental premises underpinning the Kyoto Protocol. The weight of evidence seems to suggest that that world is getting slightly warmer. However, the extent to which this stems from human activity is unclear. The rate of temperature increase seems modest — just how modest is unclear. Even vaguer are what the likely consequences of a temperature increase on human flourishing will be. There is no firm evidence suggesting that, in our lifetime, it will mean anything more than an enhanced capacity to get a good or (if one prioritizes health over aesthetics) bad suntan and an extension of the summer wardrobe period. There is some evidence that implementation of the Kyoto Protocol will result in a slight reduction in the standard of living in developed nations.

Faced with this scenario, some commentators have advised us to tread wearily and adopt the precautionary principle of international environmental law.[14] However, applying the precautionary principle in such circumstances would be 'code' for not doing anything, it is not assured that there will detrimental consequences down the track that entrench a value system whereby the interests of others are more important than that of our own. While we have a duty not to inhibit people, with whom we share the earth, from having a meaningful life, we do not owe it to others to ensure that they have a better or even equal standard of living to our own. There is no moral principle that requires us to make martyrs of ourselves — or our children or their children. Paradoxically, this is a point from which our children (and their children) will in fact take considerable delight. It means that, when it is time for them to discharge their moral responsibilities, they too will be able to do so, consistent with the maxim of positive duty and apply their talents and resources to the fullest extent possible.

Moreover, the precautionary principle, applied in the context of the Kyoto Protocol, runs foul of the principle that certain consequences should always carry more weight in one's decision making than speculative consequences. This is particularly apposite, as in the case of the Kyoto Protocol, where the worst case scenario is manageable and the prospect of it eventuating is very small. In such circumstances it would be a mistake to encumber our standard of living.

Thus, it is clear that the maxim of positive duty does not require us to implement the Kyoto Protocol. There is simply insufficient evidence to suggest that a person alive today will have his or her interests seriously set back if the Protocol is not implemented. Absent such evidence, the calculus involved in applying the maxim does not even commence.

A commitment to the environment is normally assumed, rather than established, in most commentaries on environmental law. This is regrettable. Absent a framework concerning the source and scope of our environmental duty, it is likely that unsound environmental policies and laws will be implemented. The Kyoto Protocol is an example of ill-conceived environmental policy, which has blossomed in part by the lack of normative analysis of its merits.

The strongest rationale in favour of protecting the interests of future generations stems from the maxim of positive duty. Application of this principle does not require us to implement measures such as the Kyoto Protocol which, current evidence suggests, is likely to have only a slight adverse effect in years to come.

NOTES

1. See T R Tyler, *Why People Obey the Law* (1990) where following a 1984 study of about 1,500 people who lived in Chicago, in asking about their contact with legal authorities, Tyler noted that normative issues are closely linked with compliance with the law.

2. For a good account of Hume's theory M Smith, 'Valuing: Desiring or Believing?' in D Charles and C Lennon (eds), *Reduction, Explanation and Realism* (1992) 323.

3. See chapter one.

4. It has many parallels with the issue of whether one owes a duty to the dead. See also, B Rollin, 'Environmental Ethics and International Justice' in Steven Luper-Foy (ed), *Problems of International Justice* (1988) 124; R T De George, 'Do We Owe the Future generation Anything?' (1978) *Law and Ecological Challenge* 180; and J P Sterba, 'The Welfare Rights of Distant People and Future Generations: Moral Side-Constraints on Social Policy' (1981) *Social Theory and Practice* 99.

5. R T De George, 'Do We Owe the Future generation Anything?' (1978) *Law and Ecological Challenge* 180.

6. C C Joyner, 'Burning International Bridges, Fuelling Global Discontent: the United States and Rejection of the Kyoto Protocol' (2002) 33 *Victoria University of Wellington Law Review* 2. For a discussion regarding the merits of the Protocol and the politics surrounding its implementations see the special edition of the *University of New South Wales Law Journal* (2001): S Freeland, 'The Kyoto Protocol: An Agreement without a Future?' (2001) *University of New South Wales Law Journal* 35; M Wilder, 'The Kyoto Protocol And Early Action' (2001) *University of New South Wales Law Journal* 39; L Horn, 'The Kyoto Protocol: Australia's Commitment And

Compliance' (2001) *University of New South Wales Law Journal* 42; G Rose, 'A Compliance System For The Kyoto Protocol' (2001) *University of New South Wales Law Journal* 45 and W Hare, 'Australia And Kyoto: In or Out?' (2001) *University of New South Wales Law Journal* 38.

7. M Thorning, 'A United States Perspective on the Economic Impact of Climate Change Policy' American Council for Capital Formation Center (2000) as cited in Joyner, above n 6.

8. Ibid.

9. D Wojick, 'The UN IPCC's Artful Bias: Glaring Omissions, False Confidence and Misleading Statistics in the Summary for Policymakers' (2002) 13 (3) *Energy and Environmen.*

10. S F Singer, 'Climate Change and Global Warming. Kyoto: A Post Mortem', A Better Earth <http://www.abetterearth.org/article.php/683.html>.

11. Ibid. S.F. Singer states that ultimately Kyoto is based on faulty science. 'The Kyoto Protocol, therefore, would have practically no impact on global temperatures. Even if punctiliously adhered to, it would reduce the calculated temperature rise by 0.05 degrees Celsius at most—an amount so insignificant it can hardly be measured. When confronted with that little-publicized fact, supporters of the Protocol admit that Kyoto is intended only as a first step, and that greenhouse gases will someday have to be further reduced by between 60 and 80 percent of 1990 emission levels. This fact, too, has not been much publicized by Kyoto's supporters, and with good reason: such drastic reductions would cripple the global economy. To understand the flaws of the Kyoto Protocol, it is necessary to look first at the climate science that supposedly provides a rationale for its provisions. Kyoto is not the first attempt to impose worldwide restrictions on anthropogenic emissions. In many ways, it is patterned after the 1987 Montreal Protocol, which limited and eventually eliminated the emission of chlorofluorocarbons (known as CFCs, or "Freons") in order "to save the ozone layer." By 1988, environmental pressure groups were already arguing for similar restrictions on the emission of carbon dioxide "to save the climate." As in the case of the Montreal Protocol, the groundwork for Kyoto was laid by a series of studies conducted by a U.N.-appointed group, the Intergovernmental Panel on Climate Change (IPCC). Its first report was issued in 1990 and suggested that if the concentration of greenhouse gases were to double, a global warming of between 1.5 and 4.5 degrees Celsius would follow. Those numbers were based on crude climate models whose validity had never been tested by observations—and even today, there remains no validation for the climate models that are at the heart of most claims of climate catastrophe. The IPCC maintained, however, that the model results were "broadly consistent" with observations. This claim referred to a warming trend that had begun in the late nineteenth century and continued until about 1940. That trend actually had little to do with greenhouse effects but seems to have been simply a natural fluctuation of the climate, a recovery from the preceding "Little Ice Age." Driving this point home, the global climate cooled after 1940 until about 1975—in spite of the copious emission of carbon dioxide and other greenhouse gases in the industrial boom years after World War II. By the 1970s, the persistent cooling trend had become a hot topic, so to speak, for magazines and books that fretted about a coming Ice Age, and the federal government

supported studies that calculated the economic disasters expected from a colder climate'. Similar conclusions are made by Patrick J Michaels, *The Consequences of Kyoto* (1998), CATO Institute, *at* http://www.cato.org/pubs/pas/pa-307es.html.

12. K Green, *Newest IPCC Report on Global Warming Fails to Deliver Sound Policymaking Models,* Reason Public Policy Institute (2001), *at* http://www.rppi.org/rr101.html.

13. The above account of the report by Green is taken from C E Coon, *Why President Bush Is Right to Abandon the Kyoto Protocol*, The Heritage Foundation (2001), *at* http://www.heritage.org/Research/ EnergyandEnvironment/BG1437.cfm.

14. See e.g. Joyner, above n, 6. According to Joyner, the precautionary approach advocates that governments should not use the fact that absolute scientific certainty regarding the adverse environmental effects of activities to postpone putting in place measures to prevent those effects. This strategy requires that risk avoidance becomes an established decision norm, i.e. that in the face of risks and scientific uncertainties, we must act as if there were complete scientific certainty.

Chapter Thirteen

Animals

13.1 OVERVIEW OF CHAPTER

Despite the significant level of moral advancement that has occurred over the past half century or so, there is still at least one glaring and significant shortcoming in contemporary moral theory and practice. This relates to the manner in which we condone, purportedly legitimate and encourage the horrific and brutal treatment of many animals. We eat billions of animals annually, despite the fact that animal products are not essential (and in some cases are detrimental) to our dietary needs. In the process we often farm and kill the animals in cruel ways. We intentionally inflict pain on animals in scientific experiments that have less than remote chances of success and use their skins to keep us warm and enhance our looks, despite the fact that we have an over supply of synthetic material which can satisfy these 'needs'.

Despite the so called civilisation of our time we still have no qualms about inflicting the cruel death of gentle creatures in order that we can salivate on the transient delight of a yummy burger, even though we would salivate no less on a vegetarian meal, properly prepared. Rarely is the benefits and burdens scale so grossly distorted. A moral code that accepts that it is permissible for one being to be killed so that another can enjoy the taste of its flesh is in need of significant re-wiring.

In this chapter, it is argued that there is a pressing need to improve the living conditions of many animals who have the misfortune to interact with human beings or who are caught in the cross fire of human activity. Failure to do so may cause future us to look back at in shame at our moral code.

13.2 IT IS MORALLY WRONG TO TREAT ANIMALS CRUELLY

The argument that cruelty to animals is morally wrong involves three premises. First, cruelty to people is unacceptable. There is no moral theory which condones cruelty to people. Secondly, as far as cruelty is concerned there is no morally relevant difference between people and animals. Thirdly, and hence the reason for the potential future shame, is the wholesale and unmitigated nature of the cruelty to animals. There are no meaningful counterweights to the cruelty that we inflict on animals. This reasoning is analysed against the background of both of the main streams of moral thought to highlight the fact that there is no tenable justification for the current manner in which we treat animals. I start with rights based theories.

13.2.1 Cruelty on a Rights Based Approach

Let us consider the first premise, namely that cruelty to people is morally wrong (or in the language of rights, people have a right not be subjected to cruelty). It follows from this premise that animals must have the same right unless there is a morally relevant difference between animals and humans. In terms of rights discourse, there are two different levels at which it could be argued that such a difference may exist: the definitional level and the justificatory level. I consider them in that order. If it is found that there is no difference between animals and humans at either of these levels insofar as the right to be free from cruelty is concerned, one is logically compelled to the view that such a right also inheres in animals.

Following the work of Hohfeld,[1] there is no shortage of definitions of a right which have been advanced. Some definitions expressly incorporate a reference to human beings. For example, rights have been defined as 'those minimum conditions under which *human beings* can flourish and which ought to be secured for them, if necessary by force (emphasis added)';[2] and 'as the liberties each *man* hath, to use his own power, as he will himself, for the preservation of his own nature (emphasis added)'.[3]

However, such 'loaded' definitions are not persuasive. First, it is not clear whether the reference to human kind is exhaustive, or merely illustrative, in terms of the agents in whom rights may be reposed. Even if the definitions purport to be exhaustive, they do not provide a *reason* for excluding animals from moral consideration, since they beg the question, i.e. they assume the very fact in issue. Reliance on self-evident or intuitive 'truths' can only occur in the most limited of circumstances, since their persuasion is roughly commensurate with the incongruity of an assertion to their contrary. Given that there is no patent *absurdity* in the claim that non-humans have rights, such definitions do not justify the non-conferment of entitlements called rights to animals.

This takes us to broader definitions of rights. McCloskey believes rights to be simply entitlements,[4] while in Sprigge's view 'the best way of understanding . . . that someone has a right to something seems to be to take it as the claim that there are grounds for complaint on their behalf if they do not have it'.[5] Still further, rights have been defined as claims and any entitlement to benefit from the performance of obligations.[6] Galligan defines a right as a 'justified claim that an interest should be protected by the imposition of correlative duties';[7] while Campbell notes that 'the standard view is that rights are *moral* entitlements.[8]

It is difficult to find a common thread in these definitions, so one is tempted to conclude that it is not plausible to provide an exhaustive definition of a right and that they are simply a multifarious range of claims with no common feature. However, as a common denominator I propose that a right be defined as *a presumptive benefit or protection which one can assert against others,* as such a definition seems to encapsulate the tenor of most of the other definitions of a 'right' previously discussed in this book.

To elaborate upon the specific elements of our own definition of a 'right' given immediately above, I mean that a right is 'presumptive' in that, as we saw in chapter one, it is never indefeasible or absolute. By 'benefit', I mean a positive entitlement such as the right to welfare. As for 'protection' I mean a negative entitlement, such as the right to be free from a particular violation. To this end, there would be few more fundamental entitlements which informed agents would seek to purse than freedom from cruelty. By 'fundamental' I mean that given a choice, the wish to be free from cruelty is one of, if not the, foremost protections that people can hold. This is apparent from the steps that we take to avoid cruelty. This obviously depends to some extent how one defines 'cruelty'. As is noted by La Follette and Shanks, although the legal definition of cruelty (especially to animals) varies across jurisdictions, a core aspect of cruelty is the infliction of excruciating pain.[9]

The fact that people have an intense desire to avoid pain is indisputable and that animals have the same desire is just as self-evident. Anyone who has seen the lengths that a dog will take to avoid being hit by its master will attest to that fact.

The concept of animals having rights is, however, challenged by Hart's view that a right necessarily requires that the holder must be in a position to elect whether or not to exercise the particular right in question.[10] However, the capacity for volition does not appear to be a necessary feature of a right as various classes of persons who may lack capacity in some way do actually possess rights, e.g. infants and the mentally handicapped. Even if we adopt Hart's position, while the rights of animals to other protections may be threatened, the right to be free from cruelty is untouched, particularly given the lengths animals go to avoid foreseeable pain. Some may still feel that Hart meant that the election needed to be actually expressed in some manner. However the need for a right holder to expressly assert a right is untenable, given that it would lead to the absurd view that people's rights would therefore be suspended while they were sleeping or unconscious.

Michael Tooley, in the context of a right to life, raises a similar point to Hart. He claims that human life is not intrinsically valuable and that for a person to have a right to life he or she must be capable of desiring to continue existing as a subject of experiences and other mental states. Therefore, an entity lacking consciousness of itself as a continuing entity subject to mental states does not have a right to life.[11] If we extrapolate Tooley's criteria for the existence of the right to life to an examination of whether or not there is a specific right against cruelty, for an agent to enjoy the later right it would require him, her or it to be capable of desiring the enjoyment of the benefits that are consequent upon the exercise of that right. Given that animals have a preference for a pain free existence, once again the freedom of animals against cruelty is not threatened.

I now consider the ideals that justify rights. From this perspective, animals can only be denied the right to be free from cruelty if the abstract ideal or ideals which justify concrete rights do not support such a right. This is a difficult inquiry because as I have noted earlier, rights philosophers have fared poorly when it comes down to pinpointing the exact foundations upon which rights are allegedly based—I ignore theories which assume that rights are limited to the sphere of human interests. This begs the question and, as has been pointed out by Tooley, *mere membership* of a particular species (homo sapiens) does not entitle an agent to special entitlements. Any difference in species is not of itself a morally relevant difference. To regard all human beings as possessing equal and special value is 'speciesism' (an unjustified prejudice for the human race).[12] A mere difference in species does not explain why it is permissible to kill lambs, but not children.

In order to possess superior rights it is necessary to identify what it is about humans in particular that makes them so special. Other animals have many features in common with humans in that they too live, think, feel, and so on, and some animals like dolphins even have higher cognitive functions than seriously disabled persons or very young infants. As Rachels has noted, speciesism should elicit the same censure as racism and sexism.[13] Therefore *something more* than mere membership of the privileged class is necessary to morally justify the special position we enjoy as humans. Without identifying this extra something, the preference towards homo sapiens appears to be arbitrary, in the same way as it is arbitrary to discriminate between different groups, such as black and white people, within the same race.

To this end, I focus on the rights theory of perhaps the leading rights philosopher, Ronald Dworkin. For Dworkin, rights are 'trumps held by individuals',[14] which protect them from the pursuit of common goods: 'the prospect of utilitarian gains cannot justify preventing a man from doing what he has a right to do',[15] and the general good is never an adequate basis for limiting rights. He asserts that people have rights when there are good reasons for conferring upon them benefits or opportunities despite a community interest to the contrary.

Thus, the broad ideals which Dworkin invokes to justify his rights thesis are dignity and equality. Dworkin, defines 'dignity' as 'respecting the inherent value of our own lives'.[16] He also asserts that dignity, 'like autonomy, requires a degree of general competence and, especially, a sense of self-identity over time',[17] and that although 'a person's dignity is normally connected to his capacity for self-respect',[18] it is also possessed by those who are seriously demented, because what continues to happen to such a person affects the value or success of his or her life as a whole.[19]

While in chapter one the notion of dignity was challenged, if we assume that it has a veneer of plausibility for the purposes of the discussion at hand, the key question becomes whether this notion of dignity extends to animals. A central problem with Dworkin's account is that it is extremely cryptic in that what does it exactly mean to have a sense of self-identity over time? Dworkin refuses to take up the challenge of developing the notions of dignity and equality. Even though he concedes that dignity is a 'vague'[20] ideal, he provides that he 'does not want to defend or elaborate these ideas [the notions of equality and dignity], but only to insist that anyone who claims that citizens have rights must accept ideas *very close* to these (emphasis added)'.[21]

However, in speculating on what Dworkin means by the notion of dignity, he seems to require a sense of self consciousness in that the agent has the capacity to reflect upon *its* life and history and view it is a composite whole, as opposed to a disparate set of events lacking a common focal point.

If this is so, then there is no question that animals too possess this ideal of dignity. Evidence of this can be found in animal's ability to learn from previous experiences, their desire to avoid past dangers and their enthusiasm towards situations which resemble previous pleasurable moments. In addition, experiments with apes and chimpanzees show that they engage in behaviour which demonstrates an expectation of the order of future events and an awareness of themselves being distinct entities, existing over time.[22]

Other philosophers have attempted to ground moral status on other ideals which are just as vague as the notion of dignity. For example, Michael Fox claimed that:

> A moral community is a social group composed of interacting autonomous beings where moral concepts and precepts can evolve and be understood. It is also a social group in which mutual recognition of autonomy and personhood exist.[23]

On this basis, he argued that animals are not entitled to moral concern. For Fox, autonomy requires self-awareness, the ability to accept responsibility for actions and the capacity to use sophisticated language. However, the problem with this account (apart from autonomy being an arbitrary rationale for moral standing) is that it not only excludes animals from the moral equation, but also humans with limited cognitive abilities. Recognising this problem, Fox resiled from his position and a year later accepted that 'our basic moral obligations to avoid causing harm to other people should be extended to animals.[24]

In summary therefore, it would it seem that there is no convincing reason that animals can be denied the right to be free from cruelty on the basis of a non-consequentialist rights view of morality because (a) given any reasonable definition of rights, animals do possess such rights, (b) that these rights include a right to be free from cruelty, (c) despite the fact the justification for such rights is often based on such vague ideals as dignity, animals are capable of meeting such ideals.

13.2.3 Cruelty From a Utilitarian Perspective

Although Peter Singer's stimulating book in 1975, *Animal Liberation*, is largely credited with providing the momentum for the animal liberation movement, still the most powerful moral argument for extending greater moral concern to animals is by Jeremy Bentham:

> The day may come when the rest of the animal creation may acquire those rights which never could have been withholden from them but by the hand of tyranny. The French have already discovered that the blackness of the skin is no reason why a human being should be abandoned without redress to the caprice of a tormentor. It may one day come to be recognized the number of legs, the villosity of the skin, or the termination of the os sacrum are reasons equally insufficient for abandoning a sensitive being to the same fate. What else is it that that should trace the insuperable line? Is it the faculty of reason, or perhaps the faculty of discourse? But a full-grown horse or dog is beyond comparison a more rational, as well as more conversable animal, than an infant of a day or a week or even a

month, old. *But suppose they were otherwise, what would it avail? The question is not, Can they reason? nor Can they talk? but Can they suffer? (emphasis added).*[25]

If one adopts the utilitarian starting premise that all that is relevant to the utilitarian calculus is happiness and pain, it follows that to have one's interests counted as being morally relevant the only pre-condition is the capacity to experience these sensations. Accordingly, Bentham's argument appears to establish that from the utilitarian perspective animals are entitled to *some* moral concern. The reason that the capacity for suffering and its corollary, to feel pleasure, is the decisive indicia concerning whether or not a being is worthy of moral concern, as opposed to other traits such as hair color, intelligence or strength, is because it is the minimum criterion necessary for a being having any interests at all.

Bentham's line of reasoning was developed by Peter Singer about two hundred years later. He too noted the moral equivalence between animals and human beings with limited cognitive capabilities, which he claimed stems from the basic principle of equality. He advocated that it is wrong to perform experiments on animals 'unless the experiment is so important that the use of a retarded human being would also be justifiable'.[26]

The pragmatic force of Singer's argument has been diminished due to the fact that his comments have sometimes been misinterpreted. He does not contend that less protection should be accorded to impaired human beings. Instead he makes the point that animals are worthy of far greater moral concern.

The need to confer greater protection on animals has also been de-railed to some degree by the issue of exactly how much weight should be given to the pleasure of animals relative to that of humans. Some have argued that animal interests count far less than those of people. For example, R G Frey is prepared to give moral standing to animals, but believes that animals, and 'marginal' human beings like those with impaired cognitive functioning, have less moral value because their quality of life is less than that of a so-called normal human.[27] He also argues that utilitarianism does not provide a strong justification for a wide sphere of animal rights because it is possible to rear and kill animals without suffering.

However, unless it is contended that animals are to be given virtually negligible weight in moral calculations, the argument that it is morally wrong to treat animals cruelly is unaffected. Animal cruelty would only be permitted if the high level of pain resulting from this behaviour was outweighed by the amount of happiness this generated in others. Even allowing for the fact[28] that animal suffering may be given less weight than human interests, it is simply inconceivable, for example, that the transient pleasure of eating a Battery Hen

Egg McMuffin outweighs the misery experienced by the chicken/hen, who for the duration of its two year life has been unable to spread its wings or walk and has been painfully debeaked. Accordingly, it is clear that on a utilitarian basis animal cruelty cannot be justified on the pleasure/pain calculus of that school of moral philosophy.

13.3 WHY HAS THERE NOT BEEN MORE ATTEMPTS TO PREVENT CRUELTY TO ANIMALS?

It is impossible to say, or precisely prove, why there has been not been more efficacious laws and moral standards that aim to prevent cruelty. However there are several possible explanations. These include the over ambitious nature of certain aspects of the animal rights movement, ineffective enforcement of existing prevention of animal cruelty laws, economic expediency and political manoeuvring or lobbying.

To expand, there have been loud calls at various points over the past quarter of a century for increased recognition of 'animal rights'. However perhaps these calls have been too ambitious in that too many different types of interests have been argued for animals. This is not to say that certain forms of 'human rights' should not be extended to other types of non-human species. Rather it is simply a recognition of an (albeit unfortunate) social reality.

History has shown that full moral status is not accorded quickly to repressed agents. Rather it occurs in an incremental fashion—e.g. before black Americans were given the right to vote, there was a whole range of more basic interests that they first attained; such as the right to liberty and to own property. In order for progress to made in terms of according moral status to animals in all likelihood it must also occur in a similar step-wise fashion. The most productive approach is not to aim at the outset for the widest possible range of moral interests to be accorded to animals. The arguments in favour of animals having the right not be killed for human consumption are more contentious than the claim that animals should not be treated cruelly by humans. If energy is devoted principally to these more ambitious arguments, there may be a tendency within opponents to such ideas to discard all arguments in favour of extending the sphere of animal interests.

The plight of battery hens provides an example of the enormous weight given to economic expediency in the context of our treatment of animals. A report in 1998 by the Australian Productivity Commission[29] claimed that (a) barn system egg production costs are 35% higher than that of the battery cage system, (b) a dozen eggs produced by the barn system costs $1.75 per dozen compared with

$1.25 per dozen under the caged system; (c) the displacement costs per capita to phase out the caged or battery hen system would be approximately $2.85 per resident and (d) barn systems are far more labour intensive than the battery hen system. It has been argued[30] that these cost differentials hardly justify the level of cruelty which battery hens suffer and that given that only 2,500 are directly employed in the egg industry, a move to more labour intensive, but less cruel, forms of egg production would be a boost for rural unemployment. These arguments have fallen on death ears. It seems that even minor economic efficiencies trump large scale animal suffering.

To remedy this situation we need to move towards incrementally improving the plight of animals, by gradually increasing their moral standing in the eyes of the community. The first stage of this process involves ceasing to engage in all forms of activities that are cruel to animals, unless this is an overwhelming benefit to be obtained from such conduct. This means that it is never permissible to kill animals for food using means that inflict pain on animals, given that we do not need animal products to maintain a healthy diet. Cruelty in relation to scientific experimentation should be only permitted where the objective of the research is to advance human or animal health; the potential benefits of the research are significant; the research goals cannot be achieved without animal experimentation and there is a high level of confidence that the research will achieve its stated outcomes.

Once the moral standing of animals has been elevated to a point where it is accepted that it is impermissible to treat them cruelly, the next stage involves a recognition of the fact that it is wrong to kill animals (even using painless techniques), or otherwise mistreat them, for our consumption.

Until we reach that level of moral understanding our behaviour towards animals will continue to be the shame of our generation. *Mahatma Gandhi* correctly noted that: 'the greatness of a nation and its moral progress can be judged by the way its animals are treated'. At this time, many of us stand shamed.

NOTES

1. W N Hohfeld, defined four categories of rights: claim-rights, privileges, powers and immunities. He qualifies this by stating that only a claim-right accords with the proper meaning of the term: W N Hohfeld, *Fundamental Legal Conceptions as Applied in Judicial Reasoning in and other Legal Essays,* in W W Cook (ed), (1919).

2. J Kleinig, 'Human Rights, Legal Rights and Social Change', *supra* n. 56, at pp. 44–5.

3. T Hobbes, *Leviathan* (1651) (1946) 84–5.

4. H J McCloskey, 'Rights: Some Conceptual Issues' (1976) 54 *Australian Journal of Philosophy* 99, 115

5. T L S Sprigge, *The Rational Foundation Of Ethics* (1987) 216–7.

6. G Marshall, 'Rights, Options and Entitlements' in A W B. Simpson (ed), *Oxford Essays in Jurisprudence* (1973) 228, 241.

7. D J Galligan, 'The Right to Silence Reconsidered' (1988) *Current Legal Problems* 69, 88.

8. T Campbell, *The Legal Theory of Ethical Positivism, supra* n. 52, 164.

9. H LaFollette and N Shanks, 'Uti-lizing Animals' (1995) *Journal of Applied Philosophy* 13–25.

10. H L A Hart, *Are there any Natural Rights?*' (1955) LXIV *Philosophical Review Quarterly* 175.

11. M Tooley, 'Abortion and Infanticide', in P Singer (ed.), *Applied Ethics* (1986) 69.

12. For a discussion of this concept, see H LaFollette and N Shanks, 'The Origin of Speciesism' (1996) *Philosophy* 41.

13. J Rachels, *Created from Animals: the moral implications of Darwinism* (1990), chapter 5.

14. R Dworkin, *Taking Rights Seriously* (4th ed, 1978), xi.

15. Ibid, 193.

16. R Dworkin, *Life's Dominion: An Argument About Abortion, Euthanasia, and Individual Freedom* (1993) 238.

17. Ibid, 230.

18. Ibid, 221.

19. Ibid, 237.

20. Ibid, 198.

21. Ibid, 199.

22. See P Singer, *Practical Ethics* (1991), 110–117.

23. M A Fox, *The Case for Animal Experimentation* (University of California Press, 1986) 50.

24. Ibid. For a positive argument in favour of animal rights see T Regan, *supra* n. 74, where he argues that all subjects of a life (which he defines as self-conscious beings who are capable of having beliefs and desires and who can conceive of the future and have goals) have rights. From this he believes that animals have the right to be treated with respect as does any individual with inherent value.

25. J Bentham, *Introduction to the Principles of Morals and Legislation* (1789, 1948 ed) ch 17.

26. P Singer, *Animal Liberation* (2nd ed, 1990) 78.

27. R G Frey, *Interests and Rights: The Case Against Animals* (1980); 'Moral Standing, the value of lives and speciesim' (1988) 4 Between the Species 191.

28. The rationale for this 'fact' may be that the suffering caused to animals does not continue beyond the immediate sensation of pain and is not perpetuated by fear of similar pain in the future or the sense of loss or violation caused by the particular terror.

29. *Productivity Commission. Research Report* (1996), 50.

30. Animals Australia. *Submission to the Standing Committee on Agriculture and Resource Management's Review of Layer Hen Housing in Australia.* October 1999, p. 32.

Part F

BUSINESS ETHICS

Chapter Fourteen

The Ethical Obligations of Corporations

14.1 INTRODUCTION

In this chapter I examine the moral norms that apply to corporations. Morality is important in this context not only because it guides all human conduct, but because there is a growing body of evidence that companies that 'do the right thing' make more profits in the long run. Mbare, quoting a recent study notes:

> The English Financial Times [31 March 2003], reported the conundrum that is now at the heart of every business case for CSR: does ethical behavior pay off financially? It is reported that scandals over corporate excess and fraud reveal the high cost of unethical behavior. Proving there is another side to the coin — that doing the right thing boosts shareholder value — is much harder. Yet research published by the UK's Institute of Business Ethics, comparing companies in the FTSE 250, provides strong evidence that those clearly committed to ethical behavior perform better financially over the long term than those lacking such a commitment.[1]

This chapter is about discovering which, if any, moral duties apply to corporations. Corporate ethics concerns the intersection between corporate activity and normative ethics. This of course assumes that ethics and corporate activities do in fact overlap. A tenable argument can be mounted that ethics and corporate activities are parallel areas of human endeavour, which do not intersect. In the next part of this chapter, following a brief history of business ethics, I consider whether the fusion between business and ethics belongs in the realms of reality as opposed to wishful or 'virtual' thinking.

In section three of this chapter, I provide a brief overview of moral theory. I also examine the moral rules that govern business in general. The ultimate aim of most corporations is to make money and hence there would not seem to be a relevant distinction between the ethical constraints that bind the business world in general and the corporate world in particular. Thus, in considering the ethical duties that bind those involved in corporate decision-making we examine the ethical constraints that bind businesses in general. However, in section four we shall see that very successful businesses, which normally operate under a corporate structure, have additional moral duties.

14.2 THE THRESHOLD ISSUE: IS THERE A ROLE FOR ETHICAL CONSIDERATIONS IN BUSINESS

14.2.1 A Short Look at The Short History of Nusiness Ethics

The notion that businesses have moral duties is becoming increasingly widespread. This has been partly as a result of what appears to be an increasing number of corporate scandals. As is noted by Scott Mann:

> The scandals of Enron, WorldCom, Xerox and Merck are in the headlines: massive accounting frauds involving many billions of dollars of fabricated and inflated profits, assets and revenues through which these corporations with the help of their accountants, have maintained share prices far above those justified by their true financial status, to increase the wealth of existing shareholders (including company executives) and to attract new investors. These companies have responded to the public revelations of such practices by sacking thousands of workers to "reduce their costs" (17,000 in the case of WorldCom alone).[2]

In a similar vein, Gordon Clark and Elizabeth Jonson note that, during the past two decades there has been a considerable degree of interest, at least at the theoretical level, in the concept of business ethics. The topic of business ethics has been elevated to the front pages of the mainstream media as a result of events going back to the 1980s, including the 1987 stock market crash (where billions of dollars were wiped form the resource base of investors), the recession of the early nineties and the apparent corruption in business, leading to the collapse of personal leveraged empires in Australia, the United Kingdom and the Canada.[3] Springboarding from this are concepts such as 'corporate social responsibility'[4] and 'obligations to stakeholders'.[5]

Laura Nash correctly notes that 'the topic of business ethics is acknowledged to pervade every area of the corporation just as it is a recurrent theme in media. Corporate codes of conduct are now the norm rather than the exception'.[6]

However, the link between business and ethics has a very short history. It has been recognised as a genuine form of applied ethics for little more than the past few decades. According to Aristotle, the practice of *chrematisike,* or trading for profit, was devoid of virtue and engaged in only by 'parasites'. As is noted by Robert Solomon, this view prevailed until the seventeenth century.[7] Thereafter the attitude to business quickly changed.

> John Calvin and then the English Puritans taught the virtues of thrift and enterprise, and Adam Smith canonized the new faith in 1776 in his masterwork, The Wealth of Nations. . . . The general acceptance of business and the recognition of economics as a central structure of society depended on a very new way of thinking about society that required not only a change in religious and philosophical sensibilities but, underlying them, a new sense of society and even of human nature. This transformation can be partly explained in terms of urbanization, larger more centralized societies, the privatization of family groups as consumers, rapidly advancing technology, the growth of industry and the accompanying development of social structures, needs and desires.[8]

While business has became an acceptable activity it is only recently that a 'more moral and more honourable way of viewing business has begun to dominate business talk'.[9] Although business ethics has a very short and patchy history, Laura Nash notes that some trends apparently emerged regarding the changing focus of business ethics. In the 1950s the two major concerns were price-fixing and dehumanization in the workforce. In the 1960s constraints were placed on environmentally and socially destructive activities. The 1970s witnessed concerns about bribery following the shift to internationalism, in particular to markets in Asia the Mideast? In the 1980s the focus shifted from institutional responsibility to the moral capacity of individuals. Thus, there was considerable concern at the activities such as insider trading and hostile takeovers which were marked by a high degree of greed and dishonesty.[10]

In the early 21st century, greed, sprinkled with an unhealthy dose of dishonesty, is still the main constant underpinning public disillusionment with the corporate governance of many large public companies. This disillusionment has been fuelled by a string of corporate collapses, wiping out billions dollars of shareholder investment. Notable instances being the plight of Enron, HIH and One.Tel. This is nothing new. It seems to be an almost cyclical event. For example, in the Australian context, about a decade ago even middle Australia was taken aback by the collapse of the Quintex group and Pyramid Building society. Company managers continue to be criticised for their apparent inability to look beyond the bottom line of the profit and loss statement and, in particular, how this impacts on their personal fortunes. There is also increasing disquiet regarding the huge sums paid to corporate directors, both in the form of salary and wages and severance payments.

14.2.2 The Disunity Between Business and Ethics Argument

Despite the emerging popularity of the notion of business ethics, there is little convergence in opinion regarding the precise moral duties owed by company managers.[11] In light of this, and the infancy of the concept of business ethics, many commentators still maintain that ethics does not have a role in the corporate world. The duty of a company director, so the argument runs, is to maximise corporate profits within the bounds of the law—no more, no less.

The most famous exponent of this argument is Nobel Prize winning economist Milton Friedman who in an article in the New York Times over three decades ago titled 'The social responsibility of business is to maximise profits', stated that company directors are the employees of shareholders and therefore have a fiduciary duty to maximise profits. Directing resources to charities or other social causes is akin to stealing from shareholders. He called business people who defended the notion of corporate responsibility 'unwitting puppets of the intellectual forces that have been undermining the basis of a free society'. He also accused them of 'pure and unadulterated socialism'.[12]

The notion that there may be a contradiction between commercial realities and moral norms, has been noted (though not endorsed) more recently in the context of legal practice by Justice Michael Kirby who has 'has speculated about whether it is possible to maintain noble ideas while practising in the world of commercial realities'.[13]

Thus, before launching into a discussion of business ethics the threshold issue which must be addressed is: Does ethics have any role in guiding the decision making of company managers?

14.2.3 Morality Applies to Business Because Moral Judgments are Universalisable

A counter to separateness of business and ethics argument is that it violates a fundamental paradigm of morality. As we saw in chapter one, the surface nature of moral language suggests that moral principle is applicable to all forms of human conduct, whether public or private, and provides the ultimate evaluative framework by which our behaviour is judged. The notion of contracting out of morality seems untenable. A key feature of moral judgments is that they are universalisable and it follows that in order to justify the independence thesis, it is necessary to identify a *relevant* difference between business activities and other activities which are subject to moral evaluation.

14.2.4 Exception to Universalisation—Activities with Internal Settled Rules?

A possible basis for distinguishing business from most other human endeavours—which are clearly subject to moral evaluation—is that business is a 'self contained' activity. That is, it is already governed by relatively settled and clear principles and standards. Moral rules appear to apply most acutely to govern conduct between private individuals, which is largely unregulated by other norms. Thus, it is morally reprehensible to lie, break promises or cheat on our partners, and so on.

Business on the other hand has its own settled rules, and hence, so the argument goes, there is no scope for morally evaluating activities conducted within the scope of business. The boxer who intentionally injures his opponent is immune from moral blame, even though his conduct would be clearly reprehensible if performed in a different setting. Corporate and business activities are regulated by extensive and complex legal rules and principles. Hence, just like boxing, the activities performed by corporations should not be immune from moral evaluation.

This attempt to excise corporations and business from the sphere of moral evaluation, fails because it places too much weight on the importance of the existence of established rules. The level of sophistication, organisation or system that underlies an area of human endeavour is generally irrelevant to its amenability to moral evaluation. This is shown by the fact that activities which produce undesirable outcomes, such as drug trafficking, people smuggling and child pornography do not attract moral immunity irrespective of their level of internal regulation and organisation.

There certainly may be instances where following the rules of an existing rule governed practice may provide a general immunity from moral blame. Tackling another player in conformity with the rules of soccer, refusing to pass a weak student, serving the first person in queue are all perfectly justifiable actions. However, this has nothing to do with the fact that forms of conduct are regulated by rules (of sport, academia and etiquette respectively), but rather because the rules themselves have either been designed in light of pre-existing moral norms or at least are not morally objectionable in themselves. Similarly, the only reason that boxing is morally acceptable is because the good consequences from it outweigh the bad—the need to respect the autonomy of the boxers weighs more heavily in the moral calculus than the possible harm that might occur as a result of condoning fighting in a controlled environment.

Further, those involved in generally non-offensive rule governed activities never acquire an *absolute* indemnity from moral censure. For example, it is reprehensible for organisers of a boxing context to pit a professional skilled fighter against a rank amateur or for a referee to permit a fight to continue after one boxer has been clearly rendered defenceless. Hence, even in relation to rule governed practices which are generally regarded as being morally acceptable, moral norms continue to play a supervisory role. This role is so cardinal that morality remains a constant catalyst for rule changes to the practices — to ensure that they continue to conform to changing, more enlightened, moral standards.

It follows that the mere fact that corporations have well settled rules, procedures and protocols for all aspects of their activities does not provide them with immunity from moral norms. The important question is whether corporations conform to minimal moral standards.

14.2.5 Are Moral Norms too Vague to Apply to Business?

A further rationale that has been advanced in support of the separateness of business and ethics is that morality has no role in business because it is too subjective and, given its indeterminate nature, is incapable of providing guidance concerning business practice.[14] To this, there are three counters. First, as noted in chapter one moral principles are in fact objective, capable of logical proof. The mere fact that it is sometimes *difficult* to find moral answers, does not derogate from this — in the same way that difficulties in finding cures for many physical illnesses does not mean that there are not necessarily better forms of treatments.

Secondly, for sceptics who are unconvinced about the objectivity of moral judgments, even if we accept that moral judgements are by their very nature imprecise and often indeterminate, this has not limited their application to other human endeavours and activities, such as politics, law, or even sport. Why then should the situation be any different in the case of corporate business activities?

Thirdly, the fact that the moral status of an activity has not been resolved and the application of moral principles to it has not produced clear standards of conduct pertaining to that activity, generally results in increased moral reflection and assessment upon the matter, rather than an abandonment of such discourse. For example, the fact that activities such as eugenics and euthanasia are morally equivocal has proved a catalyst for further moral dialogue and debate on such issues — not less, or none at all.

Accordingly, since there is no relevant difference between corporate and business activities and other activities which are regulated by moral principles, the business world is not outside the sphere of morality.

14.2.6 Promise to Shareholders to Maximise Profits as Basis for Rejecting Application of Moral Principles to Business?

A third possible justification for excluding the operation of moral principles to business is the argument that businesses 'owe' it to their shareholders and investors to make profit maximisation the cardinal objective.[15] 'Owe' in this context is used in a normative sense, inferring that investors and shareholders invest in business in the reasonable expectation that they will be profit focused and hence it would be morally reprehensible for businesses to act contrary to this—it would violate the moral prescription that one should keep their promises. This argument fails for several reasons.

First, few investors who put their finances into a business receive an express promise that their funds will be only used to maximize profit.[16] It could be claimed that although investors do not receive an express promise as to the manner in which their funds will be used, there is widespread knowledge in the community that the sole aim of business is to maximize profit and hence there is at least a tacit promise to this end. However, even if businesses did promise to investors to use the funds solely to advance profit, this does not justify the harmony thesis. Promise keeping is not the highest order moral requirement. It is undoubtedly morally permissible and necessary to break a promise where keeping it would result in significant harm to another person. For example, there is no question that it is appropriate to break a promise to meet a friend or colleague in order to attend to an emergency. Business, too, would be justified in breaking a 'profit promise' to shareholders where keeping the promise would violate higher order moral ideals.

In order to get at least some mileage out of the promise to shareholder argument, it could be contended that while the existence of a promise does not absolutely justify the harmony thesis, it goes at least a partial way to doing so by providing a *prima facie* reason why profit maximisation should be the main business goal.

However, even this less ambitious form of the argument fails. It is not true that one always has even a prima facie obligation to uphold a promise. The content of a promise can often affect the reason for keeping it.[17] Implicit in the word 'prima facie' is the notion that the act it relates to should be done *unless* there are other more compelling considerations. If even in the absence of other more compelling considerations, the act still should not be performed, due to its abhorrent nature, then the use of the term 'prima facie' is not only redundant, but also incorrect. Thus, a corporate officer would not have an obligation to approve the sale of dangerous goods, no matter how profitable the arrangement was to the corporation.

14.2.7 Summary of the General Link Between Business and Ethics

In all other areas of life, moral principles are the ultimate standards by which we evaluate and assess activities and actions. Business is a label, describing one of many types of human activities. Irrespective of how desirable an activity is felt to be the universalisability and pervasiveness of morality is such that it applies to properly regulate the actions performed within the relevant activity. This is so even in relation to practices such as medicine, law and charitable services.

The fact that corporate activities are not different in any relevant sense from the range of activities to which moral principles are applicable means that they too are caught within the sphere of moral evaluation. As such, moral principles are the ultimate evaluative standard of business conduct and should prevail where there is tension between them and business principles.

Having dispelled the argument that there is no role for ethics in business, I now turn our attention to the content of the ethical norms that apply in the business setting. Before doing so, it is important to note that business ethics is not a stand-alone moral construct, but that it forms part of normal ethics, the fundamental tenets of which are set out in chapter one.

14.3 APPLICATION OF MORAL PRINCIPLE TO BUSINESS SETTING

14.3.1 Types of Duties Imposed on Corporations—Proscriptions Against Causing Harm, Lying and Environmental Camage Already Legally Enforced

According to some commentators, the managers of corporations have extensive moral obligations to all those affected by corporate activities. Robert Solomon believes that 'managers of corporations have obligations to their shareholders and all other stakeholders as well. In particular, they have obligations to consumers and the surrounding community as well as to their employees'.[18] More elaborately he defines the stakeholders in a company 'as all those who are affected and have legitimate expectations and rights regarding the actions of the company, including employees, consumes and suppliers as well as the surrounding community and society at large'.[19]

The content of this obligation to all stakeholders is unclear. Nevertheless the view that corporations have wide-ranging ethical obligations is shared by a growing number of commentators and members of the public. It is an increasingly popular conception that institutions should be 'good corporate citizens' and that they have widespread 'social responsibilities'. While, the exact meaning of such phrases has not been defined the connotation is clear. Corporations should be managed in a way so that they are socially responsible and do not engage in activities that adversely impact on the interests of others.

There are a myriad of ways in which companies can damage the interests of others. The most obvious is where a corporation sells or otherwise distributes unsafe products or engages in unsafe practices which place at risk the lives and physical safety of employees. Less extreme, but potentially just as damaging, are practices which are not conducted in a sustainable manner. For example, where corporations exhaust finite resources or destroy culturally or environmentally valuable assets. It has also been suggested that corporations have a duty of candour to all people who may be inclined to invest in them. Finally, it has been suggested that corporations should not only avoid committing harmful acts, but that they have a positive duty to engage in activities that promote desirable social ends.

Thus, there are broadly four levels of expectations or duties that can be imposed on corporations:

(i) Not to directly harm people;
(ii) Not to engage in activities that are socially or environmentally unsustainable;
(iii) Not to lie or otherwise misrepresent the activities of the corporation; and
(iv) To engage in activities that are socially desirable. For short, I shall call this the duty of benevolence.

In determining the nature and scope of moral duties that apply to corporations, the starting point, as we have seen, is that all agents are subject to moral norms and evaluation. Corporations are ultimately a group of people acting towards a common goal. There is no doubt that moral liability applies not only to individual, but also group actions. Individuals cannot opt out of moral liability by engaging in activities with others. Thus, we see that each individual in a group or 'gang' of people that harms other is morally liable for the conduct. This applies irrespective of the size of the group and in some cases even entire nation states can be held to account for the conduct of individuals or groups within the state. The best example of this is the censure that is typically cast on nations which engage in unjustified war against other states, such as Germany during both world wars, Japan during the Second World War and more recently Iraq during its occupation of Kuwait. Thus, the collective decision-making and action taking nature underpinning corporate activities does not provide a relevant basis for limiting the scope of moral duties that apply to corporate agents.

Against his background, we see that the first three duties are not highly controversial. All agents have a moral duty to not engage in activities that physically harm others and not to lie to others. There is also a widespread consensus that we have a moral duty not to damage the environment, although as we saw in chapter 12 this has been over-stated. These duties apply universally and there is no tenable argument for carving out a business exemption in relation to them.

In relation to each of these areas, all western nations have wide-ranging and settled laws. These nations have highly developed and wide-ranging product liability laws (which protect consumers) and labour laws (which protect employees) and in most circumstances these operate effectively to discourage corporations form distributing goods which place at risk the physical safety of consumers or from engaging in work practices that imperil the safety of their workers. There are also strict duties on directors to accurately report on the activities of the corporation and to flag any material changes to the activities of the corporation. In addition to this there are wider-ranging laws, often imposing criminal sanctions (which are often strict liability in nature), that proscribe or limit activities that damage the environment or risk exhausting finite resources.

Underpinning and justifying these laws are the moral principles adverted to above. While the overlap between moral and legal duties that apply to companies relating to dishonesty and activities that cause direct harm to others or that damage the environment is probably not complete it is certainly extensive. It may be the case, that there are some moral gaps in laws proscribing, for example, the sale of dangerous goods, however, there gaps are not evident. If commentators wish to impose a moral duty above and beyond the legal duties that already exist in these areas it is important to note that these must be *established* by reference to the above theories and principles and not merely *asserted* as abstract and stand alone claims. Given that there is already extensive legal regulation prohibiting the first three forms of harm listed above[20] against all agents, including corporations, the focus of the rest of this chapter is on moral norms which are not legally enforced.

14.4 ADDITIONAL DUTIES IMPOSED ON CORPORATIONS—A DUTY OF BENEVOLENCE?

14.4.1 Acts and Omissions Doctrine Serves to Miminise Obligations on Corporations

The fourth and most controversial duty that potentially applies to corporations is a positive duty to be a 'good corporate citizen'. This imposes on corporations a duty to do more than to 'simply' obey the law. It seeks to impose on corporations an obligation to engage in activities that promote the welfare of the community, including company stakeholders, beyond providing high quality and safe goods and services. The content of such a duty can vary enormously.

A modest expression of the duty would require corporations to treat all their employees with concern and respect, for example by paying performance and Christmas bonuses. A far more extravagant requirement is in the form that corporations have a positive duty to enhance community and social capital by either directly engaging in benevolent activities or indirectly doing so by, for example, donating to worthy charities or social causes. A duty of benevolence is perhaps the most extreme form of a positive duty that can be imposed on corporations.

Thus, a duty to be a good corporate citizen can obviously be framed in many different ways. It is not feasible to consider each such manifestation of this duty. For the purposes of this chapter we consider the most extreme expression of this duty—that of benevolence.[21]

Recognition of such a duty is not in keeping with contemporary corporate practice. While many corporations are certainly in business of donations, often this is clearly grounded in self-interest (the clearest example of this being donations to political parties), otherwise it is considered to be an expression of extreme generosity, rather than the fulfilment of a pre-existing obligation. Additionally, given the mountain of legal rules that now apply to corporations it may seem pragmatically unrealistic and theoretically untenable to expect corporations in a highly regulated environment (where the regulation has been already driven by basic moral norms, such as proscriptions against lying —hence duties of disclosure and the like—and harming others) to do more than pursue profits and comply with the law.

As a general observation, this is correct. At the individual level, as we have seen, there are very few positive moral obligations imposed on us. This is also the case as far as the law is concerned. Thus it is rare that individuals are required to positively do an act (as opposed to refraining from engaging in conduct) to assist another.

This stems from a fundamental distinction that is entrenched in most common law jurisdictions: the acts and omissions doctrine, which is the view that one is only responsible and liable for one's positive acts, as opposed to events that one fails to prevent (omissions). This was analysed in chapter ten.

The acts and omissions doctrine has also attracted widespread appeal because it supposedly prevents our lives being intolerably burdened by demarcating the extent to which we must help others. Given the deep roots of the acts and omissions doctrine in the law, there seems little scope for asserting that corporations do in fact a positive duty to engage in social and community building activities.

This view is supported by the observations of Solomon, who states that the 'the purpose of a corporation, after all, is to serve the public, both by way of providing desired products and services and by not harming the community and its citizens'.[22] While Solomon proposes that corporations should serve the public, this duty is supposedly discharged merely by providing quality goods and services and not harming people. But cannot we ask even more from corporations?

14.4.2 Principal Duty is for Corporations to Comply With Law—Business is Morally Neutral

From the above, it follows that the starting point so far as the moral obligations of corporations are concerned is that corporations must abide by the law in their pursuit of profit. It is necessary to emphasise that engaging in business and seeking to make profits is a legitimate form or conduct and that people, acting individually or collectively, should be given the opportunity to pursue such activities. Corporate managers in the pursuit of profits do not, at least prima facie, need to keep one eye on the bigger moral picture in their pursuit of profits. They can without any moral embarrassment or guilt go about seeking to make us much money as is legally possible.

While we might hope that people would engage in somewhat more virtuous activities than chasing the next dollar, it is not easy to identify a concrete basis for imposing such a duty. A good Samaritan duty has not been justified. The pursuit of profits like watching television, writing books, walking in the park, dining with friends, playing or watching sport and driving a car is ultimately a break-even or neutral moral activity. It does not harm the agent or the wider community, nor does it necessarily either promote or diminish any person's relevant interests. Moreover, profit chasing can never fully exhaust the ambit of one's morally relevant behaviour.

Each person engages in an infinite range of activities. Some are purely for pleasure, such as watching television and playing tennis, others are functional, such as working and cleaning the house and buying shares, some are spiritual, such as attending church, others are sourced in kindness, such as babysitting the neighbours' children and engaging in volunteerism. The point to note is that even if engaging in business is a morally neutral activity, moral worthiness (if in fact we should be looking to more than morally break-even) can be yet be readily acquired through the myriad of other activities in which a person engages.

So far as business (and other non-inherently harmful activities) is concerned, people should be given as much space and freedom as possible in terms of how they go about their activities and projects. This means that corporate managers should at every point along the process be permitted to keep their eye firmly fixed on the bottom line of the profit and loss statement in making their business decisions.

Business decisions can thus be made along business lines. Corporate managers are entitled to pay employees and directors market wages, they can pursue efficiency at the expense of 'propping up' an inefficient work force and when they close down unsound branches they do not need to pay above market severance packages.

14.4.3 A More Elaborate Duty—Extreme Wealth and Maxim of Positive Duty

Despite this, there are two (related) reasons that can be advanced to assert that corporations have a positive duty of benevolence. The first is that the acts and omissions doctrine is in fact unsound.

Despite its intuitive appeal, as we saw in chapter 10, the doctrine does not withstand close scrutiny. Pursuant to the maxim of positive duty there are occasions when acting morally requires us to do more than merely refraining from certain behaviour; where we must actually *do* something. We must assist others in serious trouble, when assistance would immensely help them at no or little inconvenience to ourselves—the maxim of positive duty.

The second reason that the acts and omissions may not provide corporations with a shield to defend themselves against a positive duty to contribute to socially worthy enterprises stems from a relatively rare trait that is disproportionately enjoyed by corporations.

Corporations often are funded by thousands and in some cases millions of individuals. As a result they have an enormous resource base. This allows them to compete very effectively in the market place as the preferred provider of goods and services. This often leads to the generation of enormous profits. Thus, a distinction between many corporations and individuals is that corporations control more wealth.

This raises for consideration the issue of whether extreme wealth generates additional or special moral duties.

Generally speaking, wealth is not regarded as being morally relevant in demarcating the scope of an agent's moral rights and responsibilities. Gifts to charity and other altruist forms of behaviour are regarded as virtuous conduct, but there is no expectation on individuals to donate a portion of their resources to the more needy. While altruism can elevate the moral status of an individual it is not a necessary requirement for an individual to be a morally fit and complete agent. This is so, arguably, irrespective of the capacity of the agent to donate money and other resources.

On this view, a strong argument can be made that corporations, no matter how large and wealthy, do not have an obligation to promote the betterment of the community. Corporations are, ultimately, a collection of individuals and the profits belong to the shareholders. Their duty to assist others should not be elevated merely because their wealth derives, at least in part, from shareholding as opposed to, say, income derived from personal services.

14.4.4 Requirement to Pay Social Dividend

There are, however, perhaps two fallacies associated with the view the corporate wealth does not attract a benevolence duty. First, it is not the case that money derived by collections of individuals is necessarily disaggregated when assessing whether there is a duty to assist others in need. The ultimate group enterprise which is involved in the accumulation of wealth is the nation state. Each nation has a bottom line profit and loss statement which is largely measured by its Gross National Income (GNI). As discussed in chapter 10, there is a well-established international custom that wealthier nations will donate a portion of their wealth to developing countries. This money could, of course, be distributed to the citizens of the respective countries, but the argument that the money actually belongs to the individuals does not seem to overcome the strong expectations on rich countries to donate their wealth. Thus, at least in relation to very large institutions there seems to be a relatively well settled moral expectation that very rich institutions should donate part of their wealth to the more needy.

Secondly, even at the individual level it can be argued that there is an obligation on the obscenely rich to redistribute a portion of their wealth. It is not necessarily accurate to assert that the parameters of our moral obligations are necessarily circumscribed by an obligation not to engage in activities that harm others.[23] This is an obligation which more and more people seem prepared to fulfil. For example, a study by ACOSS published in December 2004 into the level of donations made by Australians revealed a growth in the collective sympathy gland of the community. The key findings were:

- $867.7 million was claimed in tax deductible donations in 2001–2, up by 3.5% from the previous year. This builds on a 16.2% increase in the year before that.
- 3,595,391 taxpayers—34.8% of all taxpayers—made and claimed tax deductible donations in 2001–2. 148,828 more people than the previous year.
- Since 1996, the amount donated by individual Australians as a proportion of total income has been rising and is at an average of 0.25%. It is now at its highest level since 1992–3.

- The average tax deductible donation in 2002 was $241.35.
- The average tax-deductible donation made and claimed by Australian males in 2002 was $280.38 compared to $197.23 for Australian females.[24]

Thus, a strong argument can be made that corporations do in fact have a moral responsibility to contribute to the improvement of the communities in which they operate. This obligation only crystalises when a corporation is very successful in achieving its wealth generating objective. In dollar terms it is not feasible to draw a bright line at what point this is reached. Any figure will be challenged as being arbitrary, however, I suggest that the threshold is reached once a company (or group of companies) makes a billion dollar annual profit. It should then pay a 'social dividend' of 5% for each profit dollar exceeding this amount. A billion dollars is so large a sum that it is unlikely that anyone could argue, while maintaining a straight face, that 'we need more'. Five per cent constitutes a meaningful contribution but is small enough to discourage hard work and innovation.

The obvious counter to this proposal is that it is the government's role to fund such matters and programs. However, as Peter Singer has commented (in the context of international aid) there is no evidence that an increase in private donations will diminish the amount of government support to such areas — in fact it might even result in an increase.[25] Additionally, the two processes of giving and society building are not mutually exclusive.

In terms of how this social dividend is delivered there are obviously a multitude of causes and projects that could be described as 'worthy'. To remove doubt the money should be applied to basic human needs, such as health and shelter. Thus, I propose that the social dividend should be paid directly to public hospitals and other non-profit health providers or institutions involved in providing housing to destitute members of the community. Food is obviously another fundamental human need, but the absence of people dying of malnutrition in Australia indicates that the provision of this important service is already satisfied.

It should be noted that the duty cast in this manner can be reconciled with the non-interventionist approach to corporate management set out earlier. As noted above, corporations are not required at every step to do more than is legally necessary in their pursuit of profits. However, if they are spectacularly successful in achieving this goal, they must then donate a portion of their profits. The proposal being advanced here is analogous to the duties imposed on individuals. Tiger Woods does not have to break into his golf round to visit the elderly or man a soup kitchen, but if he keeps producing outstanding golf rounds and in the process derives millions of dollars, some of the proceeds should be donated to worthwhile social causes. Framing the duty in this manner allows corporate managers and individuals to focus on what they do best, without constantly being required to have their routine and processes disrupted by pursuing socially desirable aims, which they may not have appropriate skills and judgment to identify and implement. At the same time, the community benefits if they are successful at achieving their prior orientated objectives.

14.5 EXTREME WEALTH AND DUTY TO NOT FRUSTRATE ACCESS TO JUSTICE

Wealth also confers other advantages on agents in our legal system. At the substantive level, there is widespread consensus that the principles underpinning the Australian legal system are relatively just and fair—as noted earlier, certainly it is not easy to identify laws which are demonstrably unjust.

However, this is largely meaningless if parties cannot obtain access to the law in order to assert and enforce their legal rights. The rights to be free from assault or to own property would be largely vacuous if muggers and thieves were never charged and prosecuted. As far as the civil law is concerned, laws of contract and negligence would be empty if people could not sue those who had their economic or physical interests harmed by others.

In legal systems, such as those that operate in most Western countries, where the losing party is normally liable for the other party's costs, the wealth of the potential litigants plays a crucial role in a rational assessment of whether a party should pursue his or her legal rights. Corporations often have an invisible barrier of protection from legal accountability for their unlawful acts because it is not economically viable for consumers to seek legal redress against them. It is not financially viable to issue proceedings for a $50 overcharging for a phone, electricity or health care bill. Even a 'win' in court will result in a net loss. While this is the situation even where the defendant is another individual, the problem is even more acute where the defendant is a wealthy corporation, which has the capacity to financially exhaust the resources of the plaintiff through interlocutory proceedings even before the substantive claim is determined or to engage an army of lawyers to fend of a relatively modest claim.

Thus corporations have an obligation not to frustrate access of others to the courts. This obligation can be discharged in a number of different ways. The first is to have an efficient and open internal complaints system, whereby customer complaints are handled promptly, courteously and fairly and which involves providing written reasons to customers regarding the company's response to complaints. This complaints resolution process should be publicised to customers. For matters that cannot be resolved at this level, and which end up in the courts, corporations should undertake not to initiate unnecessary interlocutory steps or engage legal counsel beyond that which is commensurate with the complexity of the matter and the monetary sum involved. To do otherwise is to use their size and wealth to achieve unjustified outcomes.

14.6 SUMMARY

Corporations, like all agents, have moral duties and responsibilities. The content of the moral obligations of corporations, however, must be established not asserted. It is empty to merely claim that corporations must be good citizens without defining the source of such a duty.

We have seen that the moral duty owed by corporations must be grounded in a verifiable normative ethic. Business ethics is the application of normal ethical principles to the business setting. An application of moral theory to a business setting where there is extensive legal regulation broadly based on enforcing basic moral proscriptions, such as the duty not to harm others or lie, reveals that company managers have relatively few moral duties over and above those to obey the law.

Corporate managers are free to base their business decisions on business criteria without having to add moral considerations into the decision-making calculus. However, where they are spectacularly successful in achieving their profit making goal the maxim of positive duty mandates that they pay a social dividend. At what profit level this duty crystalises is unclear. I suggest that the threshold is an annual profit of one billion dollars, in which case corporations should be required to donate 5% of their profit to worthwhile social causes. In addition to this, corporations should not use their wealth to effectively prevent or discourage individuals from pursuing and enforcing their legal rights. If companies observe these two duties (and do not breach any laws) they can then claim to be good corporate citizens.

NOTES

1. O Mbare, The Role of Corporate Social Responsibility (CSR) in the New Economy (2004) 10 *Electronic Journal of Business Ethics and Organisational Studies*.

2. S Mann, *Economics, Business Law and Ethics* (2003) 13.

3. See Clark and Jonson, 'Introduction' in Clark and Jonson (eds), *Management Ethics* (1995), 11.

4. See for example, S Longstaff, 'About corporate social responsibility' (2000) 40 *City Ethics* 1. See more generally list of articles by St James Ethics Centre at <http://www.ethics.org.au>.

5. *See for example,* O Mbare, "The Role of Corporate Social Responsibility (CSR) in the New Economy' (2004) *Electronic Journal of Business Ethics and Organization Studies.*

6. L Nash, 'Why Business Ethics Now', in Clark and Johnson (eds), above n 2, 25.

7. R C Solomon, 'Business Ethics' in Peter Singer (ed), *A Companion to Ethics* (1991) 354, 355.

8. Ibid.

9. Ibid, 356.

10. Nash, above n 6.

11. For an overview of some of the different theories so far as they apply to business, see Mann, above n 2

12. As cited in R C Solomon, 'Business Ethics' in Peter Singer (ed), *A Companion to Ethics* (1991) 354, 360.

13. As cited in J Cain and K Hammond, 'Tending the Bar: Lawyers are expected to act ethically. Whose job is it to ensure they do?', *The Age* (Melbourne), 18 August 2002, 16.

14. M Friedman, as cited in R C Solomon, 'Business Ethics' in P Singer (ed), *A Companion to Ethics* (1991) 354 above n 12, 1.

15. M Friedman, as cited in Robert C Solomon, 'Business Ethics' in Peter Singer (ed), *A Companion to Ethics* (1991) 354.

16. C Stone, *Where the Law Ends: The Social Control of Corporate Behaviour* (1975). Moreover, an increasing number of people want corporations to focus on matters beyond profit making. Mbare, above n 4, notes that 'The Millennium Poll on Corporate Social Responsibility, September 1999 conducted by Mitsubishi Corporation found "two in three citizens want companies to go beyond their historical role of making profit, paying taxes, employing people and obeying all laws; they want companies to contribute to broader societal goals"'.

17. C L Ten, 'Moral Rights & Duties in a Wicked Legal System' (1989) 1 *Utilitas* 139.

18. Solomon, above n 12, 361.

19. Ibid, 360.

20. This is obviously not the case in all countries, in which case there is a need to carefully consider the moral obligations of businesses in these areas. Such considerations also arise where companies from western nations operate internationally. For a discussion about business ethics in the global environment, see M Kopperi, 'Business Ethics in a Global Economy' (1999) 4 *Electronic Journal of Business Ethics and Organization Studies* . A particularly important issue in global business ethics concerns the so called 'race to the bottom'. This is the view that corporations are forced to compete with lower salaries, taxation, safety regulations and standards for environmental protection. In this kind of system, it has been argued that it is very difficult or even impossible to act in a way that would benefit not only the shareholders but all the stakeholders and the society on the whole. Given the highly regulated trading and labour market in Australia, this is not a problem at the domestic level.

21. The duty described this way accords with the meaning of corporate social responsibility adopted by the European Commission. A useful summary of the Commission paper on the topic is provided by Mbare, above n 4: 'According to the European Commission's Green Paper entitled "Promoting a European Framework for Corporate Social Responsibility" (July 2001), CSR is defined as a 'concept whereby companies integrate social and environmental concerns in their business operations and in their interactions with their stakeholders on a voluntary basis'. On a simpler note, CSR are actions, which are above and beyond that required by the law. Frederick (1986: 4) summed up the position as follows: 'The fundamental idea of 'corporate social responsibility' is that business corporations have an obligation to work for social betterment'.

22. Solomon, above n 12, 361.

23. According to Peter Singer people in first world countries on average or above average incomes should be donating about ten per cent of their income to reducing poverty, *Practical Ethics* (2nd ed, 2002) 246.

24. ACOSS, 'Facts reveal record generosity of Australians at Xmas', Media Release 13 December 2004: www.coss.net.au/news/acoss/1102745671_844_acoss.jsp.

25. Singer, above n 23, 241–42.

Chapter Fifteen

Bribery and Networking: Is There a Moral Difference?

15.1 INTRODUCTION

Bribery is widely condemned in the Western world. Significant efforts have been made in the international law arena to stamp out bribery, which is seen largely as a third world phenomenon. The cultural characteristics that have been identified as enabling bribery and other corrupt practices to flourish are:

> The cultures are 'relationship-focused'—personal connections are crucial; they are 'strongly hierarchical', valuing wide status differences; and they are 'polychronic, with a relaxed attitude toward time and scheduling.[1]

It has been suggested that these characteristics are common to developing countries.[2] The United States has recently received high praise for its determined efforts to eradicate the practice.[3] This has culminated in members of the OECD signing the *Convention on Combating Bribery of Foreign Public Officials in International Business Transactions* in December 1997.[4] Article 1(1) of the Convention states:

> Each Party shall take such measures as may be necessary to establish that it is a criminal offence under its law for any person intentionally to offer, promise or give any undue pecuniary or other advantage, whether directly or through intermediaries, to a foreign public official, for that official or for a third party, in order that the official act or refrain from acting in relation to the performance of official duties, in order to obtain or retain business or other improper advantage in the conduct of international business.

Thus, the Convention targets the person giving the bribe, as opposed to the receiver. The reason for this is that OECD members are the largest exporters of global trade and business and it is from these nations where most bribery money comes from.[5]

In contrast to bribery, networking is standard business practice in most Western nations. Despite the moral gulf (in terms of prevailing community sentiment) between the two practices it is difficult to find a principled and logical distinction between them.

In this chapter I examine the nature of bribery and contrast it with the practice of networking with a view to discerning whether the different moral and legal treatment of the practices is based on principle or simply cultural preference, or perhaps even a sense of cultural elitism or imperialism.[6]

The normative analysis is undertaken in section three of this chapter. In the next section I set the framework by defining the key terms.

I argue that bribery and one form of networking (expenditure networking — which involves spending money, normally in the form of providing services, on clients) both have the affect of distorting the proper functioning of the market economy by encouraging business decisions to be made on the basis of economically irrelevant considerations; namely, the thickness of the paper bag or the opulence of the corporate box. Expenditure networking is a little more subtle than bribery, but this is a difference in degree only — not nature. Thus, on a strictly *economic analysis*, both practices are equally wrong.

However, there is perhaps a moral distinction between the two practices. Viewed more broadly, there is at least one important incidental good consequence stemming from networking. It encourages and fosters companionship. As noted in chapter two, studies have shown that social involvement is integral to human happiness. Thus, it may be that this good effect of networking outweighs the economic downside associated with it.

15.2 DEFINITIONS

15.2.1 Bribery

Bribery is an offence at common law. A good starting point for considering the nature of bribery is to examine the manner in which it has been defined by the courts. The offence of bribery was initially confined to judicial officers, it now applies to all public officials. The development of the offence is summarised in *R v Glynn*[7] where the New South Wales Court of Criminal Appeal, made the following observations:

> A convenient starting point in an understanding of the essential nature of the common law misdemeanour of bribery is the pithy treatment of the definition of

it in Burdick, The Law of Crime (1946), Vol 1, par 288. There is no difference in this respect between the common law of England and that of the United States. So far as material Burdick states (at pp 426–427):

> "According to Coke . . . the crime of bribery was limited to the acceptance of a bribe by 'any man in a judicial place' (Coke, III Inst 145). . . By the time of Hawkins, the law had extended and he said that 'bribery in a strict sense is limited to judicial officers, but in a large sense it is sometimes applied to the receiving or offering of any undue reward, by or to any person whatsoever whose ordinary profession or business relates to the administration of public justice, in order to incline him to do a thing against the known rules of honesty and integrity'. . . But the view that bribery applies only to judicial officers, or to persons concerned in the administration of public justice, also became regarded as too narrow. The next step was to apply the offence to all public officers, and Russell's definition modified Hawkins by saying that 'bribery is the receiving or offering any undue reward by or to any person whatsoever, in a public office, in order to influence his behavior in office, and incline him to act contrary to the known rules of honesty and integrity' (Russell on Crimes (9th ed), Vol 1, p 319) . . ."

The evil to which the common law is directed is that of public officers being bought to act other than honestly and impartially in the performance of functions within the ambit of their office.

Thus, the paradigm case of bribery is a payment of money to an official in order to confer favouritism to the briber.

Unlike the criminal offence of bribery, in the business setting the notion of bribery extends beyond payments to public officials. It also includes payments to individuals in private business, such as company officers.

For the purpose of this discussion, I use the term bribery in a generic sense to refer to both the public and private business setting. As was noted by Philips in *Bribery*,[8] bribery means receiving any reward by a person who has *official duties* in order to influence his or her behaviour and incline him or her to violate an official duty of office. These duties need not necessarily derive from public office. They also arise out of the duty of fidelity and good faith implied into all private employment relationships and derive from private office—for example, being a company director.

15.2.2 Networking

Net-working has been variously defined. A standard definition is that offered by the Macquarie Dictionary which states that to network is 'to form possibly *advantageous* associations with other people (emphasis added)'.

At the extremes, there are two forms of networking. The first can described as simply 'mingling networking'. This involves actively seeking out the company of people that one believes may prove to be useful business or professional contacts at some point in the immediate or distant future. Examples of this are where a person joins a professional association in order that he or she can make contacts with other people in that industry or joins a local sporting club in the hope that by expanding his or her sphere of contacts that some of them will include professional or business associates.

At the other extreme is 'expenditure networking'. This involves providing services or goods to prospective clients, while at the same time socialising with the client. This differs from mingling networking in that it involves monetary expenditure by the agent which is aimed to directly confer *tangible benefits* to the agent. Commonly the money is directed towards paying for tickets to a sporting or cultural event. Often it goes well beyond this to include food, drink, travel and accommodation.

15.3 MORAL EVALUATION OF BRIBERY

Despite the widespread condemnation of bribery, it has been noted that some good consequences may stem from it. For example, it has been suggested that bribery generates new jobs[9] and supplements the income of lowly paid workers (for example, police and other mid-level government officials).[10] However, these considerations are all short-term economic benefits which are clearly outweighed by the considerable costs and long term inefficiencies caused by bribery.

To this end, Niilante Wallace-Bruce identifies several negative effects of bribery:

> The first, few would dispute that corruption reduces official government revenues. As people bribe their way through government processes, they are able to avoid the payment of tax and other charges which should have gone to government revenue. Second, transaction costs for the corrupter increase as a consequence of corruption. . . . For example, German officials have estimated that the German economy loses DM50 billion per year as a consequence of inflated contract prices and loses additional tax revenue as a consequence of bribes. . . Third, it has been shown that . . . where there is marked corruption in a country, foreign investment tends to decrease, which in turn leads to slower economic growth. . . Fourth, corruption distorts global business generally because transactions are not made on the basis of supply and demand and the efficient allocation of resources. . . As the recent histories of Nigeria, Indonesia and the Democratic Republic of Congo (formerly Zaire) have demonstrated, when corruption becomes pervasive, it can bring a country to its economic knees (references omitted).[11]

Similar sentiments were expressed by the Commonwealth Attorney General, Daryl Williams, in his second reading speech regarding the Criminal Code (Bribery of Foreign Public Officials) Bill 1999. He stated:

> It is important that Australia should support the OECD's initiative to combat the bribery of foreign public officials and take a principled stand against corruption. ... There is good business sense, as much as morality, in introducing this legislation. Bribery distorts attempts at international competitive bidding, bribes themselves are non-productive and are therefore paid from profits and bribes distort trade in that contracts are not based on merit and can lead to production of poor quality goods and services. In the aid context, bribery can lead to a very poor selection of projects, and this can in turn lead to diversion of resources away from areas of greatest need.[12]

The main thrust of these comments is that bribery is bad because it prevents the proper operation of the market economy. Basic economic theory suggests that in order for the market to operate most efficiently business should be directed towards the person or entity that is best able to produce the relevant goods or supply the desired services. In this context, the most meritorious business is measured by two principal criteria: price and quality — not according to how much it is willing to pay 'on the side' to win the business.

15.4 MORAL EVALUATION OF NETWORKING

15.4.1 Mingling Networking

From the view point of mainstream moral theory, mingling networking is not objectionable. There is no demonstrable basis for assuming that the practice of mingling networking reduces the happiness of the agents involved.[13] Hence, it does not offend the utilitarian ethic. Likewise concerning a rights based theory of morality. A 'right not to be approached by insincere or disingenuous people' is certainly not part of mainstream of moral discourse, and there is no obvious basis upon which such a right could be founded.

However, there is one non-consequentialist moral theory upon which mingling networking appears to run foul. Theoretically mingling networking can be criticised on the basis that it violates Kant's categorical imperative that people should always act as if every action were to become a universal law. It follows that we should treat others as ends given that that is how we regard ourselves. To treat another person only as a means to achieving what we want is to treat the person as a thing or tool and not as an agent. Given that we do regard our own functionality to others as being the criteria of our worth, we would not be prepared to prescribe using others as a universal norm and hence we should not use others.

According to this view, there is nothing inherently wrong with joining sporting or professional clubs. However, according to Kant motive is everything. People should join tennis clubs if they enjoy tennis and they should join the local law society because they are interested in promoting the objectives of the society. If in the process of participating in these activities one happens to *incidentally* form relationships which prove to be advantageous in the business or professional sense all the better. However, it is morally objectionable, so the theory runs, to seek out others with the express objective of attempting to *use them* for personal advancement. The appropriate foundation for friendships and relationships is a genuine interest and concern for the other person, not 'what's in it for me?'

Kant's theory has been subject to a number of criticisms. However, as we have seen, one unassailable aspect of his theory is that moral judgments are universalisable. A judgment is universalisable if the acceptance of it in a particular situation entails that one is logically committed to accepting the same judgment in all other similar situations.

However even if we accept this, it does not necessarily follow that it is morally offensive to engage in mingling networking. For it is not contradictory for an agent to hold the view that it is appropriate for other people to use him or her as ends; particularly where this does not (as is normally the situation with networking) simultaneously disadvantage the agent. Thus, a business person may be happy to socialise with people that he or she is aware are indirectly seeking to gain some commercial advantage from him, such as a contract for the provision of service. After all, there is no threat to any of his or her tangible interests.

Further, even if we do adopt Kant's maxim, at the pragmatic level it does not appear to provide a workable or coherent foundation for proscribing mingling networking. There are an almost infinite number of reasons that people form friendships and other relationships. Most commonly friendships start on the basis of a common interest or experience, for example, the parties may work together, share an interest in tennis, have a similar dress sense, or share political values. Arguably, all friendships commence with at least one party seeking, or at least stumbling upon, a pleasurable social experience with another person. Sometimes the experience is simply companionship (that is, someone to talk to—irrespective of the subject matter of the dialogue), at others times it is the opportunity to engage in a social pastime such as golf or chess, on other occasions it is simply the opportunity to discuss relevant issues with another person. Friendships form when the parties become aware that there they have more in common than one or two common interests, and form a genuine interest in each other—which transcends their sphere of common interests. The important thing to note here is that there is no obvious limitation—apart from the desire to engage in conduct which is aimed to directly harm the other person—concerning the nature of permissible motivations for seeking out the company of another at the pre-friendship stage. Thus, the desire to speak to another concerning mutual business or professional activities would appear to be no less admirable than the other reasons which motivate us to seek other human contact.

15.4.2 Expenditure Networking

However, as is noted above, activities classified as networking in Western business culture go far beyond the casual conversation at the local tennis club. They include the concept of seeking out and entertaining prospective and existing clients. In this regard, three professions which are more active than most are accounting, law and medicine. Law and accounting firms spend large sums of money providing prospective clients and established clients (who they want to keep as clients) with tickets to the best sporting and cultural activities available. A seemingly endless food and drink budget are normally an incident of this—not to mention the company of representatives of the firm. On an even grander scale are the pharmaceutical companies that wine, dine and entertain the medical profession. Treating in this context often goes beyond the best corporate box in the house and extends to a weekend or longer 'conference' at a suitable beach or ski resort. Once again, plenty of company representatives provided.

In terms of the nature of the entertainment involved, it quite often involves a sporting activity, such as a corporate box at the tennis or football, or cultural activity, such as tickets to the ballet or opera. However, ultimately, the type of entertainment is limited only by the tastes of the prospective client.

In order to evaluate the moral status of this practice a starting point is to ascertain the objective behind it. Why do businesses wine and dine prospective and established clients? In relation to established clients one reason is, no doubt, to thank clients for their custom—an act of gratitude. In respect of prospective clients it provides an opportunity to meet and develop a relationship with the person who makes decisions about the purchase of services or goods, to get to better know their business and to develop a relationship based on trust. It is a form of payment in exchange or compensation for the person giving up his or her time to meet with the hopeful new supplier.

However, another (maybe predominant) reason must be to attempt to influence the future business decisions of clients. Let us suppose that following extensive qualitative studies on the effects of networking that it was established that expenditure networking had absolutely no bearing on client's purchasing decisions. How many businesses would still engage in the practice? The answer is probably about zero. This response admittedly involves a degree of speculation, but we take a fair degree of confidence in it from the absence of social workers, public school teachers, trolley boys (and girls) and philosophers gracing the inside of corporate boxes—no matter how sparking their personalities. Unless Marketing Directors have been able to pull the wool over the eyes of corporate decision makers one is entitled to assume that expenditure networking occurs because there is a return on the investment in the form of business from those in receipt of the entertainment.

If networking was abolished, surely some business people would still wish to pursue existing relationships with clients due to the fact that something akin to a friendship has formed. However, in such circumstances the relationship would not be so one-sided as is the case with networking. Human relationships do not operate on the basis that one party is *always* treating the other. Most relationships involve some degree of reciprocity—that is, your shout today, mine tomorrow—or at least that is how it roughly works. As a general rule, relationships are only one-sided for one reason: where the party (always) treating wants something from the other party.

Most businesses are normally on the look out for a wider client base. Consequently to attempt to influence another business to purchase your services or goods is not necessarily undesirable. In fact, all business should seek to influence the purchase of their goods or services through the provision of accurate information to the market about price and quality so that the allocation of resources (through purchasing decisions) in any particular market can occur efficiently. However, there are limits to the means that can be legitimately employed to secure more work. The principal means adopted in our economic system for expanding the scope of a business is advertising. Personal referrals, especially in the professions, are also a valuable tool. Direct approaches ('cold calling') to prospective clients is another common marketing tool.

These are all part of a robust economic system which encourages competition. These marketing tools allow businesses to provide *information* to the market concerning why their product should be preferred to that of their competitor. However, expenditure networking is an attempt to influence the market on the basis of an economically irrelevant consideration—the ability of the business to wine, dine and entertain other people. The size and position on the ground of a law firm's corporate box has nothing to do with the firm's capacity to provide accurate, sound and timely legal advice.

Thus, expenditure networking is an attempt to gain a market advantage on the basis of criteria which has nothing to do with the merits of the business. This is bad for the same reason as bribery—it distorts the efficient operation of the relevant market and in turn the economy. Contracts for the provision of goods and services should be directed towards the organisation which can most efficiently and effectively discharge the contracts.

Expenditure marketing is more subtle than bribery. The consideration or benefit conferred to the other party is not as obvious and the exact favour being sought is not as defined. However, this is a distinction in degree, not nature. Further, moral norms, unlike many legal ones, cannot be circumvented by use of technicalities.

It follows, that on the basis of a strictly economic analysis expenditure networking is wrong. However, on a normative analysis this conclusion does not necessarily follow. Morality and economics are not necessarily harmonious. Moreover, moral principle trumps business practice. Economic principles are important in guiding human behaviour, but moral principle is applicable to all human conduct, whether public or private, and provides the ultimate evaluative framework by which our behaviour is judged.

Thus, even though expenditure networking leads to some market inefficiencies this does not necessarily mean that it is morally wrong. It may yet be the case that the incidental good consequences outweigh the damage done to the market place. The incidental good consequences we refer to are the increased level of human contact that is inherent in all forms of networking.[14] Networking is a forum in which individuals who otherwise would not socialise are brought together. Obviously it is impossible to quantify the level of good that this causes. However, recent surveys tend to show that the most important things to happiness are not centered upon financial concerns, but rather social interaction.

Contrary to economists' belief that income (together with leisure) is the source of all utility, as we saw in chapter two evidence shows that companionship, which does not pass through the market, has higher utility and contributes more to well-being than does income. The number of friends one has is a much better indicator of overall happiness than personal wealth. People are far more likely to achieve happiness by spending time with friends and family than by striving for higher income. Once one is beyond the poverty level, a larger income contributes almost nothing to happiness.

Thus, a strong argument can be made out that the inefficiencies stemming from expenditure networking are outweighed by the good in the form of the increased social interaction that stems from the practice. The persuasiveness of this argument depends on a number of assumptions and considerations. First, it assumes that if networking was prohibited then business people would not spend this time socialising in any event—probably a safe assumption given the ever increasing hours spent at work. Secondly, it is important to note that the more effective that networking actually is the harder it will be to balance the other side of the utilitarian scales. Hence, we are left with the paradoxical view that the less effective networking actually is in securing contacts the more justifiable it is.

15.5 CONCLUSION

Bribery and expenditure networking have far more in common than has previously been observed. The objective of both practices is the same: to gain a market advantage by providing a 'sweetener' to a person responsible for delegating the provision of goods or services. The effect of both practices is the also the same: to distort the pure operation of a market economy by encouraging business decisions to be made on the basis of irrelevant criteria—either the size of the brown paper bag or the opulence of the corporate box.

However expenditure networking has the incidental positive side effect of drawing people together in a congenial social setting. Bribery has no such redeeming feature. Socialising with others is integral to human flourishing. Hence, it may well be that this incidental good outweighs the harm caused to the market.

The scales are too finely balanced to make a confident call—unlike the other matters discussed in this book.

NOTES

1. R Gesteland, *Cross-Cultural Business Behavior* (1996) 101.
2. N Wallace-Bruce 'Corruption and Competitiveness in Global Business—the dawn of a new era' (2000) 24 *MULR* 349, 351.
3. Ibid.
4. Other notable international developments are discussed by Wallace-Bruce, ibid.
5. See Wallace-Bruce, above n 2, 368.
6. For an argument along such lines, see C Hotchkiss, 'The Sleeping Dog Stirs: New Signs of Life in Efforts to End Corruption in International Business' (1998) *17 Journal of Public Policy & Marketing* 108.
7. (1994) 71 A Crim R 537, at 541–42.
8. M Philips. *Bribery* (1985).
9. P Phongpaichit, et al, 'Guns, Girls, Gambling, Ganja: Thailand's Illegal Economy and Public Policy (1998).
10. V Tanzi, 'Corruption around the World: Causes, Consequences, Scope, and Cures' (1998) 45 *IMF Staff Papers* 572–73 as cited in Wallace-Bruce, above n 2, 357.
11. Wallace Bruce, above n 2, 359.

12. Commonwealth, Parliamentary Debates, *House of Representatives*, 3 June 1999, 6044 (Daryl Williams, Attorney-General).

13. In the short term it may reduce the happiness of the networker, by taking him or her away from the time that would have otherwise been spent with family and friends. However, this is no different to all work activities. Presumably, as with other work activities, the networker believes that on balance the time spent networking others is commensurate with the importance of work to his or her overall happiness.

14. This is in contrast to bribery which by its nature is not a socially inclusive activity. However, it should be noted that attempts have been made to spell out other good consequences of bribery. For example, economic models have been developed which seem to demonstrate the efficiency benefits that could be derived by companies giving bribes: Vito Tanzi, 'Corruption around the World: Causes, Consequences, Scope, and Cures' (1998) 45 *IMF Staff Papers* 559, 578, 581–2 cited in Wallace-Bruce, above n 2, 350.

www.ingramcontent.com/pod-product-compliance
Lightning Source LLC
Chambersburg PA
CBHW021403290426
44108CB00010B/358